D0396536

Redeeming Justice

REDEEMING JUSTICE

From Defendant to Defender, My Fight for Equity
on Both Sides of a Broken System

JARRETT ADAMS

CONVERGENT

NEW YORK

Published in the United States by Convergent Books, an imprint of Random House, a division of Penguin Random House LLC, New York.

CONVERGENT BOOKS is a registered trademark and its C colophon is a trademark of Penguin Random House LLC.

Library of Congress Cataloging-in-Publication Data
Names: Adams, Jarrett, author.
Title: Redeeming justice / Jarrett Adams.
Description: New York: Convergent, 2021.
Identifiers: LCCN 2021004332 (print) | LCCN 2021004333 (ebook) |
ISBN 9780593137819 (hardcover) | ISBN 9780593137826 (ebook)
Subjects: LCSH: Adams, Jarrett. | Lawyers—United States—Biography. |
African American lawyers—United States—Biography. | False imprisonment—
United States. | Discrimination in criminal justice administration—United States. |
Race discrimination—Law and legislation—United States.
Classification: LCC KF373.A29 A3 2021 (print) | LCC KF373.A29 (ebook) |
DDC 340.092 [B]—dc23
LC record available at https://lccn.loc.gov/2021004332
LC ebook record available at https://lccn.loc.gov/2021004333

Printed in Canada on acid-free paper

crownpublishing.com

9 8 7 6 5 4 3 2 1

First Edition

Book design by Diane Hobbing

To the strength of the Black women—to Sugar, Honey, and Peaches, for never giving in, and refusing to let me give up!

CONTENTS

I—Fall

II—Rise

I.
Fall

1.
Life after Justice

November 2018

I walk through the woods with Kerri O'Brien, a local television news reporter who for the past three years has been covering the case involving my clients. I wear a dark suit and hold a leather binder. I squat and twigs snap under my dress shoes. I rub my palm on the ground and think about the men I'm representing.

On April 25, 1998, Allen Gibson, a white police officer in a small Virginia town, entered these woods behind an apartment complex and surprised Terence Richardson, twenty-eight, and Ferrone Claiborne, twenty-three, in the middle of a drug deal. The officer drew his gun, the two young men wrestled with him, and the gun went off, shooting Gibson in the stomach. Terence and Ferrone fled the scene. Shortly after, a state trooper discovered Gibson on the ground, bleeding, severely wounded. In his weakened condition, the officer managed to describe the drug deal and his attackers: two Black men, one with a ponytail, the other with dreadlocks. Later that afternoon, Gibson died in the hospital. On a tip from a witness, police picked up

Terence and Ferrone and charged them with the murder of Allen Gibson. Open and shut. End of story.

Except not one word I just told you is true.

Terence and Ferrone were nowhere near these woods at the time of Gibson's shooting. Police picked them up in separate locations, on opposite sides of town. Neither had a criminal record; neither had ever sold drugs. Investigators found no trace of their fingerprints, hair, or DNA at the crime scene, and neither wore a ponytail or dreads. Which should have raised a question: In the course of approximately thirty minutes, how could they have murdered a police officer, removed all the evidence, fled the scene, gotten rid of the drugs, changed, disposed of their clothes, gone to separate locations, and *cut their hair*?

Police rounded up and interrogated nearly every young Black male in Waverly, Virginia, determined to find two men to charge for the killing of the officer. They had a crime. They needed two criminals. It is still unclear how my clients' names came up, but two days later police arrested them for the murder of the police officer. Fearing the death penalty and strongly encouraged by their lawyers, Terence and Ferrone pleaded guilty to lesser charges, Terence to involuntary manslaughter, Ferrone to accessory after the fact to involuntary manslaughter, a misdemeanor.

Despite being innocent, Terence and Ferrone made this choice because it was the only one offered them. Across America, in cities and in small towns—and especially in this small town—they saw that the police didn't dispense equal justice to Blacks and whites. They had seen Black people routinely railroaded, sent to prison, put to death for nothing. When the same system came for them, Terence and Ferrone pleaded guilty to lesser charges to save their lives.

For members of the town's white establishment, it wasn't enough. They saw the punishment as a slap on the wrist. They wanted more. They wanted Terence and Ferrone's heads.

Because Gibson's shooting was linked to a drug deal, the FBI came in. The feds interviewed a parade of informants, making deals with several people in exchange for their testimony. A false portrait emerged of Terence and Ferrone as drug kingpins, even though neither had any history of drug dealing and police never found drugs in their possession or records of any large transactions or cash deposits.

In 2001, a jury in federal court additionally found Terence Richardson and Ferrone Claiborne guilty of conspiracy to sell crack cocaine. In a rare legal action, the judge used their previous murder charge and guilty pleas as a cross-reference to enhance their drug sentence. The judge sentenced them to life in prison.

Twenty years later, Terence and Ferrone sit in federal prison for a crime they didn't commit.

I know what my clients are going through. I know they sometimes scream at the top of their lungs until their voices give out and then they continue to scream silently. I know they feel as if the walls were closing in on them. I know how with each day that passes they become diminished, feeling another piece of their humanity peeling off, like dead skin. I know exactly how they feel.

In 1998, I was falsely accused and ultimately wrongly convicted of rape. I was sentenced to prison for twenty-eight years. I, too, had done nothing. I, too, got terrible legal advice.

Unlike my clients, I made a catastrophic mistake that set the whole thing in motion, putting me on the path I'm on today.

I went to a party.

Three of us—three Black kids from Chicago—drove to a college campus in Wisconsin. At the party, we each had a consensual sexual encounter with the same girl, a white girl. Her roommate walked in, called her a slut, and stormed out. These were the facts. But the girl later said we raped her.

As a man raised by four strong, prideful women—my mom, grandmother, and aunts—I still have no idea or sense of how difficult it is for any woman to come forward after she has been raped. I cannot imagine the humiliation, shame, anger, and fear a woman must feel having to relive the details of her attack as she files a police report and submits to a rape kit test. As a lawyer, I know the statistics for false rape accusations. According to the National Sexual Violence Resource Center, only 2–10 percent of women falsely claim they have been raped.

My accuser falls into that 2–10 percent.

The police believed her. They charged us with rape, and we went to trial. I thought that if I told the truth, I would be safe. I trusted in the truth and in fairness. I believed in justice. After all, that's what trials are about—justice, right?

Not necessarily. Particularly if the accused is poor, uneducated, and a person of color. In too many cases, justice doesn't prevail, even if the accused is innocent. Some days, justice doesn't even make an appearance.

At my trial, the prosecution's insistence on getting a conviction at any cost and deep-rooted prejudice barred justice from the courtroom. Justice never had a chance. I never had a chance. The prosecutor looked at me and at Dimitri Henley and Rovaughn Hill—the friends on trial with me—and called us "three Black men from Chicago." We had no names, but the all-white jury knew us. They'd seen "us" on the news. They'd read about "us" in the newspapers. We were criminals, drug dealers, gangbangers, rapists, killers. We were *them*. Three nameless Black men from Chicago. It didn't matter that the prosecution presented no real evidence, that the so-called victim's story made no sense. The truth didn't matter. Like my clients Terence Richardson and Ferrone Claiborne and so many young Black men, I was convicted.

After nearly ten years, with the help of the Wisconsin Innocence Project (WIP), I was exonerated and released from prison. The court dropped all charges against me, and my record was expunged. I was free. Well, not quite. Ten years behind bars took its toll. I needed to adjust to the world outside. I found that reentering society was almost as difficult as surviving prison. A mash-up of emotions assaulted me—anger, despair, frustration, confusion. Eventually, thanks to the kindness of my mother, my family, co-workers, teachers, the commitment and hard work I put into therapy, and my faith, I emerged from a place of darkness and came to a place of healing. I also confirmed my path in life. In prison, I became a jailhouse lawyer, helping inmates with their legal issues. I made a vow to myself that once I got out, I would go to college and law school and become an actual, card-carrying attorney.

After my release, I began working on that promise. I felt as if I were on a mission and that God had answered my prayers. He gave me a second chance. Now I live to exceed His expectations. I work and live at warp speed.

"What drives you?" people ask.

Two emotions fuel me every day, motivating me to wake up at dawn and keep charging until I collapse from exhaustion late at night.

First, fear. Fear drives me. I'm afraid of not doing the right thing, of wasting time, of disappointing others, and of disappointing myself.

Second, commitment. I have made a commitment to serve those behind bars who have been locked up for minor crimes, serving unconscionably long sentences, and those who have been wrongly accused, people like Terence and Ferrone. I am fighting to set them free. The process takes perseverance, patience, and time—literally years, and sometimes even decades.

One day, as I was explaining a legal procedure to Ferrone, he suddenly blurted, "Had I known that by pleading guilty to save my life, it would've *cost* me my life . . ."

His voice, laced with pain, trailed off. But those three words seared into me.

Had I known.

I wish that I, too, had known.

Had I known how badly the odds are stacked against us. *Had I known* that I needed a good lawyer to represent me. *Had I known* how long it would take to reverse an unjust conviction. I want my clients' families and even their future generations to *know*—what our broken criminal justice system can do to them. I vow to litigate and to educate. This is my promise. This is my life after justice.

In this country we have two criminal justice systems—the one you can afford and the one you can't. If you are unfortunate enough to find yourself without the means to afford at minimum competent legal representation, you will discover, as I did, that justice will be banned from your courtroom.

At best, achieving justice becomes a chess match, a game of strategy. You looking ahead several moves, positioning your pieces, sometimes lulling your opponent to a false sense of security before you attack, before you win.

As a lawyer, you play a high-stakes game.

You play, literally, for people's lives.

Who wins?

In prison I learned it's not the lawyer who has amassed the most or "best" evidence. Sometimes it isn't even the one who's right.

The one who wins, I learned, is the one who tells the best story.

2.
The Neighborhood

November 1985

I am five years old.

My parents have split up. Years from now, I won't remember the divorce. I'll only remember shapes, shadows moving rapidly past me, flickering on walls, voices raised, doors slamming, crying. And I'll remember silence. Not *quiet*, but silence. There is a difference. Quiet calms you; quiet comforts you. Silence is stark and cold and terrifying. Silence rips into you. After my father leaves, that's what I remember most—the silence. My brother, five years older, remembers him, feels hurt, feels loss. I don't remember my father at all.

My mother works for the U.S. Department of Housing and Urban Development, down by O'Hare Airport, an hour-and-a-half drive from where we live, the South Side of Chicago. After the divorce, my mother rises at four thirty, gets ready for work, wakes me up, drops me off at my grandparents' house around five thirty, and drives to her job. She picks me up after work, around seven thirty at night, and we go back to our house. I get ready for bed while my mother takes a bath. One night, I hear a shriek coming from the bathroom. I bounce out of bed and nervously open the door. I see my mother in the bath-tub, her head bent over, her shoulders shaking. I see that she is sob-bing.

"What's wrong?" I ask her.

"Nothing," she says, turning away quickly. "Nothing."

I know she can't tell me, but I can guess—the divorce, the drive, money being tight, and maybe at night the silence.

Not nothing.

I close the door, go back to my room, slide into bed, and stare at the ceiling.

Many nights, I lie awake like that, listening to the sounds of the house, the squeaks, creaks, settling noises, squirrels scurrying on the roof, people out on the street, a laugh, a holler, a bottle shattering, and sometimes, the worst sound of all, my mother crying behind the bathroom door. On those nights, I whisper a prayer: "Please God, I promise I'll be good, if you just stop my mom from crying."

My grandmother Lane and my grandfather Buddy live in what our family calls the Big House, a rambling, two-story fortress spread over a corner lot backed up to Chicago State University and tucked in tight to the DMV. When I'm outside, my grandmother always warns me to watch out for crazy drivers who take the corner too fast or nervous teenagers taking their driving tests.

Lane and Buddy call me their miracle grandchild. I want to know why. I'm five, but I'm intensely curious about everything. I reject those adult clichés—"Don't ask so many questions," "Do it because I said so," and "I'll explain when you're older." I'm old enough now. I want answers.

Buddy sighs and sets me on his lap. He has a favorite chair, a well-worn La-Z-Boy recliner, set up in front of the TV so he can watch his beloved Chicago Cubs. He speaks directly to the Cub players as if he were in the dugout and they can hear him. He cheers loudest for the Black players—Shawon Dunston, Leon Durham, and especially Big Lee Smith, the most intimidating relief pitcher in the game.

"He lives right near us," Buddy says. "South Side. I've seen him."

My grandfather grins with a familiarity suggesting that "I've seen him" means he and Big Lee are practically best friends, possibly drinking buddies. At five, I believe it. I believe everything Buddy says. My grandfather has stepped into my father's absent shoes and become my father figure, the major male presence in my life, an actual World War II hero, and my hero. Sometimes while watching the Cubs, I ask if I can hold the medal he received in the war, and Buddy will allow me to play with his Purple Heart.

My family comes from the Deep South, our legacy birthed and bred in the cotton fields of Mississippi. History records that our country officially abolished slavery with the Thirteenth Amendment in 1865, but I know for a fact that many Black people—including my family—continued to live a life of de facto slavery, picking cotton under the oppressive rule of racist cotton farmers for seventy-five years afterward, until the early 1940s. Protected by the local police and a legal system that wasn't enforced equally for Blacks and whites, the cotton farmers brutalized their workers by day and preyed on young Black women at night. Buddy and Lane did that work for years. By the time their daughters were teenagers, they reached their breaking point and declared they'd had enough of the backbreaking, demeaning, low-paying, and dangerous life in Mississippi.

In 1943, Buddy went north to join his brother in Chicago. Shortly after, my grandmother made the same journey with their seven children. Almost as soon as my grandfather settled at his new address on the South Side, he received a letter embossed with a government seal: his draft notice. The army didn't care that he was in his early thirties, the father of seven, and his family's primary breadwinner. Buddy soon found himself in uniform, a private in the U.S. Army, crammed into the cargo hold of a transport plane with a platoon of Black soldiers, all flying overseas to fight in World War II.

Buddy fought at D-day in the Allied invasion at Normandy, part of the initial surge of the 320th Barrage Balloon Battalion, an all-African-American unit that hit the sand first. The 320th sent up hydrogen-filled balloons designed as cover to protect the Allied infantrymen from being mowed down by enemy aircraft fire as they charged onto the beach. My grandfather's platoon succeeded in sending up the balloons, but they did without any cover for themselves. Enemy gunfire raked through them. Only my grandfather and one other soldier survived.

A bullet pierced Buddy's chest right next to his lung. Eventually, a medic found him bleeding in the sand and managed to get him to a hospital where doctors determined if they removed the bullet, he would bleed to death. Unable to treat him, the army shipped Buddy to a stateside hospital. He not only made it back in one piece but came home a hero. He eventually got out of bed and walked out of the hospital—carefully. He knew that any strenuous activity could dislodge the bullet and cause it to puncture his lung.

Buddy took a job at a meatpacking plant and lived hard, except for an aversion to climbing stairs, which he took slowly and deliberately. He refused most medication, instead using drink to dull any pain he felt around his chest. He loved to dance, loved going to nightclubs, and he loved his wife, my grandmother Lane. Soon they had their eighth child, my mother. "My miracle child," Buddy called her.

"And that's why I call you my miracle grandchild," Buddy tells me as I sit on his lap, getting ready to watch the game.

Nothing against any of my cousins, but I feel a special bond with Buddy. He keeps his eye on me, even when he seems to focus all his attention on the Cubs, and I keep my eye on him. Seventy years old and he's up at the crack of dawn, puttering around the house, tending Lane's rosebushes, or mowing the lawn. The Big House's big corner lawn has grass that's as manicured and as green as a golf course. Buddy is always busy. Aunt Sugar says, "Daddy, Buddy, you never sleep. You need to sleep."

Buddy says, "Sugar, if that bullet moves, I'll have plenty of time to sleep."

In the fall, Buddy drives me to school in his beloved Oldsmobile, light blue and clean, the size of a boat. I'm too short to see through the windshield, so he has me sit on the center armrest. He's not breaking the law. Children under eight don't have to wear seatbelts. I sit on that armrest proudly, riding shotgun, on the same level as my grandfather.

When the bell rings at the end of the day, I see the Oldsmobile parked outside my elementary school and Buddy, all six feet four of him, leaning on the hood, waiting for me. He grabs me when I come out of school, scoops me up, kisses me, and plops me down on that armrest, my special seat. When I get older, enter first grade, then second grade, I start to feel embarrassed seeing my grandfather outside school. I finally break the news to him one afternoon.

"Man, Granddad, why you always waiting for me after school? And don't kiss me in front of my friends. I want to walk home with them."

Of course, I can't know that I've hurt his feelings just by growing up. He stops coming around in his Oldsmobile after school, but he still watches over me. As I peel away from my friends walking home and approach the Big House, I see him standing in the picture window, waiting for me to arrive, some days his Purple Heart wrapped around his wrist.

My grandmother Lane oversees the comings and goings in the Big House like a benevolent general. She controls the kitchen and nurtures her eight children with nothing but love. As for me, I know I get into things that deserve a spanking. But nobody raises a hand to me. Not as long as my grandmother stays within shouting distance.

Lane always has something on the stove or in the oven. In the summer, she leaves the screen door open, and when I turn the corner onto our street, the smell of freshly baked butter cookies hits me so hard my mouth waters. My grandmother is so good in the kitchen she has taken a job as a cook for one of the local schools.

I want to learn. I start asking questions about how she made this dish and why she put that ingredient in that pot. Before I know it, Lane puts me to work. She teaches me the names and varieties of vegetables, and I taste each one raw and cooked. She teaches me the difference between pots and pans, instructs me about burners and the oven. She introduces me to spices. I sprinkle salt, pepper, paprika, cayenne appropriately over our food, and soon she has me standing on a chair, stirring a stew or a casserole. Before long, I'm stationed next to her, her sous chef, chopping, dicing, concocting a thick beef stew, chicken noodle soup, and, my favorite, chili.

After teaching me to cook, my grandmother teaches me to read. I'm intensely inquisitive, some say annoyingly nosy because I want to know—why? What does this say? What does that mean? After making dinner for sometimes a dozen people, my grandmother relaxes by reading *Our Daily Bread,* a pamphlet of Bible verses. She begins by reading a verse to me, and then she starts having me read the verse to her. At first, I struggle to sound out the words, but I learn quickly, retain everything, and soon I can read the verses to her fluently. Reading provides me with even more questions to ask, countless questions, a torrent of questions, probably driving my grandmother crazy.

"Look it up in a *book,*" she usually says.

She gives me books, sends me off to read them and report back to her. When we run out of books at home, she takes me to the library. Thanks to my grandmother, I develop what will become a lifelong love of reading. I don't know then that reading—and writing—will one day save my life.

My grandmother also makes sure that I accompany her to church. I don't mind. I like going to our small local church a few blocks away, and I definitely like sitting next to her. She understands children and knows how restless and bored I get during the services and sermon. She takes her seat in her regular pew, and I eagerly scoot next to her. She tries not to laugh. She knows what I'm after. She keeps a virtual candy store in her purse and parcels candies into my eagerly awaiting palm during the service. The candy comes with a cost, though. I have to agree to attend church without complaining, read the hymns aloud and enthusiastically, and promise to give the idea of faith at least some thought.

When summertime comes, the kids in our neighborhood don't go to camp or take music lessons. We climb the fence and sneak into the pool at Chicago State, which is closed for the summer. Then the summer before I enter fourth grade, my brother Jamal teaches me to play basketball.

We have no parks with hoops, no inside gyms, no rec centers, so we have to improvise. We lift a discarded wooden crate out of the dumpster behind a grocery store, saw out the bottom, and nail the crate to a light pole in an alley near the house, between a row of garages. We sweep all the debris out of the alley, Jamal rounds up a few of his friends, and we play two-on-two or sometimes three-on-three games of crate ball. The game resembles "army ball," a vicious version of basketball that feels closer to tackle football. You fight for position, literally, and if you call a foul, you better be bleeding. I learn inside moves, how to muscle up bigger guys, create a variety of effective fakes and a serious handle that allows me to maneuver in very tight spaces, and because it's ridiculously hard to make a shot into a crate, I develop an extremely soft touch on my mid-range jumper. I go from being the last guy picked to a gritty point guard, someone you want on your team.

My mother keeps me busy by putting me to work at church. I serve on the usher board, and she gets me in the "Sunbeams Choir," a group of kids that meets every day for practice. I don't know what strings she pulls, because I cannot sing. At all. Despite my off-key voice and hopeless sense of tone, I stay in the choir for the rest of the summer.

I am unaware of their motives then, but my mother and my aunties know exactly what they are doing. They are determined to keep me occupied at all times. They triple-team me, these smart, strong, caring, spiritual women: Honey, the thicker-set, softer-spoken, oldest sister; Sugar, tall, thin, an ebony-skinned beauty, unafraid to express an opinion; and Peaches, my mother, the baby of the family, quiet, but clear and direct. They warn me, even at the age of nine, to stay close to the house, announce where I'm going, watch my surroundings, and always avoid putting myself in any compromising situations, especially with the police. They impose a strict rule at night: as soon as the streetlights come on, I have to come inside. *Don't give them a reason,* my mother says. She repeats that phrase as often as "Brush your teeth" and "Wash your hands."

My mother, aunties, and grandmother insist that they have to know where I am at all times. I don't understand. Not at first. But these women know the history of young Black men in our city, in our country, in our society, and on the South Side. They tell me about a neighborhood only a couple miles away, Greater Grand Crossing, where the largest and most elaborate amusement park in the country opened in 1905—White City. The city gave the park that name because of the thousands of white lights that adorned the buildings in the park. But they could've given the park that name because they allowed white patrons only—except for a game called the African Dip. In this "game," park goers threw balls at Black men sitting on flimsy chairs above a water tank, aiming to hit them in the head. If they succeeded, the person working the game would tip the chairs and dunk the Black men into the water.

After the Depression, the park closed, and the city built a public housing project on the land called Parkway Gardens. By the 1970s, whites had moved out of the neighborhood, the city cut off funding, and Parkway Gardens fell into disrepair. In the early 1980s, gangs came into the neighborhood, bringing with them drugs and guns. The gangs took over Greater Grand Crossing and started moving into our part of the South Side.

Toward the end of the 1980s, I hear about a drug called crack coming into our neighborhood. I notice more and more families without fathers, and I see more kids my age coming to live with their grandmothers. Then I see grandmothers moving out as the neighborhood begins to deteriorate. Stores closing up and buildings becoming dilapidated. On summer days now, my grandmother keeps the screen door closed. I hear about people stealing cars on the street and houses being broken into. I hear about a guy on our street who got shot in the neck. A charge of energy crackles through our grid of a dozen or so blocks—an undercurrent of nervousness and fear. My mother, my aunties, and my grandmother huddle over coffee or tea at the kitchen table, whispering urgently about the state of our neighborhood and its uncertain future. They use a phrase I overhear too many times to ignore—"disposable young Black boys."

They talk about kids—sons, grandsons, and nephews of women they know—who have had interactions with the police. Young Black boys getting picked up for crimes they didn't commit, or being picked up just because they were out at night. That's all they did. *They were out at night.*

That can't be right, I think. That's not normal.

It isn't right. And it is normal.

I begin to see that young Black boys my age fall into two categories.

Those who are sheltered, overprotected, and kept inside the house, safe.

And those who are out on the streets, exposed, in danger.

My mother will do anything she can to keep me in that first category.

Right before my tenth birthday, my grandfather dies.

His death, the loss of our patriarch—Buddy, my buddy—leaves a gaping hole in my heart and in our family, a presence that I know cannot be replaced.

He dies from cancer, of all things, not from the bullet lodged in his chest.

To this day, I remain inspired by his toughness and his spirit. If I feel a cold coming on or have a slight fever, my instinct is to get into bed. Then I think of Buddy. This man walked around with a bullet in his chest. He kept his motor running, no matter what. Nothing slowed him down. If he felt pain, he never complained, never showed it. He'd take a shot of whiskey and keep going. I keep seeing images of myself with him—sitting on the armrest next to him in his beloved pale blue Oldsmobile; sitting with him in his recliner, watching the

Cubs; playing with his Purple Heart, rubbing the ribbon, pressing the embossed face on the medal, George Washington's face, our first president. The army gives you a medal for getting hurt and for making it home. For surviving. My grandfather and his Purple Heart taught me this: a hero is someone who *survives*.

A year later, Lane goes with him.

My grandmother, the matriarch, the glue of our family, the woman who taught me to read and to cook, and who insisted that I have faith and keep my faith, dies of a broken heart. She succumbs to life without Buddy. That may not be the official medical diagnosis, but that's how I see it. That's what I believe.

My godmother, Sugar, steps up as best as she can. I know money is tight for my mother, and Sugar, who has a good job as an auditor, contributes to our household. My mother still makes that killer drive to work way past O'Hare, but even with financial help from her family she struggles to make ends meet. And I still hear her crying in the bathtub. One night, her sobs don't stop and her crying turns into something deeper, more primal. When she gets out of the bath and puts on her robe, I pad into her bedroom and quietly ask what's wrong. I have some sense of the answer, or answers. Money troubles, raising two kids as a single mom, feeling lonely and exhausted, and losing both of her parents in the space of a year. I'm ten years old and I cannot fathom the emotional upheaval she must be feeling, but I am in no way prepared for her response.

"Life is so hard," she says, breaking into a wail. "It's too much."

I think of Buddy on the Normandy beach, bleeding but surviving. I picture threading the ribbon of his Purple Heart through my fingers and I say, "You can't give up. You can't."

I don't know if my mother hears me. But she looks at me and sighs so heavily her shoulders shake. She pulls me into her and hugs me. I hold on for my life—for her life. Eventually, she releases me, calms herself, and swipes at the tears on her cheek with the back of her hand. She puts on a tiny smile, kisses me, and goes into her bedroom. I don't remember hearing her crying in the bathtub again.

The neighborhood turns hard, grim, dangerous. For practically my whole life, gangs have roamed the streets, but I've never felt afraid. The gangs now seem angrier, a current of rage and violence thrumming through the clusters of kids, most of them older, some I know or have seen around. Rivalries emerge. A kid selling drugs on one corner competes with someone else on the next corner. I see beatings, I hear gunshots. I see vacant houses with plywood nailed over windows. I see cars abandoned on the street, stripped, hollowed out. Someone even tries to steal my mother's car. She hears a loud noise outside and, without even thinking, runs into the garage, grabs a strung-out-looking intruder by the sleeve, forces him into a corner, and calls the police. He tears himself away from her and runs off. A few days later, the same guy breaks into another garage. The car's owner appears with a gun and shoots the thief in the chest.

Then I witness two incidents—one involving drugs, the other violence—that suggest the neighborhood has turned so dramatically it may never turn back.

One cold winter night, a family down the street holds a wedding reception at their house for their daughter and new son-in-law. They invite everyone in the neighborhood, a common practice.

I go to the reception with some friends. On our way out, I see a guy smoking what looks like a cigarette. Either the guy smokes too much or the cigarette has been laced with something toxic, because he starts to convulse. Someone tends to him and my friends and I walk away. The guy recovers, but the next day the neighborhood buzzes with speculation about what the guy had been smoking and his spastic reaction to the drug.

"He's on that crack," a friend says. Turns out, the guy was smoking a "wicked stick," a cigarette stuffed with crack and dipped in embalming fluid.

"I keep hearing about that," I say.

"It's serious, man. You get hooked. You get crazy. It's real bad."

I bank the memory. A few months later, on a summer night while friends and I play Piggy outside on our street—a version of baseball played with a bat and a tennis ball but without running bases—a car roars around the corner; then another car follows on its tail. We scramble out of the way, dash onto lawns and porches, and then the first car slams into a tree. The car's doors fly open. The guy who smoked the wicked stick at the wedding reception jumps out, and a gun clatters onto the street behind him. The second car screeches to a stop, two guys burst out and start chasing the wicked stick guy. Seconds later, police cars, sirens blaring, race down the block and skid to a stop, and cops flood the neighborhood. I don't know if the police or the guys from the second car catch the wicked stick guy, but from this point on—every day, sometimes every other hour—police come around. They hassle every young Black man they see. They hassle my friends. And one afternoon, in broad daylight, they hassle me.

"You look like somebody," they say. "A person of interest, a guy involved in a shooting."

I shake my head, scared mute. Somehow that convinces them.

"You can go," one of the cops says. "This time."

After these two incidents, change in our neighborhood goes from incremental to pervasive. The streets become home to crack dealers, gangbangers, hustlers, invasions by cops. The night, once filled with the sounds of crickets and cats and barking dogs, becomes filled with an orchestra of gunfire.

One day, my mother hits my brother and me with news.

"I'm selling the house," she says. "We're moving out. The neighborhood is no longer safe. The schools have gotten terrible. I want you in a better school."

My mother, always thinking about me, my safety, my future, vows to stay one step ahead of the violence and deterioration we see all around us. So we move. This will be our first of many moves.

Overall, I attend five different schools in seven years. I am always the new kid. I adjust, or try to. I find my place, make friends, settle in, and then I move again and begin all over at a new school. I play down the classroom smarts. Smart kids are rarely popular. Smart kids get shunned. If you're smart—or different—you eat alone. Even though I change schools often, I rarely eat alone. I'm social, good at sports. I survive. But I have my secret. I can retain information quickly and easily; my mind seems to allow knowledge to flow in and lock it away. I don't let anyone know that. That would be revealing a superpower.

One day, I bump into my father on the street. I've heard he works in the neighborhood. I haven't sought him out, but I see him working construction, pouring concrete. I hesitate when I see him, and then I slowly approach. I feel awkward. As I walk, my awkwardness and hesitation turn into resentment. He looks up and stares at me, and I wonder for a split second if he even recognizes me. I want to shout at him, *why did you leave?* But when I reach him, I go uncharacteristically quiet. I look at the concrete he's pouring, my eyes riveted on the sidewalk. My sudden shyness stifles me at first. Because if I'm honest, I want to know him. I hate that he left. I feel my mother's pain, her heartbreak, her loneliness, and I blame her feelings and our struggles, financial and emotional, squarely on him. But he's my father. I'm drawn to him. I want to know him.

Gradually, I start to speak to him. We don't really connect—I don't feel particularly comfortable with him—but we talk, casually. After that first time, I find myself running into him more often. The more I see him, the more I observe his work ethic. He's always working, hard. He reminds me of Buddy—that motor, that drive. You get up, you shake off whatever cobwebs have formed in your head from the night before, and you go to work. No matter what. You go to work.

We move to another house on the South Side, and then to another, my mother trying to keep ahead of crime and the crack epidemic, always in search of a better school for me. We move so much I feel like an army brat. Then my brother gets his own place, and James, a good man who will become my stepfather, moves in.

Around my junior year of high school, my mother says that she has arranged for me to attend a high school near my father, out in the suburbs, and my father will take me in. I spend my last two years of high school commuting between my parents, keeping clothes at both places, living weekdays in the suburbs with my father, our relationship tentative, our conversations minimal, and weekends with my mother. I stay on the move, meaning partying, sometimes outside the city. My mother would worry sick if she knew. So I don't tell her. What she doesn't know won't hurt her.

I coast through senior year, as most high school seniors do, my future out of focus. I go to prom, walk at my graduation, and then, poof, high school ends and reality arrives like a slap. I have made plans for after the summer: I've registered for courses at a local community college, and I've sat down with a recruiter from the National Guard to talk about enlisting. Other than that, my future remains murky. Only two types of recruiters come to our high school, those from colleges who go after the handful of elite athletes, and those from the armed services who go after decent students from poor families. These uniform-wearing recruiters pitch us the security and adventure of life in the military. That seems to be my only choice. My path. Black kids have to be elite athletes or off the charts academically to be recruited for college. If you're Black and a good student, if you're smart and normal, you are ignored. I am ignored.

After high school, culture shock slams me. I suddenly have to figure out how to make a living—and a life—immediately, without guidance, counseling, or help. I've gone from being a high school student to an instant adult. I haven't had time to figure out what I want, what I want to be, or who I am—except I know I need my own place and some cash flow. All I know for sure is that I want to settle down; I want to stop *moving*.

Over the summer, I work two jobs. I bag groceries at the Shop 'n Save near my father's house, and I work for a temp agency, selling bottles of cologne wholesale with a crew of guys, including two who become my main partners on the weekend. There's Dimitri Henley, a friend from one of my previous schools, and Rovaughn Hill. Rovaughn, a year older, has a car that works—barely—and receives the lowdown on every party within a three-hour radius. It's the summer between the end of high school and the beginning of young adulthood, or, as I see it, my last two months to party before I have to get serious about life. So we hit every party we can; my only real concern is that on long trips Rovaughn's car will break down in the middle of nowhere.

But sometimes I picture my mother, my aunts, and my grandmother sitting around the kitchen table at the Big House, sipping coffee, talking, worrying, fearing—for me.

"When you're a young Black man, you don't give the police a reason."

Disposable young Black boys.

Those words burn into me like a tattoo.

3.
The Party

September 1998

A friend of Rovaughn's tells him about a freshmen pre-orientation party on the campus of the University of Wisconsin–Whitewater, this knowledge as good as a personal invitation.

Rovaughn, Dimitri, and I have spent the summer road-tripping to parties, including some on college campuses. We've blanketed the state of Illinois, traveling to the University of Illinois campus, two hours away in Champaign, and to Southern Illinois University in Carbondale, *five* hours away. Driving that far for a party means nothing to us. We'd rather be on the road for half a Saturday night than stay on the South Side. We feel safer on the freeway in Rovaughn's clunker than cruising the city streets, looking for a house party. And we prefer parties on college campuses where the beer and spiked punch flow abundantly and people pass joints freely. Let's be honest. I'm seventeen, red-blooded, male, and like every young man my age I'm looking for fun. Meaning: women. I'm not traveling five hours to Carbondale to sit with a bunch of guys and talk about the Bears' chances this year.

This night in early September, we map our route and determine it'll take a good hour and a half to get to the Whitewater campus. I pack up a few bottles of cologne, figuring I'll pass them out as party favors. College kids like free stuff. Who doesn't? Then we set our alibis for the night. I tell my father I'll be sleeping at my mother's, and I tell my mother I'll be sleeping at Dimitri's. We've planned to pull an all-nighter—drive the hour and a half to Wisconsin, slide by the party, head out by two, three, depending how it goes, stop at the all-night Waffle House on the way back. We'll reach Chicago before dawn, at which point I'll slip into bed at my mother's house, nobody the wiser, no harm, no foul. Sneaking out to a party is commonplace, a rite of passage.

We don't speed.

In Rovaughn's clunker with its conspicuous red doors, you can't. The last thing we want is for the highway patrol to notice three young Black men driving a funny-looking car on an interstate. I hear my mother's voice: *Do not give them a reason.*

"My mother would kill me if she found out about these trips," I say to the car.

"At least," Rovaughn says.

I shudder and try to laugh. But I don't think twice about our plan to go to Whitewater. I'll be back in my bed before my mother wakes up Sunday morning. I've done it before. Probably do it again. Although as I flip mentally through a calendar, I think, maybe not. This road trip may be my last. A couple more weeks and I'll be starting classes myself, trying to figure out my future.

It takes us an hour forty to get to the Whitewater campus. We follow a sign and pull in to a parking lot near a cluster of high-rise dormitories that look like modern apartment buildings. We slowly get out of Rovaughn's car, Dimitri scanning the grounds. I stretch, trying to shake off the ride. "That car makes me feel like an old man," I say, bending my knees, my joints squeaking.

"I need to locate my friend," Rovaughn says. "Want to find out where the party's at."

"The party is *here*," Dimitri says, gesturing toward the edge of the parking lot.

I see where he's looking. A group of kids outside a dormitory, laughing, smoking cigarettes, passing a joint. Another group walks past them; then more kids emerge, everyone heading into the dorm.

"Let's follow them," I say. "They look like they know where they're going."

We catch up with that group, everyone friendly, talkative, all of us entering the first floor of the dorm and continuing down a hallway, where the party seems in full force. Kids lean against walls, drinking from red cups, some passing a bottle of liquor, others passing a joint. Music blares from one open dorm room. Laughter and a hum of excitement spill out of another. I take a few steps past the doorway and see people standing around a table, watching a girl trying to lob a Ping-Pong ball into a red cup. She arcs it, the ball lands with a splash, applause bursts from the crowd.

"What is that?" The words escape from me, asked to the room.

"Beer pong," a guy answers, brushing past, giggling, tipsy, clutching his red cup.

I watch the girl playing beer pong for a few more minutes, still trying to figure out the rules of the game; then I accept a joint someone passes to me. I inhale deeply, take in what I immediately identify as good college-grade weed, a cut above the usual stuff we get in our neighborhood. I take one more toke, and then somebody else offers me a red cup filled with punch. I shake my head, exhale a light brown cloud from the joint, and say, "No, thank you."

I admit that I like weed, but I don't really drink, and I never mix the two. I get ill, violently ill. My system can't handle them together. I nod to no one, feeling pleasantly light-headed, and ease out of the beer pong room. I sidestep a couple making out in the hallway and see a tall Black kid coming my way, the first Black face I see, the only Black student I see on this campus. I reflexively slap his hand, and we talk for a minute or so. He plays baseball, he says, and asks if I'm on an athletic scholarship.

"Nah," I say. "I don't go here. I'm visiting. Here for the party."

"Good place for that," he says. "Good party school."

"Nice to know," I say, and then I hear what sounds like Rovaughn's voice coming from a nearby dorm room. I say goodbye to the baseball player and follow Rovaughn's voice, laughing now, and I walk into a dorm room. Dimitri sits on a chair across from a guy who's plugging in a Sega Genesis console on his desk.

"Hi. Jarrett Adams," I say to the guy holding the Sega, offering my hand.

"Shawn Demain," he says, shaking my hand. He smiles and nods at the video setup. "You want to play?"

"Absolutely." I grin. "You interested in cologne?"

I hand him a sample bottle of the watered-down crap I've brought along.

"Any good?" Shawn says, opening the top, sniffing the cologne.

"Nah," I say.

Shawn laughs. "Least you're honest. Appreciate that."

He fires up the game, *NBA Jam*, and hands me a controller. We go at it, Dimitri and Rovaughn watching, urging me on, caught up briefly in the South Side of Chicago versus University of Wisconsin–Whitewater basketball championship. Shawn, of course, doesn't know whom he's up against. I'm good at video games, but mainly I'm good at winning. I like competition. I would've done well at lobbing Ping-Pong balls into red cups of beer after all those years I spent arcing shots into rickety wooden crates nailed up on light poles in alleys. It's the drinking part I'd fail at.

For a while, we stay like that, arranged around Shawn's room, talking, laughing, four young men hanging out in a college dorm room, drinking a little, my attention focused on playing *NBA Jam*. I do see that a small plastic bag of weed has materialized. Dimitri reaches for his wallet and pulls out some rolling papers. Maybe it's the soft buzz from the weed or the booze or the combination of the two, but the four of us talk easily, comfortably, even personally. Shawn talks about making the jump from high school to college, coming into a new environment away from home, finding your place, meeting new friends, feeling nervous, wondering if he's up to the academic challenge. I relate, I say, and describe the adjustments I had to make every time we moved. The new kid.

"Five times," he says. "That's a lot. Was it tough?"

"I mean, yeah, but I had no choice. You have to adjust."

Shawn nods and Dimitri and Rovaughn cheer as my pixelated Scottie Pippen soars above the rim and executes a reverse slam dunk.

Shawn's room appears to be party central. Every thirty seconds someone walks in, hangs out for a minute, then walks out, looking for someone else. Shawn has a calm, genuinely patient, mellow nature. I can tell people like being around him.

"You seem to fit in fine," I say.

"So far. Still. Change is hard."

I nod, riveted to the game.

"All beginnings are difficult," I say.

I read that in a book, but even now, sitting in a dorm room on a college campus, I don't want to let on to Shawn, or for that matter to Dimitri and Rovaughn, that I read *books*. A lot of them.

We remain in Shawn's room for a while, the party traffic never letting up, a constant flow of people coming in and out. We're comfortable here, all of us, and for now nobody suggests we go anywhere else. I certainly don't want to leave Shawn's room yet. I am *on* this game, a terror with this controller.

"Whoa, you keep winning," Shawn says. "You own this game."

I laugh and keep playing, and I do just that, I keep winning. Then, for one moment—a glimmer, a flash—I wonder, what about me? Could I see myself here? Would I fit in? Could this be my room? Could I be starting my life here? Could this be my future?

A commotion at the door. Laughter. Voices. I don't look up. I'm vaguely aware of more people coming into the room. Then, of course, you can't miss them. Their presence fills up the room. They command the room.

Two young white women. Freshmen. Roommates. Laughing. Flirting.

One roommate giggles, peers over my shoulder at the game, and rubs her hand over my hair. The other—I'll call her only the young woman—is even more flirtatious. She laughs and sits on Dimitri's lap.

I reach the next round in the game, a round that demands concentration and dexterity, and I'm *into* this game, dominating it, the controller practically attached to me like part of my hand, even though behind me, in my peripheral vision, I see Dimitri, chewing on a straw, and the young woman tugging on the straw playfully, whispering something, and Dimitri laughs. I don't know how much anyone has had to drink, but the smell of alcohol hovers in the air.

More laughing from Dimitri and Rovaughn, and one of the girls says we should all go to her room. An invitation to a private party. I don't say anything, but I hear movement behind me, and Rovaughn and Dimitri and the two girls move toward the door.

"Jarrett," someone calls, "come on."

"I'm still on this game," I say. "I'll be there in a few. I have to finish this game."

A trail of laughter, of voices. The girls and my friends parade out of Shawn's room, leaving me in a wake of perfume, of cologne, of alcohol, of flirtation, of promise.

We hang for a while, Shawn and I, playing the game, until another ten minutes pass, and I win. I shoot my hands up as if I were signaling a touchdown.

"Unreal," Shawn says.

"Beginner's luck," I say, and we laugh.

"Come on, let's go downstairs, hang out, have a smoke," Shawn says.

"Sounds good," I say, pushing away from the Sega console and the desk. "Let me go get Dimitri and Rovaughn. Where they at?"

Shawn starts tidying up his desk, putting away the controllers. "Upstairs," he says. "Two flights up. The room is right off the exit of the stairwell."

"Okay, thanks, I'll go get them."

"See you downstairs," Shawn says. "And, hey, thanks for the cologne."

I head out of his room, bypass the elevator, and take the stairs two at a time. I come out of the stairwell at the end of a hallway. Right away, I hear music coming from the room closest to me. I knock on the door and wait. No response. Maybe they can't hear me over the music. I knock again, hesitate, ease open the door, and walk into the room.

I need a second to adjust to the low light. The room is dark but backlit by a pool of light spilling onto the floor from a streetlamp. I close the door behind me and take another step in. I see three people in the room—the young woman, Dimitri, and Rovaughn. What happens over the next few minutes has altered my life forever. Each one of us has a consensual sexual encounter with the young woman.

At one point, the door suddenly opens.

The roommate comes into the room. She gasps, then starts to speak.

"I can't believe you," the roommate says, her voice rising. "What are you doing?"

And then, almost as if a wave of anger surges through her, in a ferocious afterthought she says, "You're having sex on my *bed*? That's my bed. You're a *slut*."

The roommate storms out of the room, banging the door shut behind her. The young woman pushes off the bed. She whirls on the three of us.

"Act like nothing happened, okay?" she says.

Then she repeats herself, almost as if she were scrambling to gather her thoughts. "If anyone asks, just act like nothing happened."

She goes after her roommate, a few doors down the hall. I can hear her pounding on this other door and shouting, "Hey!"

Then I hear the roommate's voice, slightly muffled, coming through the closed door. The rooms are so close together and the walls so paper thin that I hear the conversation clearly.

"Don't open the door for her," the roommate says to someone inside that room. "She's a slut. She's on my bed with these guys, having sex—*on my bed.*"

"Wait," the young woman says, then shouts into the room. "Are you mad at me? Don't be mad at me. Let me in. I want to talk. Come on. It's not what it seems. Don't be mad. Please. Don't be mad at me."

Silence.

Dimitri, Rovaughn, and I don't look at each other. We don't speak. We don't stir. We barely breathe. Seconds pass. I count in my head: one, two, three.

Then footsteps. The young woman charges back into the room.

"She's mad at me," she says. "She's upset."

Then she says again, "If someone says anything, act like nothing happened, okay? She's so mad at me."

"Okay," I say. "Cool. Look, I told Shawn we'd meet in the smoking area. Let's go downstairs."

We all leave the room. I hustle out of there, bounce out of her room, Dimitri and Rovaughn on my tail. We take the stairs, the same way I came up, go past Shawn Demain's room, and go outside to the smoking area. We find Shawn among a few other people. He greets us, passes a joint. Then I see that the young woman has joined us, followed close behind. We all make small talk. Nothing seems strange, or strained, or off, in any way. We talk, we laugh, we smoke. A bunch of people mingling at a party, passing the time.

Then the roommate and another girl, someone I haven't seen before, walk into the smoking area. The roommate stops and stares at the young woman. She narrows her eyes and points her finger at the young woman, stabbing the air.

"There she is," the roommate says. "Right there. And those are the Black guys she was with—having sex on my bed. Unreal. She's a *slut.*"

The young woman stands. "I don't need this," she says. "I'm leaving. I'm done. I'm not gonna stay around this."

She goes.

I never see her again that night.

A joint comes my way. I cup it and take a hit, my last of the night. We stick around talking with Shawn and a few other people, laughing and hanging out for another forty minutes or so. By now, it's close to three in the morning and the group in the smoking area has thinned out. Dimitri, Rovaughn, and I go back to Shawn's room, and he and I exchange contact information.

"I'd like to stay in touch, man," I say.

"Definitely," he says.

"Let me know when you got other parties going on. Homecoming, stuff like that."

"I will. You have to come up for homecoming."

"You'll be all settled in by then," I say.

He grins and we shake hands. Dimitri and Rovaughn say their goodbyes, and we climb inside Rovaughn's clunker as the party fizzles out. He eases out of the parking lot, and we head toward the expressway, the Waffle House, and back to Chicago. I calculate I will be back in my bed, if all goes well, by eight in the morning. My mother won't know that I've been out all night. She won't suspect a thing.

"I'm starving," someone says.

"I could eat a horse," someone else says.

We go quiet then, maybe all of us replaying parts of the party in our heads, maybe imagining a stack of waffles or pancakes swimming in maple syrup, maybe anticipating the ride back to Chicago, arriving home, getting back to our basically uneventful lives. We cannot fathom the events that lie ahead. We're three teenagers heading home from a road trip.

Three disposable young Black men.

"Good party," someone says.

It's at the Waffle House, I believe, that Dimitri realizes he doesn't have his wallet.

4.

Intake

With two weeks left before school, Dimitri, Rovaughn, and I hit up a couple more parties, including one at Northern Illinois University, a little over an hour away. Rovaughn still drives, his old beater barely making it there and back. September surprises us with a heat wave, extending summer a couple extra weeks, and then we come to the last of our road trips. As my grandfather might say, I experience a sudden case of the blues. I've got to start piecing stuff together, I tell myself.

Slowly, I do. I don't feel I have my future figured out completely, but I have a vague plan. I request more hours bagging groceries at Shop 'n Save. I need to bank as much cash as possible. I have to pay for books and new clothes and put away enough for first and last months' rent and a security deposit for an apartment I'm picturing. I scratch out some numbers on a legal pad and figure out that the financial aid I've received will cover my first-semester classes and fees. If I ace my courses, I will earn a scholarship for the rest of my community college. Forget about joining the military. Visiting all these college campuses has stirred something in me. I don't have a career goal in mind yet, but I know I want to get a college degree. I don't want to spend the next seven years wearing a uniform.

Late September arrives. The famous Chicago winds kick up, the days turn chilly, the leaves start to fall. I circle the day of orientation on my calendar, a week or so away. Going to the store for my mother, I run into Dimitri, who works for UPS. We talk about life now and in the future. We don't talk about the summer. The summer seems like a distant memory.

One day, a Tuesday, I go to campus and purchase my books for the semester. I come home, cradling the stack of books in my arms, and see a business card tucked into the corner of the screen door. I push open the door with my shoulder, put down the books, and pluck out the business card. On it I read, "Chicago Police Department, Robbery/Homicide Division," and after that the name of a police officer.

I frown at the card, thinking the police have made a mistake. They have obviously come to the wrong house and stuck this card into the wrong door. Then I flip the card over and see my name.

"Why did they write down my name?" I say quietly. I turn the card over, stare at it, then turn it back to my name. What could this be about?

I search my memory.

Then it dawns on me. Over the summer, I noticed an uptick in gang shootings in my mother's neighborhood. The police must want to know if I've seen or heard anything. They want me to help them.

I look at the number on the card. I dial it on the phone in the kitchen.

An officer answers. I ask to speak to the officer whose name is on the card.

I wait on hold for a short time. I pace. I twist my fingers through the phone cord. A police officer comes on the line. I tell him my name and describe the card I found stuck in the screen door. He's friendly. He thanks me for calling.

"What is this about?" I ask him.

"Better if you come down here and we talk in person," he says.

"Okay," I say. "I'll be right there."

"No."

I'm thrown.

"No?"

"We've got—it's too busy right now. Better to come—Thursday."

"Thursday? In two days?"

"Yes. Thursday. That'll work. That's better."

"Okay, I'll come Thursday." And then I say again, "Can I ask—what is this about?"

"Informational. We wanted to ask you a few questions. That's all."

He's so vague, I think. I don't understand why he won't tell me more. But I don't press it.

"Do I need to bring my mother?" I ask.

"How old are you?"

"Seventeen."

"When's your birthday?"

"Couple months. November 19."

"You don't need your mother. You're fine. So, okay, we'll see you Thursday."

"All right. Oh. Any particular time—?"

Click.

The line has gone dead.

Thursday.

I sit at a table in a cold barren room across from two police officers, the man I spoke to on the phone and a woman with short blond hair and filmy blue eyes. They offer me water or a soda, but I decline. I try to get comfortable. I can't. I shiver and feel claustrophobic. The male police officer nods at the woman officer.

"This is Sergeant Scout. She came down from Wisconsin."

She doesn't say anything. She stares at me. A probing, unsettling stare.

"Okay," I say.

"We just want to clear you out of this thing," the male officer says. He semi-smiles. An attempt, I believe, to put me at ease.

I am not at ease. I should have brought my mother, I think. She doesn't even know I'm here. I didn't tell her, or my father, or anyone else.

"What thing?" I say.

Sergeant Scout folds her hands on the table, leans in, and says, "The incident in Wisconsin."

Again, that stare.

"What incident in Wisconsin?" I say.

"Did you attend a party in Wisconsin?" the male officer asks. "At a college?"

"Yeah. I did. It was maybe six weeks ago."

"What happened at that party?" Sergeant Scout asks.

I shift in my chair. I really don't know what she's talking about.

"What happened—?"

Sergeant Scout starts peppering me with questions. She asks the questions so fast I hardly have time to answer them. One after another, after another, after another. She pummels me with questions. Whom did I come with? Whom did I see? What time? What did you do? Where? When? Who, who, *who*? Finally, she slows down and asks, "Did you and your friends meet any girls at the party?"

"Yes."

"What about these girls you met?"

I wait, confused.

"I don't understand. What about them?"

"One particular girl. You met one particular girl, didn't you?"

"I—"

"You met one *particular* girl."

"I mean—"

"Did you and your friends have sex with her?"

"I, well—"

"Did you have sex with her? Jarrett, did you have sex with her?"

I take a deep breath and exhale. Words, sentences, paragraphs, come gushing out: everything that happened, every detail, every moment I can remember. As I speak, I think what my mother, my aunts, and my grandmother have told me over and over about dealing with the police, what they have drilled into me. Be calm, be polite, tell the truth.

Most of all, tell the truth.

"Yes, I did have a sexual encounter with her," I say. "We all did. All my buddies, the three of us, had sexual encounters with this young woman. Yes, ma'am. It was consensual."

"How did you get up to her room?" Sergeant Scout asks.

"We were downstairs in this guy's room. We were hanging out. I was playing a video game. This girl came in with her roommate. She was there for a short time, and then she invited us up to her room."

"Were you drinking?" Sergeant Scout says.

"I wasn't, no."

"Were you smoking marijuana?"

Tell the truth, I think. Tell them the truth and it'll be fine.

"Yes," I say. "We were smoking marijuana."

"And then you went up to her room?"

"My buddies did first. I went up later."

"You went to her room?"

"Yes."

Sergeant Scout unfolds her fingers, grips the side of her chair, and leans back. She doesn't move a muscle, but she looks right into me, right through me.

"Why would this *white girl* from up in Wisconsin, the first time she meets you guys, three Black guys from Chicago—why would she *consent* to have sex with you?"

"I don't know," I say. "Because we were kids. We were at a party. We were smoking marijuana. Drinking. Probably because of all that."

Sergeant Scout pauses for what seems like a minute.

"Well," she says.

She glances at the other police officer and then turns back to me.

"I want to let you know that since you've admitted to placing yourself at the scene, you're going to be charged with party to a crime of sexual assault."

I feel my mouth open, close, snap shut.

"Sexual assault," I manage to say. "I don't understand—"

"Rape," Sergeant Scout says.

"Rape?" I say. "There was no rape."

The male police officer suddenly stands. Sergeant Scout keeps looking at me, and then she stands so deliberately it looks like she's moving in slow motion.

"You said I'll be charged," I say, but I can't finish the sentence. I feel as if I were in some kind of dream.

"You'll be hearing from us," the male officer says. He opens the door and stands to the side, indicating for me to leave. I peek at my watch. I've been sitting here for two hours. I stand and walk past the two police officers, avoiding eye contact, not sure what to do, where to go, or whom to talk to about this.

I can't tell my mother, I know that. She has spent her life trying to keep me away from trouble, from the police. Now I've spent two hours with the police, accused of something I didn't do, something I don't even understand.

They were trying to scare me, I think. I know the truth. Nothing happened. There was no sexual assault, no rape, no nothing. I told them the truth.

"If you tell the truth," my mother always says, "you'll be all right. You'll be safe."

I have told the truth. Nothing can happen to me. I know that.

I don't tell my mother or anybody else in my family. Instead, I do what so many seventeen-year-old kids would do. I tell my friend James, who lives next door to my father. He's older than I am, and he's had some experience with the cops. I tell him everything. I tell him about going down to the police station and the two cops who interrogated me.

"This dude and this woman cop," I say, "they were talking about a rape. There was no rape. There was no nothing."

"They were fishing," James says. "They don't have anything."

"They knew about us, though. They knew we went to that college, to that party. How did they find us?"

It dawns on me then.

Dimitri's wallet.

They must have found his wallet.

"Look, man," James says, "they were just trying to get information out of you."

"Yeah," I say. "That's what it was. Had to be."

Then he echoes my mother.

"As long as you told them the truth, you don't have anything to worry about."

Three days later, when I get home from work, I go next door to talk to James again. Suddenly we hear cars roaring up the street, then doors opening and slamming. I look out the window, and I see six police cars parked in a semicircle outside my father's house.

"There's police all over the place," I say.

I start for the door.

"Don't go over there, man," James says, his voice even, grave. "Do not go over there."

"I didn't *do* anything," I say. "I need to *explain*—"

I feel my teeth grinding as I speak.

"They don't know you're here," James says. "You need to wait until they leave. Then go turn yourself in, with a lawyer."

"A lawyer—"

"Listen to me."

I don't listen. I feel so adamant, so angry, so violated.

"I'm going over there right now," I say. "I'm going to straighten this out."

I bolt out the door. The police see me and come toward me.

"We have a warrant for your arrest," an officer says.

I start to explain that they've made a mistake, that I'm innocent.

The police swarm me.

They handcuff me.

I start to scream, but the words stay caught in my throat. The world starts to whirl. My legs buckle. I look up from the ground and see my neighbors gawking at me. "What did he do?" they ask each other and the cops.

Nobody asks, "Why are you taking him in? What is he accused of?" They assume I'm guilty of—something.

Then I think of my mother, and a tremor of shame slices through me.

A hand clamps onto my head, presses down, and stuffs me into the backseat of a police car. I crane my neck to look back at my father's house, where I have lived, off and on, for the past two years. The car starts to pull away, and I see more and more faces I know, neighbors, friends, gawkers, watching me ride away in a police car.

What did he do?

This can't be happening, I think. This isn't happening. This is a movie. I'm watching myself in a movie. Then, incredibly, I think about the chores I have to do, the errands I need to run, the books I just bought for my first semester at college. I have so much to do. I have to get back. I have to go home.

Mom.

I should've called you. I did something stupid. I made a mistake. I went to a party. I need to tell you what happened. I need help.

I look back at my father's house, and I imagine him there. He stands outside his front door. He waves frantically, helplessly. I keep looking at him as he gets smaller and smaller, and then I can't see him anymore.

The police march me into a cell at a holding facility.

"You'll be transferred to Cook County Jail, processed, then extradited to Wisconsin," an officer tells me.

I hear these words and they stick, as information entering my head always does, but these words don't seem real. I can't commit to them. They are words meant for someone else. I want to spit them out, send them back, but then I hear the clang of metal bars closing in on me. I turn in the tight, closet-sized space and see a concrete slab, a mattress as thin as a wafer, no pillow, no sheets, no blanket. I pace, then sit on the concrete slab. I drop into a fetal position. I want to sleep, but I know when I wake up, I will still be here. Knowing that fills me with panic. I bolt upright and get to my feet, and I start to pace again.

"Hey."

An officer stands outside the cell.

Heavyset, white, his face round and red.

"We're transferring you to County," he says. Then he smiles, his grin dark, judgmental. "Why y'all go up there to Wisconsin and rape that little white girl? They don't play in Wisconsin. They gonna hang you in Wisconsin."

"I didn't do that," I say. "I didn't do anything. She's lying. She's making it up."

I rush to the bars, grip them with both my hands.

"Look at me. I'm seventeen years old. I've never been in trouble in my life. I've never been in jail. I don't have a record. You're not going to find my name in your system, because I've never done *anything*."

I feel the heat rising. I fear it will burn a hole through my throat.

"Sir, listen to me. Please. Do you think that for the first time I'd ever get in trouble, I'd drive almost two hours out of state, to Wisconsin, to rape a white girl? You think that's what I'd pick to do?"

The officer pauses, studies me. He speaks softer now, his tone gentler. "I'm just saying, man, they don't play up there. You better get yourself a good lawyer."

Later, the police drive me to Cook County Jail.

"For your intake," a police officer says.

The word "intake" flitters away. I focus only on "Cook County Jail."

If you're a Black male and live in Chicago, you've heard all about Cook County Jail. You know its reputation, and you've heard the stories.

Cook County Jail—a monolith sprawling over nearly one hundred acres—is the largest jail in the United States, housing ten thousand inmates, double its capacity, 75 percent of whom are Black. What happens at Cook County stays at Cook County, but the rumors have spread throughout the South Side—guards brutally beating inmates, random, middle-of-the-night, vicious strip searches, stabbings and fistfights, filthy conditions, rats biting prisoners while they sleep.

These images dance through my mind, visuals I try to blink away as the police lead me inside, to Unit 11, a maximum-security unit for people facing murder and rape charges. I walk in, handcuffed, barely moving, my head lowered, downcast, trying to avoid eye contact, re-lying on my peripheral vision to see my way, my mind flailing to grasp this reality—that I am actually *here*, in this place, this cold, dirty-walled cellblock, or pod, crammed shoulder to shoulder with humanity. Fifty men glaring at me in a space fit for twelve, sizing me up, all of them older, hardened, some of them already sentenced to life in prison. They pelt the air with questions.

Who are you?

What did you do?

How old are you? Shouldn't you be in juvie?

I answer with silent questions of my own.

Why has this happened?

Where am I?

Where is God?

Who am I?

They herd us toward a detention cell. A bullpen. As we walk, a guy in his twenties, nervous, fidgety, whispers to me, "Your first time in here?"

I nod. I can't seem to find my voice.

"Me, too. Man, they got me for driving with a suspended license. I'm in for a traffic ticket. You believe that?"

He ducks his head, looks quickly left, then right, as if searching for an escape route. "I shouldn't be in here," he says.

"Hold up," a guard shouts.

We all stop.

"Line up against the wall," the guard says.

We have very little room to maneuver, but I do my best to squeeze in toward the wall.

"You know the drill," the guard says.

"What drill?" the guy who spoke to me asks, standing two people away.

"Everybody get naked," the guard shouts.

I keep my eyes front as I hear grunting, belts being unbuckled, clothes being removed, shoes pulled off. Slowly, flushing with embarrassment, I undo my belt, step out of my shoes.

"Kick your clothes away," the guard says, then shouts, "*You!*"

I look to my right and see everyone standing naked, except for the guy who spoke to me. He wears his undershorts.

The guard screams, "I said, get naked!"

He picks up someone's work boot and guns it at the guy. The boot smashes the guy in the head. His head jerks back, hits the wall.

The guard screams, "Didn't I say get naked?"

I hear the guy whimpering, see him getting to his feet, fumbling to remove his undershorts. I look straight ahead, don't move an inch. We stand here in a line, naked, vulnerable. I feel dehumanized. Then the guard tells us to lift our genitals as ten or so officers advance to inspect us. The lead guard tells us to turn around, bend over, and cough, and the guards shove rubber fingers inside us.

"Clean, no weapons," someone says, a voice muffled in a chorus of coughs. The guard tells us to turn back around and pick up our official Cook County Jail uniforms.

"Don't put your clothes on yet," the guard shouts. "Go this way."

Holding our balled-up clothes to our chests, we walk zombielike into another room. We stand clustered together, as motionless as we can. A new emotion passes through the room—dread, and for me the added terror of not knowing.

"Oh, no," someone says, as a man in a blue smock comes into the room. Not a guard, I think, and then the same guy whispers urgently to the room, "The dick doctor."

"Looking for STDs," someone says to the guy who'd been hit by the boot. "Infections."

I don't like how this sounds. I want someone to fill me in, but the dick doctor approaches me first. He holds a Q-tip.

I'm not sure what he's about to do, but as a reflex I bite my lip a second before he sticks the Q-tip into my penis.

I gasp and tears come, and then he withdraws the Q-tip, which hurts worse. An electric shock of pain pulses through me.

I don't remember how I arrive at the next phase of the intake, but I am in a room with several showers and I wander under one. A trickle of ice water squirts down my back. I shout and whip around, and someone trains a hose on me, dousing me with disinfectant. I back up beneath the shower, the frigid drip biting into my skin.

Six hours later, I get dressed in my Cook County Jail uniform, and two guards escort me down a hallway, past a rumbling soundtrack of jail bars clanging, shouts, screams, hoots, and guffaws of voices from countless invisible men. I feel out of my body, as if I were not really here. It's as if I were watching a black-and-white documentary of this scared, clueless kid walking inside some dreamlike prison camp. Or worse. I'm not comparing myself to my ancestors, but I capture a snapshot of them in my mind, imagining for one small second, what it must have felt like in the bowels of a slave ship.

A guard hands me a cup, a small plastic toothbrush, a travel-sized tube of toothpaste, and a tiny bar of soap, then closes me in a cell with another man, an older, heavyset Latino who speaks no English. I sit down on the slab that is my bed. My heart feels as if it were rocking in my chest. I've read about people having panic attacks, and I wonder if that's what's happening to me. I exhale, close my eyes, bend over, and try to catch my breath. Breathe, I tell myself. Jarrett, breathe.

Staring at the floor of my cell, I realize I've lost track of time. I lift my head and look over at my cellmate, the older Latino man. We make eye contact. He nods. I nod back. I wonder who he is and why he's in here. I'm sure he wonders the same of me. I take another deep breath, attempting to calm myself, and I close my eyes. A moment later, I hear a noise, paper crinkling. I open my eyes, and the Latino man is standing next to me. He holds a sandwich in a paper wrapper— bologna, lettuce, tomato. My mouth waters. I'm famished. I haven't eaten since—I can't remember when. My cellmate pulls the sandwich apart and offers me half. I look at him, fight back the tears that fill my eyes. I take the half sandwich he offers and I say, "Gracias."

"De nada," he says.

Every hour a fight breaks out. Rival gangs go at it. Guys brutalize each other in the TV room, slashing each other with hidden shivs, throwing chairs, slamming heads onto the floor. Bloody ambushes are carried out in the shower. The bank of pay phones becomes a battlefield. Prisoners rush the phones to make a call. Other prisoners attack, fight them off, fists fly, pounding heads, breaking noses, fingers turning into claws, ripping faces, gouging eyes. For these first two days, I stay as far away as I can, leaving my cell only when a guard forces me to.

I count a number of people locked up in here who are dope fiends or certifiable, or both. People shriek at each other, at themselves, at the ceiling, at horrors only they can see. Inmates strip naked and curl into fetal positions on their cots, howling, crying. One guy, coming off a bad drug trip, claws at his forearm, tearing at it, peeling off the skin. At night, in the darkness, sound itself becomes both brutal and horrifyingly beautiful. Inmates shout, swear, sing, rap, attack the bars of their cells with cups, fists, bodies. I feel as if I've gone from high school to hell.

Miraculously, nobody bothers me. I speak to no one, keep to myself. More than once an inmate asks, "How *old* are you?" When I say, "Seventeen," I mostly get looks of surprise. "You're in the wrong place," people say. "You shouldn't be in here. This is no place for a kid." Looking so young, I think, keeps me out of danger.

We shower irregularly. Once or twice a week, I'm told, but I'm not sure that's the exact number. I know I missed the day the guards handed out towels, so even if I got to shower, I wouldn't know how to dry off. Forty-eight hours in here and I feel dirty, light-years away from normal hygiene, the daily rituals we take for granted—showering, washing up, shaving. Those feel like luxuries I have lost, belonging to somebody else in a different world. Taking a long, hot shower anytime I want? I would give anything for that right now.

Mostly, I sit in my cell and wait—in silence, trying to sort out my thoughts. I've stopped praying, stopped asking God *why*. I know I won't get an answer. I feel too confused, my mind having dissolved into a state of shock. On occasion, though, I hear my cellmate, the older Latino man, murmuring Spanish that I believe may be his prayers. If ever there were a time that I should pray, now would be that time. But I can't. I just can't. Other than that question—*Why?*— I have no idea what I would ask God, what my prayer would be.

I know, too, that I should call my mother, but I can't do that either. I tell myself that I don't call because I want to protect her. She's so fragile I fear she'll fall apart when she finds out I'm in here. I honestly believe she could have a nervous breakdown. I want to spare her feelings. I try to convince myself of this. I almost succeed. The real reason I don't call her is because I am filled with shame. What would I say to her? How would I explain this? I can only imagine how disappointed she'll be, how devastated.

I sit in this cell, frozen, immobile as a statue. My spirit feels gutted. This must be what depression feels like, I think. I always thought depression was a mental state. I never knew that it was also physical, a kind of weight crushing through you, laying you out, splintering your will. I can't eat, I don't sleep, I can barely move.

On my third night in Cook County, after lockdown, a sheriff's officer rattles my cell. Lying in his bed, my cellmate awakes, grunts.

"Adams," the officer says.

I lift myself out of my bed.

"Yes?"

"Go call your mother."

He opens the cell, pulls me out, closes the door behind me.

"Your mother and your aunts have been calling here nonstop for three straight days. They think something happened to you. They called the *sheriff*. Get on the phone and talk to them."

He leads me to the phone bank, to the battlefield. But this time of night, I am alone. I look at the phone, then back at the officer. I don't move.

"Call your *mother*," he says, handing me the phone.

My hands shake as I dial my mother. She answers.

"Mom," I say, collapsing onto the concrete floor.

"Wait, wait, *wait*, I'm going to patch in your aunties."

A few seconds pass, and then I hear Sugar, Honey, and my mother, talking over each other until my mother takes the lead.

"Your father called me," she says, breathlessly.

I can hear the tears in her voice.

"Are you all right?"

Her question comes out as a plea.

My lip quivers.

"I'm fine," I say.

"What's going on?" Sugar says. "Why are you in there?"

"I can't—"

I swallow; then I speak in halting sentences.

"I don't have all the facts," I say. "I can't explain everything. I go to court in a few days and I'll know more—"

"Court? For what?"

My mother's voice rises higher than I've ever heard. It sounds like a shriek.

"I'm being charged from a case out of Wisconsin."

I exhale and then I speak rapidly.

"We went to a party there, me, Rovaughn, and Dimitri, and this girl up there, this white girl, you know, she accused me—us—of rape."

My mother starts to cry.

"Rape," she says. "No."

"Mom, I didn't, I would never—"

Her voice stiffens, goes eerily calm. "When were you in Wisconsin?"

"It was back in the summer. We drove up there."

"I never knew."

"I know. I never told you."

Sitting on the floor, I hug my knees to my chest. Tears start filling my eyes, but I cough, fight them off. I will not cry on the phone with my mother. That will break her. That will destroy her.

"A lawyer," someone says, Sugar or Honey, I can't tell.

"We can't afford a lawyer," my mother says, her voice thin, distant.

"I know," I say. "But I didn't do anything. I swear. This whole thing is made up. This girl is lying. If I tell the truth, I'll be all right."

"I never knew you went out like that, without telling me," my mother says. "I'm—surprised."

She means "hurt." I hear the ache in her voice.

"To Wisconsin," she says, a finality to her tone.

"Jarrett," one of my aunts says, "God has a reason."

I pull myself off the floor.

"I know," I say, "but for the life of me, I can't think of one single reason right now."

"You pray and you keep praying."

"I will."

"You have to."

Then nobody speaks. For a few seconds, I hear only their breathing, their sighs, their tears.

"I don't know if I can come down there. I don't know if I can see you there," my mother says.

She sounds so brittle, so sad.

"You shouldn't come down here," I say. "I'll call you. I'll keep you informed. I promise."

"I don't want to see you like that," my mother says, and she begins to sob.

"I know, I know." I look at the officer, who has turned away from me, giving me this time, all the time I need.

"I have to go," I say. "The officer says I have to get off the phone."

"Call us," Honey says.

"You keep praying," Sugar says.

"I will," I say, but I honestly don't know if I will, or can.

Then I hear a muffled sound I know. My mother's crying has gone into another gear. I can picture her sobbing, swaying. I can't stand seeing her like this, even in my imagination.

"Mom," I say. "I love you. Don't worry. We'll straighten this out."

But she's gone.

I say goodbye to my aunts and hang up the phone. The officer leads me back to my cell. He opens the door, and I make my way to my bed, feeling disoriented. My arms seem to be swimming through the air as if I were trying to poke my way through a dark maze. I get to my bed and sit down, my breath coming quicker, almost in spasms.

"Amigo."

My cellmate, the older Latino guy, stands a few feet away. He looks at me, his face lined and bruised from age and hardship, but his eyes are clear, kind. He takes a few more steps and hands me a towel.

"Toalla," he says.

I hesitate, then take it from him. I sigh. I can now shower. I can dry myself off. For that one tiny moment—the first in days—I feel human.

My shoulders rock as the sobs come and the tears gush down my cheeks.

Two days later, at six in the morning, an officer rattles my cell door.

"Wake up," he says, "you have court."

I force down breakfast, a plate of lumpy gray gruel dotted with something yellow and runny that may or may not be scrambled eggs. An hour later, two officers bring me out of my cell and chain me to a line of inmates. Tethered leg to leg, the thirty of us shuffle through a series of tunnels, my legs aching, the metal links banging into me as we walk in an underground chain gang. We arrive at a small detention cell that fits twelve people tightly. Officers unclasp the chains, and the thirty of us shove and elbow our way into this dimly lit, claustrophobic cage. An officer tells us that we will wait here until somebody calls our name. Then we'll leave this bullpen, go into another bullpen, and then into the courtroom. If we need to use the bathroom, we tell an officer who will escort us to one of two commodes that sit out in the open, outside the bullpen, right in front of the group. I pray that I don't have to use the bathroom.

In the bullpen, I struggle to find room enough to exhale. I'm shorter than nearly all the other inmates, but the hours I played basketball in the alley with my brother and his friends have taught me how to maneuver for position against bigger guys. I stand shoulder to chest, back to back, and butt to butt, claiming my space in this scrum, waves of hot, vile breath blowing on my neck and face, mixed with the smells of urine, vomit, liquor, sweat, body odor, and recent defecation. I pinch my nose with my fingers, try to shut out the smell. I can't. I squirm and I start to feel the walls closing in, terror rising inside me. I play mind games to distract myself, add numbers in my head, make a mental list of the chores I still have to do, daydream, fantasize that I'm far away from here, on a desert island, in a school classroom, anywhere but here. Mostly, I stand in position, in the present, and wait. And wait. And wait. Ninety-nine percent of the time you spend in jail, you wait. I wait all morning, trapped here, crushed here, waiting all told for four hours, and then finally, mercifully, somebody calls my name.

An officer takes me out of this bullpen and into another bullpen, this one feeling like heaven because only ten inmates wait here. Another half hour passes, and a young man in a rumpled suit appears, trains his eyes over all of us in the bullpen, and calls my name. I get the sense that he has gone through this procedure hundreds of times. A lawyer, I think. "Clearing the bullpen," someone behind me says. An officer repeats my name. I follow him and the lawyer to a small room with a table. The officer closes the door. I sit down across from the young man in the suit. He stares at me with grainy eyes. It looks as if he's been up all night.

"I'm from the public defender's office," he says. "You're here for an extradition hearing for some charges out of the state of Wisconsin. Do you want to waive your rights to a hearing and just be extradited?"

"I don't—I mean, I don't know what that means. I don't know what to do."

The public defender sighs massively, impatiently. He looks so tired. He finally speaks in a monotone. He sounds robotic.

"Do it this way," he says. "Waive your rights. It speeds things up. You want to move this along, right?"

"Yes," I say.

"Are you guilty of this rape charge?"

"No, sir. I did not rape anybody. This girl *lied.*"

"So, okay, here's what you do. You're going to go inside the court-room in about an hour. You're going to tell the judge that you want to be extradited as soon as possible because you know you're innocent and you want to face the charges. You want to get this over with, right?"

He has no idea. I want this to be over so bad I can literally taste it. I want to get back to my life. I want to go home.

"Tell the judge what I said. You got that?"

"Yes, sir."

That's what I do.

An hour later, I tell the judge that I'm innocent and I want to be extradited. He shows no expression.

Three weeks later, an officer leads me through the underground tunnels below Cook County Jail and brings me outside to a window-less minivan that's idling and belching brown exhaust fumes in a parking lot. I climb inside the van, and the guard chains me to a metal bench alongside two other prisoners. After a few minutes, officers bring two more prisoners into the van and chain them to the bench across from me—Rovaughn and Dimitri. We greet each other like long-lost friends, which in a way we are.

Seeing them, I feel relief and a sense of normalcy. Calm descends over me. We talk, the three of us. We joke about how ridiculous we look in our prison uniforms and we laugh—we actually *laugh.* We honestly don't comprehend the gravity of our circumstance. Despite being chained to a metal bench in a van, I believe that once we get to Wisconsin, this unfortunate episode, this misunderstanding, will be resolved. I believe that in this windowless minivan we're taking a ride to freedom. I believe we're riding to justice.

5.

The First Trial

A week later.

I sit next to my court-appointed attorney, an older white man with stringy uncombed brown hair, a beer belly, wearing an ill-fitting sport jacket and pants that don't match. My mother drilled into me a belief that appearance matters, that you get only one chance to make a first impression. I don't believe my attorney got that message. But I don't have a choice. I'm seventeen years old, wearing a Jefferson County Jail jumpsuit, about to hear a court official read the charges against me and a judge decide how much bond he will post. Even though we've just met and hardly spoken, I have to trust my attorney. I have to believe in him. I have to believe in the system, a system I don't understand. My attorney doesn't know me, has no sense of who I am, no idea of the egregious and false charges against me. The court has chosen him from a list and given him my name randomly.

I look to the side of the courtroom and see Dimitri, Rovaughn, and their attorneys. This time, the three of us share no feeling of joyfulness, or reunion, or camaraderie that we had a week ago in the van. I sense only gravity, even a sense of doom. I don't know what to expect from this arraignment, but I feel nervous. I look back at my attorney. He doesn't look at me. He picks at a stain on his tie with his fingernail.

I have spent the last week in a cell at Jefferson County Jail. After we pulled up outside the building in the windowless van, officers unchained Rovaughn, Dimitri, and me and took us in three separate directions. I arrived at a small holding cell, officers instructed me to strip naked, and once again I went through the intake process. As I stepped out of my shoes and began to undo my pants, I realized that before I got arrested, I'd never gotten naked in front of so many men in my life.

This time, though, after I put on my official Jefferson County Jail jumpsuit, I received my own soap, toothbrush, toothpaste, and towel, and a guard led me to my own cell on the second floor of a clean, bright pod. Over the next week, I see a stark difference between Jefferson County Jail and Cook County Jail. In here, there's a lack of violence, improved food, even a lack of fear while making a phone call. Compared with Cook County, Jefferson County is summer camp. The difference makes me hopeful. I have not yet prayed, but I feel myself working up to it. I want to believe that God could be sending me a sign, that maybe He is about to let me off with a warning.

Now, in court, I look over at the prosecutor, a white man, forties, close-cropped military haircut, well dressed, perfect posture. He reminds me of a motorcycle cop or someone recently out of the service, no-nonsense, prepared, tough. I look over at my attorney, and I start to wonder if in addition to being distracted by the stain on his tie, he's completely overmatched by his opponent, the prosecutor. *Our* opponent. I shiver suddenly from worry, and then I hear, "All rise," and everyone in the courtroom stands as Judge William Hue walks in. Judge Hue commands the courtroom. An older white man with gray, nearly white hair, Judge Hue looks distinguished and serious, carrying himself like a college professor.

He takes his seat, the rest of us follow, and then Judge Hue asks someone to read the charges against Rovaughn, Dimitri, and me. I don't hear whether a man or a woman speaks. I only hear the charges in a neutral, disassociated voice.

"Five counts of first-degree sexual assault."

Five counts *each*.

According to sentencing guidelines, if convicted, I could receive 25 years in prison per count, a total of 125 years.

Then I hear, "One count of false imprisonment."

I've never heard of that. What does that mean? I turn to my lawyer for an explanation. He looks straight ahead, avoids my eyes.

My mouth goes dry.

My breath comes fast.

Six charges against us.

And then I see her, walking into the courtroom.

The young woman.

I had no idea she would be here. I had no idea I would ever see her again, that I would have to face her, that I would be forced to look at her. Of course, it makes sense, but I never wanted to be in the same room with her again, any room, especially a courtroom. I feel blind-sided.

The young woman takes her seat on the stand. I refuse to look at her. But in my peripheral vision, I see her raise her right hand, and she promises to tell the truth, the whole truth, nothing but the truth, so help her God, and then I look directly at her. I stare at her. She won't look at me.

The lawyers begin asking her questions. They ask her to describe the events of that night. "The night she was raped," the prosecutor says. The night the three of us raped her.

"I was at a party," she says. "I was, you know, partying, and then I went back to my dorm room, and all of a sudden I turned around and there were these three Black guys behind me—"

"Did you know them?"

"No. I had never met them. I'd never seen them before."

"Then what happened?"

"They forced their way into my room. They put on a CD. Rap music. Very vulgar rap music."

I look at my attorney. Anyone could read my expression—do you believe this crap?

"What happened next?" the prosecutor asks.

"They turned the lights off," she says, and stops, her voice halting. "They, uh, began to sexually assault me. That's really it. That's what happened."

I shout inside my head, "What about your roommate?"

The questions keep coming, swirling in circles inside my head, a scramble of letters, of words.

You didn't mention when your roommate walked in, barged right in in the middle of this nonexistent sexual assault? What about her calling you a slut? What about you running after her?

Then a lawyer from our side takes over the questioning.

"Did any of these men threaten you with violence?"

"No."

"Did any of them *use* violence?"

"No."

"Did any of them threaten you at all?"

"No."

"Did you see a weapon, any kind of weapon?"

"No."

"Then why did you have sex with them?"

"I was scared."

"Did you tell them to leave?"

"No."

"Why not?"

"I don't know. I couldn't think. I was *scared.*"

"Look."

Judge Hue shuffles some papers in front of him and leans forward in his chair.

"I'm not the presiding judge in this case," he says. "I am going to bind this over for trial and let the trial judge figure this out. But I'll tell you right now, based on the testimony I've heard, I don't see any false imprisonment here, and this isn't first- or second- or even third-degree sexual assault. If you ask me, and again, I'm not the presiding judge on this case, you guys have some problems with this. There are holes in this case. You have to fill in the holes."

I glance at the prosecutor, and I can sense an energy shift. *You have to fill in the holes.* I imagine him chewing on those words, swallowing them, digesting them. I can feel it. On our side of the table, the lawyers exhale in triumph, especially after the judge admonishes the prosecution. But I don't feel triumph. I look back at the prosecutor's determined eyes. He knows he's lost this round, but he hasn't lost the fight.

Someone on our side argues for no bond, but Judge Hue decides on twenty thousand dollars, an amount I know my family cannot afford.

The arraignment ends and I return to my cell. The door clangs shut behind me, the familiarity of that sound startling me. I don't want that sound to be familiar. Human beings adjust to our conditions. We adapt to the most horrific, abusive, inhumane circumstances. We are built to survive.

At Jefferson County Jail, gossip crackles through our small pod. Inmates coming and going to status hearings held every thirty days as we await our various trials distribute news and information like candy. I hear that Rovaughn's family has put up their house, posted his bail, and hired an experienced trial attorney. A week or so after that, another inmate brings me news of Dimitri.

"Your man posted bail," he says.

"What? No way. His family doesn't have twenty thousand dollars."

"They contested the amount; court reduced it to fifteen."

"Still—"

"I don't know, man. Somehow, they scraped together the funds. He's out on bail."

"They must've sold everything," I say.

I could never raise that kind of cash, I think. We just don't have it. I have no choice. I will have to stay in here until the trial.

I call my mother and explain what's going on. She confirms that Rovaughn and Dimitri have bonded out. "I'm hopeful," I tell her. "The judge seemed to be on our side." I neglect to explain that Judge

Hue will not be the presiding judge for my trial. I tell her that I won't be in jail here in Wisconsin much longer. I'll be home soon. Maybe I'll be home for my birthday or Thanksgiving.

I'm wrong.

The judge sets our trial date for March of the following year, six months away. Six more months that I sit and wait, locked away in a jail cell.

My lawyer and I confer exactly twice in the months leading up to the trial. We meet first, shortly after the arraignment hearing, "to strategize," his term, in a glass-enclosed booth outside the pod at Jefferson County Jail. He wants to go over the police report with me and zero in on my side of the story.

"You mean the truth," I say.

I don't wait for him to respond.

"Look, man," I say, "we put ourselves in a bad spot. She invited us up to her room. We all had a *consensual* encounter. But for the most part we were all sitting around, laughing, being stupid, and then her roommate walked in. They had an argument, the roommate left, and the young woman went after her."

The lawyer frowns. "She walked out, went after the roommate?"

"Yes."

He flips through the police report, scans pages, traces paragraphs with his finger.

"This says you guys grabbed her and held her back."

I start to lose it.

"Are you listening to me or reading the report? Listen to me. *Listen* to me, man. We never held her back, grabbed her, forced her to do anything. *We never* did that."

He looks at me, confused.

"So, she walked out of the room?"

"Yeah."

"Why would she come back into the room?"

"Well, she wouldn't, if she was being *raped*."

He frowns again, tries to get comfortable in his plastic chair, riffles through the report again.

"Then what happened?"

"We all went downstairs to this smoking area. Her, too. We hung out there for a while and eventually we left."

"That was it?"

"That's all."

I don't know what else I should say. I don't know that I should create a timeline, that the order of events is crucial. I don't mention that an eyewitness exists, Shawn Demain, the guy I played a video game with in his room and who spent the entire time with us in the smoking area after we came down from the girl's room and who saw us talking with her. She didn't seem threatened or scared then. I don't suggest questioning him. I don't suggest hiring an investigator.

I don't do any of this, because I simply don't know I should. I'm still a kid, eighteen years old, having had zero experience with crime, or defending myself at a trial. I have put everything in my lawyer's hands. I put my life in his hands. I don't know any better.

"All right," he says. "I'll keep you posted."

He packs up his papers, stuffs them into his briefcase.

That was *strategizing*? I think.

Our time has ended. A guard approaches, tells me I have to return to my cell. I nod and start to leave, and then I turn back to my attorney.

"I have confidence in you," I say. "I have to. You're all I've got."

I see my attorney once more before jury selection—the second time in eight months—and that's by accident. I see him walking the opposite way about to enter the corridor, and I yell at him across the pod. I hadn't seen or spoken to him in months. I want to know what's going on. Where are we? Had he forgotten about me? He makes his way to me and we speak, briefly. He assures me that my case has not fallen through the cracks. He's on top of it. He's ready for trial.

To me, he seems overloaded. Despite his bulk, he appears always to be on the run, shuttling from client to client. After these two conversations, I get the feeling that he wants to close my case as quickly as possible because he gets paid only once a case has been resolved. He doesn't bill by the hour, nor has my family given him a hefty retainer for his services. For him, as for all court-appointed attorneys, it's a numbers game, trying to clear as many cases as he can. He has an impossible job. As an inmate says to me, "He's trying to empty an ocean with a spoon."

The day before the trial, my attorney goes through jury selection. I change out of my orange jumpsuit, put on the one suit I own, and go with him to a conference room at the back of the courtroom. He explains that the three defense attorneys and the prosecutor will choose twelve jurors and two alternates from a pool of about forty people. I will sit next to him and observe the process of selection known as voir dire, which means literally "to speak the truth."

The jurors come in one at a time. The attorneys and the prosecutor refer to the questionnaire each juror has filled out and then ask a series of basic questions to determine if the person can be fair and unbiased such as "What do you do for a living?" and "Do you have any police officers in your family?" and then one question that jolts me: "Has anybody in your family or any of your friends been accused of sexual assault?"

Nothing they ask appears to be a trick question, but I know that the defense and the prosecutor each have been given three opportunities to strike a witness, meaning they can each disqualify three people for no reason.

After a parade of six or seven white people, an Asian woman comes in. The prosecutor strikes her. Several white people follow her, and then a man of Indian descent comes in. The prosecutor strikes him. After a couple of hours, the prosecutor and the defense attorneys settle on a jury. It dawns on me then that all of them, including the alternates, are white.

The prosecutor thanks the last juror candidate and murmurs to my attorney, "I'll see you in court tomorrow." He leaves, closing the door behind him. I wait for a second, and then I say, "Why are there no Black people on the jury?"

My attorney looks at me uncomfortably. He yanks up his pants. His hefty belly protrudes through his shirt.

"What do you mean?" he says.

"I thought I was supposed to have a jury of my peers. How can this be a fair trial without any Black people?"

"Well," his says, after another hitch of his pants, "according to the Constitution, we do have a minority on there."

"Who? I didn't see a minority. He struck every person of color."

"There are a couple of women."

I'm stunned.

"A couple of *women*?"

"Yes, women are considered a minority."

I start to raise my voice.

"How is that a minority? That's gender. That's not race."

He finishes tucking in his pants.

"You should've been there when they wrote the Constitution," he says.

As I walk into the courtroom, I see my mother, Aunt Sugar, and her husband, Bill, who is my godfather, and Aunt Honey. The moment my mother sees me, her shoulders tremble, and she begins to cry. I shake my head. I have caused her so much pain. I turn my head away because the last thing I want to do is fall apart before I even get to my seat. I whistle out a slow breath to calm myself. Then I pray for the first time in months. I pray to God to end this for her, now.

I sit next to my lawyer, in a row with Dimitri, Rovaughn, and their representation. Rovaughn's lawyer, Boyle, reminds me a little of Judge Hue—an older white man dressed in a sharp, neatly pressed suit. He moves and speaks with purpose, as if he knows the answer to every question he asks. It's clear he didn't come off a panel list of attorneys provided by the court. No wonder Rovaughn's family had to mortgage their house to afford him.

Dimitri's attorney bears some similarity to my attorney. He looks bored. Sitting in the courtroom, counting the hours until the trial ends, banking his time so he can get paid. Tapping his legal pad nervously with the eraser end of a pencil. *Let's move this along*, I read in his eyes. I see no motivation to win. Forget motivation. Does he have the skill to win?

Yet we're all accused. We're in this together. We can ride Boyle's coattails. At least that's what I hope we can do. Because at this point, even though I know we're innocent, as I look at the all-white jury and at the steely-eyed prosecutor, who either avoids making eye contact with us or looks at us dismissively, a sense of crippling fear presses in on me. I've seen too much, heard too many stories—on the street, in jail, from my friends and family. If you're Black, being innocent doesn't matter. At all. Unless you're willing to mortgage your life savings.

The judge, a white woman in her creased black robe, enters, and everyone in the courtroom stands. I take a quick scan of the faces. Other than the folks related to me and my friends, I see no other person of color. Not one other Black face. The lawyers are white. The judge is white. The jurors are white. Our accuser is white.

The trial begins. The prosecutor presents his opening statement to the jury. Since the arraignment hearing months ago when Judge Hue admonished him to fill in the holes in the case he'd presented, he's clearly spent some time closing up those holes. The prosecutor has come up with a clear, direct tactic. A theme. He presents that theme to the jury.

Fear.

That's the message the prosecutor delivers. That's what he hammers at relentlessly. Fear.

"You will see that this girl was scared," he says, pacing in front of the jury. "She didn't know these three Black men from Chicago. They came up behind her and they scared her. She was *scared.*"

You would be, too, he implies without saying those words aloud. He doesn't have to. I see the jurors following him with their eyes. I can almost identify their own fear. Their fear of us. Of me.

"You're also going to hear that her roommate walked into the room," the prosecutor says. "But her roommate didn't know what was going on. It was dark. She couldn't see what was happening. The girl didn't say anything to her roommate—because she was *scared.* The roommate left. Then you'll hear that the girl walked out of her room, went down the hall, and then came back toward her room to leave the building, to get away from these men. But one of these men was in the stairwell and forced her back into her room, where the three men gang-raped her."

I look at my lawyer. He's staring off into space. I cannot believe that he is not appalled by the ridiculous, false narrative that the prosecutor spins in front of the jury.

I grab a pen and write on the legal pad in front of me.

"Lies," I write. "Never happened. *Lies!*"

I slide the pad in front of my lawyer.

He looks down. He sniffs, then turns away to watch the prosecutor.

The jury can't be buying this crap, I think.

I look over at them.

They're riveted.

I don't really focus on the rest of the prosecutor's opening statement. I know that he continues to hammer home his theme of fear through practically every sentence. I stop counting how many times he says, "She was scared." Finally, he finishes his opening and takes his seat. Boyle, Rovaughn's attorney, smooths his tie and begins his opening remarks to the jury. He's respectful, passionate, convincing.

He challenges the prosecutor's version of the events. He suggests that the story the jury hears will at times not make a lot of sense. He cautions them that when what they hear doesn't make sense, they have the responsibility to question it, to cast doubt. Sometimes, he suggests, people come to conclusions based on hearsay, based on prejudice, based on race. He concludes that you, as a jury, cannot come to a conclusion based on race. You have to listen to the facts, to what happened.

He sits down and the judge calls on Dimitri's attorney to make his opening statement next. The attorney passes.

The judge calls on my attorney to make his opening statement.

My attorney stands, hitches up his pants, and says, "Well, when it comes to my client, Jarrett Adams, you'll see the same thing that Attorney Boyle said."

He sits back down, heavily. That's it.

I want to grab the legal pad in front of me and tear it in half.

The prosecution calls their first witness, Sergeant Scout, the officer who interrogated me in Chicago. She brushes past me, sits on the witness chair, swears to tell the truth. The prosecutor asks her to give an account of the events after the night in question.

"We got a call," she says.

The prosecutor interrupts. "Who did you get the call from?"

Sergeant Scout gives a name I hadn't heard before.

"The accuser's friend," she clarifies. "She told me that this young lady had been raped on campus and that she was at the hospital having a sexual assault exam. So, I went over there."

"And what do you do there?"

"I interviewed her. I started to put things together, you know, about what happened."

"What did she say?"

"She said she was raped by three Black men she never met before. Two or three Black men. She wasn't sure."

I look at the jury. I want to shout, "Remember what Boyle said. She would know that detail. This doesn't make sense!"

"Then what did you do after you interviewed the young lady?"

"I went back to campus and started talking to people who were at the party that night."

"What did you find out?"

"It was three Black men who came onto campus. They were cologne salesmen from Chicago."

"They weren't students?"

"No."

"Did you talk to the girl's roommate?"

"Yes."

"What did she say?"

"She said she came into the room and saw her sitting on the bed with a Black man but she couldn't see what was going on. It was too dark."

"No further questions."

Boyle walks over to Sergeant Scout. He looks at her and pauses. He seems to study her for a long time before he speaks.

"Did you have a chance to talk to these young men?" he asks.

Sergeant Scout shifts in her chair.

"I talked to two of them."

"Mr. Hill. Rovaughn. And Mr. Adams. Jarrett."

"Right."

"Let's start with Mr. Hill. What did he say?"

"He said he was there and that all three of them had a consensual sexual encounter with the girl."

"And Mr. Adams? What did he say?"

"He said he was there, but he denied having any involvement in anything."

I nearly spring out of my chair. She's lying. I told her the same thing. I told her the truth.

I start to scribble that on the legal pad, but I stop because I catch a glimpse of a sneer forming on Boyle's face. He knows Sergeant Scout is lying. He steps in closer to her. He's crowding her now like a boxer pressing his opponent into the ropes. I can feel her discomfort from here. Then Boyle speaks, softly, intimately, as if they were the only two people in the courtroom.

"That's what Mr. Adams said?"

"Yes."

"Okay, well, I'm assuming you recorded your conversation with Mr. Adams, right?"

"No. We didn't record it."

"No? They had recording technology available, right?"

Sergeant Scout squirms in her chair. She looks as if she'd rather be anywhere but sitting on a witness stand being questioned by Boyle.

"Well, I mean, yeah, they did," she says.

"I don't understand why you didn't record it," Boyle says. "How do you explain this? If someone says she was raped and the person she accuses says it was a consensual encounter, how do you make a charge of rape? How do you do that? It wasn't because they were Black, was it?"

"I object. Relevance," the prosecutor says.

"Sustained," the judge says.

Boyle backs off, but I can see that his point has landed with the jury.

"No further questions," Boyle says, and turns the questioning over to my attorney.

My lawyer basically does nothing. He has Sergeant Scout repeat answers to three questions she's already answered.

Sergeant Scout leaves, and then the young woman takes the stand.

The prosecutor leads her through her version of the events of that night, of how she had never met us before, how we all came up behind her, pulled her into her room, put on a vulgar rap CD, cut out the lights, started to dance with her and grope her, and forced her to have sex with us. She describes how her roommate came in at that point and that one of us grabbed her by the arm. She recalls her roommate saying to her, "What are you doing on my bed with them?" She describes storming out of the room after her roommate to explain, then coming back into her room, escorted by me. She says I made her get on the floor and have sex with me and my friends, and when it was over, we fled the building. She says she called her friend and asked him if she could come over to his place because she had been sexually assaulted.

Her story is ludicrous.

According to her, we began the rape, stopped, allowed her to walk out of the room, have an argument with her roommate down the hall, come back, and *resume.*

I look over at the jury, thinking, you can't be buying this, can you?

Boyle begins his cross-examination.

He speaks kindly.

"At this time, how long had you been on campus?"

"About a week," the young woman says.

"Just for clarification, you're in the room and you said that they were groping you, but nothing was going on sexually at that point. But then your roommate comes in and says you were having sex on her bed?"

"No, no, I was, you know, just on the bed at that point."

"You were scared for your life, though, right?"

"Yes. I was scared for my life."

"So, you didn't want to be in that room, right?"

"No, I didn't want to be in there."

"But when your roommate walked in, she thought you were having sex."

"Yeah."

"But you were scared for your life."

"I was. Yeah."

"Then the roommate left and you went after her, right?"

"Yeah."

"Did anyone grab you and tell you not to go? Did anyone stop you?"

"No."

"Okay. So, you're knocking on this door, down the hall, and you say, 'Help me. Help. I'm being raped.' Is that what you said?"

"No."

"But you were so scared. You were scared for your life. Why didn't you say that?"

"I mean, I don't know. I just—I didn't know what to do."

Boyle stops, looks at his notes, at the transcript. "So, you're knocking on the door, and you're saying, 'It's not what it seems.' What did you mean by that?"

"Oh, well, you know, I didn't want her to think that I was having sex on her bed with those guys. That's not what I meant. I didn't want her, you know, I was just so scared. I really didn't know what I was saying. I was so scared."

"Okay," Boyle says. "There's an exit right by your room, down at the end of the hall. Why didn't you go down that way?"

"I don't know. I was just—scared."

"Right," Boyle says. "As you walked down the hall, you passed a room that had 'RA' on it. Do you know what that means?"

"Yes. Resident assistant."

"Did you know the resident assistant was in that room?"

"I didn't know."

"Why didn't you knock on that door if you were scared?"

"I, uh, I'm not sure. I don't know."

Boyle nods, looks at his notes, then peeks up at her. Her face has gone pale.

"A phone call came into your room. Do you remember that?"

"Yes. I remember."

"Who was on the phone?"

"My friend. She was calling me from my hometown."

"When you were on the phone with your friend, was this before or after your roommate came in?"

"I don't recall."

"Okay. All right. But you were in the room, right?"

"Yes."

"Obviously. You took the phone call. And these guys were there, right?"

"Yes."

"And you didn't want these guys in there, right?"

"No. I didn't want them in there."

"Did you tell the person on the phone—your friend—that you needed help?"

"No."

"You didn't say, 'Help me'? Nothing like that?"

"No. I didn't. I, uh, no, I didn't."

"Why didn't you?"

"I was scared. You know, they were right there, and I was talking on the phone."

"In fact, there were other calls that came into your room, too."

"Yeah. There were other calls—"

"So, you're in there this entire time, there are phone calls coming in, all while this gang rape is going on."

The girl says nothing.

"Right?" Boyle says.

"I don't. I can't. I was so scared."

At this point, Boyle spins away from the witness stand and turns in my direction. For the briefest instant, I lock eyes with him, and maybe I imagine this, but I see a glint, the briefest spark of light. And I read something else in his expression. An emotion. I see power, even dominance, and I know we've won. I have been watching a lawyer at the top of his game executing a precise and lethal cross-examination. A master tactician. It's as if I've been watching a lumberjack chopping down a tree, swinging his ax into the trunk, taking one cut, and another, and another. Slowly, methodically attacking the base of that tree until, finally, the tree begins to topple and fall.

I don't understand, nor could I possibly predict, the profound impact that Boyle's questioning will ultimately have on me. But in that instant, as he and I exchange that fleeting look, I feel that power. I glance at the jury, and I see them all looking over at us, at Rovaughn, at Dimitri, and at me. They look concerned, and while I don't dare allow myself to interpret their collective look with any certainty, I believe they're looking at us with sympathy.

Boyle's convinced them, I think. They believe him. They believe us. We've won.

———

Two more people take the witness stand, the young woman's room-mate and the friend who called her on the phone. The roommate appears fidgety and speaks in a monotone. I believe that she has been coached. Her answers come out vague, minimal, and without expression, as if she were struggling to remember her lines in a play. Even though she previously indicated that she saw her roommate engaged in a sexual act when she walked into the room, she now says that it was too dark to see anything specific. She seems to be following the timeline the prosecutor proposed. Boyle doesn't challenge the room-mate. I get the sense that he doesn't feel he has to.

Next, the friend who called on the phone testifies that the girl never said or even suggested that anything might be wrong during the phone call. She says only that the girl didn't really want to talk.

"I thought maybe she was tired from too much partying," the friend says.

The prosecution rests, and one by one our lawyers rest. The judge then invites the prosecution to present its closing argument. The prosecutor huddles at his table with the accuser and another lawyer he's working with. After intense whispering and nodding, he asks the judge if he may approach the bench. The judge agrees, and the prosecutor, and Boyle, moving quickly to catch up, walk up to the judge.

"Your Honor," the prosecutor says, "after consideration, we want to amend the charges from first degree down to third and fourth degree."

"You're certain about this?"

"Yes, Your Honor. We're not going to go forward with first-degree charges."

Boyle's face burns. He stammers, then goes into a full-on rage.

"No, Your Honor, *no*. I vehemently oppose that. The prosecution knows that this girl has changed her testimony from what she said on the police report. They know they have not met their burden. Your Honor, I'm asking you to declare a mistrial with prejudice right now and let these young men go home and live their lives, because, Your Honor, respectfully, this whole thing is a complete and total *sham*."

"Mr. Boyle, please calm down."

Boyle dips his head, nods, appears to count to three, composes himself.

"Yes, Your Honor. I apologize."

The judge pauses, looks at the prosecutor, at Boyle, at the jury, at us.

"Let me consider this," she says.

She calls for a short recess. She practically catapults out of her chair and speed-walks into her chambers, her robe flapping behind her like a cape. After ten minutes, she returns, again walking briskly. She sits down, leans forward, folds her hands, and speaks somberly.

"I've heard the prosecution and I've heard the defense. Given the prosecution's decision not to go ahead with the first-degree charges, I am declaring a mistrial—without prejudice."

A massive exhalation of air—a monumental sigh—whooshes through the courtroom.

My mother, my aunts, and my godfather stand and hug each other, and my mother swipes at tears trickling down her face.

Mistrial without prejudice.

I need to know what this means. I start to ask my lawyer, but he's standing, hands on hips, hovering over Dimitri's lawyer, the two of them listening intently to Boyle. Boyle gestures wildly, and then turns toward the three of us.

"We need to meet. I have to explain what just happened," he says.

Boyle and the two other attorneys arrange for an empty conference room. Escorted by a security guard, we enter the room and close the door.

I speak first. "What does mistrial without prejudice mean? We won, right? It's over."

"Yes and no," Boyle says. "Yes, we won. No, it's not over."

He pauses, gathers his thoughts, and then continues.

"The judge declared a mistrial without prejudice. She didn't declare a mistrial *with* prejudice, which is what we wanted."

I narrow my eyes. "What's the difference?"

"With prejudice means the charges are dismissed permanently. Without prejudice means you can be tried again."

"But, oh, okay," I say, stammering, "why would the judge do that? It was clear. She was lying. I could see that the jury was sympathetic—"

Boyle holds up his hand. "I know. But the judge has to play by the rules. She agreed to the prosecutor's request and she amended the charges, but if they bring charges again, and they could, that has to be done in front of a new jury."

"So, we could be right back here," I say.

"They may drop it, but I wouldn't count on it," Boyle says.

"I thought—"

I stop. My throat feels dry. I swallow.

"I thought we won," I say. "I was ready to celebrate."

I look at Boyle and then stare at my attorney. He seems to have momentarily lost the ability to speak.

"I want to go home," I say.

But I don't. I return to Jefferson County Jail. My bond remains in place. Unless my family can scrape together the fifteen thousand dollars, I will stay locked up in here as long as I still have potential charges pending. My attorney suggests that I appeal the amount of the bond. Thirty days later, he motions the court to reduce it. Given the mistrial, the court agrees to lower the bond to ten thousand dollars. My mother draws from her retirement account, my aunties chip in, and together they raise the money for the bond. I'm released from jail.

I move back to Chicago, into my mother's house. I spend my first day in the city wandering the neighborhood in a daze, getting my bearings. My life feels like a fever dream. Slowly, as the hours of the day tick away, I settle into a kind of comfort zone and I begin to breathe. I'm home, I think. This past year has been a crazy, nightmarish mistake. We won. The judge saw that the young woman lied. I know we didn't get that "with prejudice" designation and that the prosecution can come back at us with new charges, but I can't think about that. I have to move on with my life.

I pick up where I left off. I buy a car, a boxy burgundy Chevy Caprice with a rusted-out body but a good engine. A guy in the neighborhood sells it to me for thirteen hundred dollars, a fair price. I give him a five-hundred-dollar down payment and set up an affordable payment plan, but I can't actually drive the car yet, because I can't afford the insurance. To make sure I don't succumb to temptation, my mother keeps the keys.

"You are not driving that car," she says. "I'll give you the keys when you get insurance."

"Can't I take the car on a short trip, to the store, or over to Sugar's—?"

"Absolutely *not.* You get stopped by the police and you don't have insurance? Jarrett, never give them a reason. You know that."

I look into taking classes at the local community college. I get a job at Midway Airport as a baggage handler. I start seeing friends and begin dating, no one seriously, but I quickly create something of a social life. I pay off the car, purchase the insurance, and collect the keys from my mother.

One of the first days I have the car, I pick up a friend. As we head toward Ninety-Fifth Street and King Drive, a cop pulls us over—the way I see it, for driving while Black. My friend unrolls his window, and the cop smells marijuana. Anybody would. My friend smokes pot like Snoop Dogg. The cop notices a nub of a joint behind my friend's ear. He accuses us of driving under the influence, although neither of us has been smoking. He issues two citations: one for driving without a seat belt, the other for marijuana.

"Welcome home," my friend says after the cop drives away.

"There is no escape from this crap," I say.

"You got that right," my friend says, pulling out a joint he has tucked behind his other ear. I stare at him.

"What?" my friend says. "I'm stressed."

A month passes. Then another. I try not to think about that night in Wisconsin, the party, the trial. I especially try to blot out the horrific memories of Cook County Jail. I want to simply live my life. Pick up the pieces. I just want to *be.*

One day, as I walk down the street near my mother's house, a car pulls over. I look at the driver and Dimitri smiles back.

"Dimitri," I say. "Hey, man, what's going on?"

I look around, concerned that someone might be spying on us. As part of our bonding-out agreement, the court instructed the three of us not to have any contact.

"Nothing much," he says. "Staying out of trouble."

"Me, too. I got a job at Midway, wrestling people's luggage. Looking to start up with classes at community college."

"I've been working, too. I made manager at UPS."

"The big time. Now you don't have to wear those shorts."

We laugh.

"Hey, man," Dimitri says. "That night? I swear—I will never put myself in a situation like that again."

"Ever," I say. "Just want all this to be concluded. Final."

Dimitri nods, drums his fingers on the steering wheel. "Okay, well, we already broke the bonding-out agreement."

"I know," I say. "But, hey, it was great seeing you."

"Same here, Jarrett. Keep your nose clean."

"You as well," I say. "You as well."

A month later, a letter arrives at my mother's house.

A summons to appear in court.

My hands shaking, I speed-read the letter once; then I read it slowly. I fold the letter carefully and force myself to sit at the kitchen table.

I have been charged with five counts of second-degree sexual assault.

In case I don't understand the letter, my attorney calls next, detailing the charges and telling me when I have to appear in court.

A matter of days.

Aunt Honey, Aunt Sugar, and Bill drop everything and arrange to drive me to Wisconsin. My mother informs my father. I overhear her on the phone, her voice cold, distant, edgy. Because I had been staying at his house the night of the party, she blames him for what happened to me in Wisconsin. She blames him for allowing me to sneak out, for letting me go to parties. By now, I've confessed to going to parties everywhere, all summer, across state lines and in the most dangerous neighborhoods in the city.

"You can't blame him," I say. "You can't blame anyone except me."

And then I say to myself, "That's not true." I do blame myself, but I also blame everyone. Every*thing*.

The young woman. The State of Wisconsin. The prosecutor. The police. Society. The criminal justice system. The media. Our country's untold history. Bigotry.

And being Black.

That's not my fault. I'm proud of being Black.

But it's to blame.

My aunts, my godfather, and I prepare to make the five-hour drive to Jefferson County, Wisconsin, for my second trial. As we get set to leave, my mother pulls me to the side, away from everybody, and asks me to sit with her.

"Jarrett," she says, "I can't do it."

"What do you mean?"

"I can't go back to Wisconsin. I can't watch you go through that again. And *I* can't go through that again. It's too much for me."

I take her hands.

"Mom, we won before; we'll win again."

She grips my hands so hard I feel she may tear my flesh.

"You don't get it, do you?"

Her eyes glisten. I can practically feel her heartbreak.

"You seem to think that this is about *truth*. You think this is about what's right? It's not. It is not about what's right. You're *Black*."

"I know, Mom—"

"You don't."

She shakes her head so slowly she looks as if she were moving in stop-action.

"You ever hear of Emmett Till? They teach about him in school?"

I search my brain.

"No."

"I didn't think so. Emmett Till was a fourteen-year-old Black boy from Chicago. He went to visit his family in Mississippi. He was in a grocery store and someone said he whistled at a married white woman. White *girl*. She was twenty-one years old. You know what her husband and some other white men did to this fourteen-year-old Black boy? They shot him. They mutilated him. Then they lynched him. The courts in Mississippi brought his killers to trial. You know what they did to those killers? *Nothing*."

I want to object. I want to say, "I'm not Emmett Till. That was then."

But I hold my tongue.

I look at my mother, see the tears drowning her cheeks, and I get up, put my arms around her, and hold her, using every ounce of my strength not to cry. I hold her, rock her gently. I know now what she's thinking: I can't go back to Wisconsin and watch my own version of a lynching. Your lynching.

My son's lynching.

6.

Let Them Hang Themselves

The drive from Chicago to Jefferson County Courthouse in Wisconsin takes five hours but feels more like ten. I sit in the backseat, tucked into a corner, my face pressed to the window, watching the barren wintry countryside of Wisconsin float by—endless icy fields vanishing into snow-packed rolling hills. As we drive, nobody speaks. The silence underscores what I feel—an impending sense of dread.

Before we left, my aunts spoke to Dimitri's parents. They've all booked a motel not far from the courthouse, which is where we will stay during the trial. We'll check in there after Dimitri and I meet our attorneys at the courthouse. I can almost hear my lawyer's lame catchphrase—"to strategize." He wouldn't know a strategy if it slapped him in the face.

Inside the courthouse, I see Dimitri, his parents, and his attorney. I look around, eager to see Rovaughn and Boyle, the only lawyer on our side who had a clue at the previous trial. He had more than a clue. He had a strategy.

I greet Dimitri and his folks. "Where's Rovaughn at?" I ask.

Nobody answers.

"Let's find a quiet place to talk," my attorney says. "Let's go out in the hall."

"Here's the thing," my attorney says when we've found an empty part of the hallway. "We had an option—"

My attorney starts there, then slams his mouth shut.

"What option?" I ask.

"Rovaughn's lawyer—Boyle—filed a motion in appellate court saying that he shouldn't be tried because of double jeopardy."

I recognize the term from watching *Law & Order*. I'm not sure what it means.

"What is that?" I say.

"Since the first judge called a mistrial, Boyle is saying that Rovaughn can't be tried for the same thing again. He's appealing this whole thing."

I catch Dimitri's eyes. He nods. We're on the same page.

"That's a good argument," I say. "Why don't we join in on that double jeopardy?"

"Well, here's our thinking," my lawyer says. "You guys are good kids. You're out there, living your life, keeping your noses clean. We want to get this over with as soon as possible, right? No telling how long this double-jeopardy appeal will take. And he might lose. Then he's right back at the beginning. Square one. We're getting a jump."

"I know, but—"

He interrupts me. "This is a slam-dunk case," he says. "We know the girl is lying. It's obvious. The evidence supports you. The judge at the arraignment saw that, the judge in the first trial saw that."

"So, we're *not* going to join up with Rovaughn and his attorney in this double-jeopardy motion?" I say.

"No," my lawyer says.

"Can we talk about it?"

"It's too late to join his motion," my attorney says.

"That ship has sailed," Dimitri's attorney adds.

My stomach flips. I feel a shadow of dread passing over me.

"What *is* our strategy?" I say, quietly.

My lawyer shifts his weight. Tucks in his pants. Absently rolls his palms over his belly.

"We think"—he looks at Dimitri's lawyer for approval—"we're sitting pretty here. Her story is so full of inconsistencies that the best strategy is to go with a no-defense strategy."

"Let them hang themselves," Dimitri's attorney says.

I hear my mother's words. *Emmett Till. Lynching.* In one second, I go from feeling dread to feeling petrified.

I start to argue with the attorneys. I want to tell them that their no-defense strategy sounds like a terrible idea, but before I say anything, an officer of the court descends on us, calls my name, and sweeps me away to a remote corner of the hallway.

"We're revoking your bond," he says.

"Why? For what?"

"You received a traffic ticket."

I search my memory.

"I don't remember—"

"Seat-belt violation," he says.

"*That?* That was total bull—."

"That's on you. You broke the agreement of the bond. We're going to have to take you into custody."

"Are you serious? The night before the trial? I'm going to *jail*?"

"You can bond back out."

I look at my aunties, who have now formed a semicircle around me. They've overheard the officer. They look stunned, devastated, impotent.

"How much would this bond be?" Sugar asks.

"Ten."

"Ten *thousand*?"

Someone loses it. One of my aunts, Bill, I don't remember. They see red. They raise their voices. They don't curse, but they yell. Someone shouts, "That's just another way for you to suck money out of people who don't have it."

"I'm sorry," the officer says to me. "You'll have to stay in County until you bond out. Or—"

"Or?"

"Until the trial is concluded. Until you get sent back home or you get sent, you know, away."

The second trial begins. I take my seat next to my attorney and shiver.

"It's so cold in here," I say, but nobody hears me.

The cold brings a feeling of icy inevitably. A litany of clichés rushes through my head: the fix is in, it's rigged, and most of all the all-white jury will *inevitably* convict a Black boy if a white girl claims he raped her—every single time. Clichés are born from the inevitable.

You think this is about the truth?

I hear my mother's voice. I see her face—anguished, shattered, the ridges in her forehead gouged into gullies, her eyes dark, hopeless.

I'm on *trial*.

The realization slaps me.

This is it. Determining my innocence or guilt.

Looking around, I'm struck by how much a courtroom resembles a church. Attendees sit in pews. Witnesses, accusers, and the accused swear on a Bible. The judge wears a robe. Everyone in attendance follows rules of decorum—speaking to each other reverently, in whispers, bearing witness. In so many ways, a trial feels like a religious service.

Then why do I have such an unholy feeling?

The second trial progresses at two contradictory speeds—breakneck and achingly slow. I sit through another jury selection and watch the defense attorneys and the prosecutor select another all-white jury— seven men, five women. A new prosecutor has been brought in for this trial, a heavy hitter, a man with major political aspirations. Stylish and well-groomed, a loud and proud proponent of law and order, he will eventually go on to be a judge. I can imagine his campaign slogan on TV screens throughout the state: *Vote for me. I close cases. I put criminals behind bars.*

Before the jury comes in, the prosecutor approaches the judge, a white woman, impatient, hard looking, severe. She reminds me of a high school vice-principal.

"Your Honor," the prosecutor says. "We want to go with second degree."

The judge flattens her hands on her table and says, "Well, did you get over some of the obstacles the previous prosecutor faced? Did you fill in those holes?"

"I did, yes, Your Honor."

"I want you to be sure. I'm not going to stop this trial."

"You won't have to."

"You don't want third or fourth degree?"

"No." He bends back a finger, ticking off the charge, showing his certainty. "We have *force,* Your Honor. From her testimony, she says she was trying to leave, she was trying to go out the hallway exit, but someone escorted her back into her room. That's force right there."

"Okay. Second degree. That's what you're going with in front of the jury?"

"Yes, Your Honor."

"You're ready to go?"

"More than ready, Your Honor."

The bailiff leads in the jury. They barely glance in our direction. Their attention seems fixated on the floor as they take their spots in the jury box. Our lawyers make their opening arguments. Their words sail by me. I cannot escape the feeling of doom that continues to roll in my stomach. Then the prosecutor digs in. He calls the same people to the stand that we heard from six months ago—Sergeant Scout, the young woman, the roommate, the friend who called on the phone. Their accounts of the night, while similar to what we heard in the first trial, have been embellished, dramatized with color and lurid detail. The young woman describes one or two of the Black men coming out of the stairwell, bringing her into the room, holding her down, one grabbing an arm, another, a leg.

None of this happened. All lies. But my attorney doesn't object, doesn't challenge her, doesn't point out that she has changed her testimony from the first trial.

I feel desperate. I grab the legal pad and scribble a series of questions. I slide the pad in front of my lawyer, jab my finger at what I've written. He ignores me, looks away, appearing to concentrate deeply on the young woman's testimony. Still, he says nothing. *Oh, right,* I remember. That's his strategy—the do-nothing defense. Do nothing, say nothing.

How can this possibly work?

Maybe I'm wrong. Maybe the jury sees through all the lies, all the inconsistencies. I look over at them, try to make eye contact with—anyone. Nobody looks at me. I am invisible.

Next the roommate testifies, and then the friend who called on the phone comes to the stand. Because my attorney has ignored all the questions I've written, I tap him on the shoulder and whisper urgently, "Ask her about the phone call. Get details."

He does cross-examine her; he does ask her about that call.

But that's it. He asks two or three more irrelevant questions before sitting down.

I can't watch this. I close my eyes and slump in my chair, dejected.

My lawyer is inept. Unprepared. Useless. Incompetent.

I thought you had to be intelligent to go to law school.

The young woman's lies pulse red, blinking as if in a neon sign—"I'm not sure if it was two or three. They each held me down. I was scared. I was so scared."

The dread drips over me, clings to me. I lower my head and I shiver.

It's so cold in here.

So very, very cold.

———

The trial spills into day two. On the second day, my father comes to the courtroom, coiled, angry, restless, and possibly drunk. He sits by himself, muttering, enraged at the way the trial proceeds and angry, I believe, at himself for not being able to afford a good attorney. I can hear his voice behind me, offering a running commentary of outrage—"This is *crap*"—first speaking low, then abruptly raising his voice so everyone in the courtroom can hear. Once or twice, court officers remind him to keep his voice down or he will be expelled from the courtroom.

The prosecution rests, and the judge asks our attorneys if they want to present a closing argument. My attorney rises at my side and says, "No, Your Honor, we're going to rest." I look at him—his rumpled suit, stained tie, one shoe with the laces undone, and I want to scream. Then I want to laugh. This can't be real. This cannot be happening.

The judge calls on the prosecutor to present his closing argument. He approaches the jury. He seems cool and confident, bordering on cocky. Why wouldn't he feel that way? He must feel like a politician whose opponent has dropped out of the race. He's running unopposed.

The prosecutor begins his closing. He doesn't even attempt to hide an undertone of racism.

"She was so *scared*," he says to the jury, enunciating the final word. "These three Black cologne salesmen from Chicago had no business being at that party. They drove all the way up here to *stalk their prey*. And they found their prey that night. This girl. This innocent college student. They found their prey, went up to her room, and sealed the deal."

Stalked their prey.

The jury looks at me.

I know that I'm not going home that day.

The jury deliberates for less than two hours.

As they file back into the jury box, I try to read their faces, but no one, not one person, will even look in my direction.

The judge calls on the foreman.

"Foreman, has the jury reached a decision?"

The foreman stands and says, "Yes, Your Honor."

I lean forward. I stare at one juror, then another and another, try-ing to make eye contact with someone, trying to connect, one human being to another, but no one will look at me.

The foreman reads the verdict.

"Guilty on all five charges."

The room detonates.

My aunts and godfather and Dimitri's family howl and scream and sob.

Dimitri collapses, goes facedown onto the table in front of him, his shoulders convulsing as he cries uncontrollably.

My father shouts over all of this, his voice roaring, "This is BULL—," hollering the phrase over and over, leaping up, waving his arms, thrusting his fists into the air until two security officers corral him, tell him to leave, threatening to throw him in jail. He barrels toward the door, punching the air, screaming over his shoulder.

I can't speak. I sit frozen in my seat. I refuse to cry. Then a ball of rage rises within me. I whirl around to my aunts and my godfather, who are all crying, and I say, "I'm sorry. I'm very sorry. I want to apologize for bringing this on you, on my mother, on our family, but I will not apologize for a rape I didn't commit. I will not do that. I will not apologize for that."

The judge, glaring at me, slams her gavel, dismisses the jury, orders the bailiff to clear the court. Then she ducks into her chambers, dis-appearing through a small, secret door behind her.

Through the din, I hear someone say—my lawyer perhaps—that Dimitri and I will be sentenced in a few weeks. I hear myself apologize again to my family, and I feel my chest heaving, fighting back tears of my own, and then I find myself sitting across from my lawyer in a small windowless room with peeling paint.

"I want to talk to you about sentencing," my lawyer says.

"Guilty on all five counts," I mumble.

The words—the realization—ice me.

"We can talk about the notice of appeal, but for now she's preparing to drop the sentence on you and let me tell you, you really don't want to piss off this judge."

"Piss her off?"

"Look, things got a little raw there at the end, you know, when you spoke to your aunts."

He pauses to clear his throat. His face reddens.

"I seriously think you should apologize to the judge. Show some remorse. Could go a long way."

"Show some remorse? For *what*? I didn't do anything."

"She's a tough judge. No-nonsense. If you apologized—"

"I did apologize—to my family. I hurt them. I didn't hurt anybody else."

"I'm just saying."

I sigh so deeply it sounds like a shout.

Finally, after an endless and painful silence, I say, "What do you think the sentence will be?"

My lawyer adjusts his sitting position. His size overwhelms the chair.

"I think you get twenty years."

"Twenty years?"

I gag on the words.

"You might get her to go for less, if you apologize."

I ignore that.

"What about Rovaughn and his appeal?" I say.

"Waiting for the decision to come down."

I lean my elbows on the table and stare at him. "Why didn't you join in on his motion?"

He attempts to shrug.

"Easy to second-guess that now. Monday-morning quarterback. We'd be having a different conversation if we'd won, right? Well, anyway, if he wins the appeal, you guys will be released right away."

I stare into him. He can't look at me directly.

"Are you sure?"

"Oh, yeah, that was always our safety net."

I don't believe him. I don't believe a word that comes out of his mouth.

"That doesn't make any sense," I say.

Another brutal, uncomfortable pause. And then my lawyer peers at his watch, grunts, and pushes himself away from the table.

"Well, I have to run," he says. "It's Miller Time for me."

I don't sleep the night before my sentencing. I allow time to pass, counting the minutes in my head. Nothing seems real. None of it. In the morning, I move in slow motion. I pick at my food, push it around with my fork. I can't eat. I can barely walk into the courtroom. I feel numb. Then, as the minutes tick by, I feel—dead. I have not been shot, or stabbed, or hit by a car. But as I sit in the courtroom, waiting to hear a judge assign how much time I will be confined inside a box with bars for a crime that never happened, I feel as if I were not me, that I no longer exist.

People mill about the courtroom as we wait for the judge to walk in. I see my family huddled in a corner. Gloom lines their faces. My father, silent, dejected, listens in on my aunts' and stepfather's conversation, an observer, a bystander. He seems broken. He seems ashamed, not of me, but of himself.

A man suddenly appears in front of me. I recognize him as one of the girl's relatives, maybe an uncle.

"I want to tell you something," he says to someone near him. "My wife and I are givers. We try to open our hearts to the less fortunate. We adopted two colored kids. They're in middle school now."

He lowers his voice.

"I'm afraid to leave them at home with my wife," he says.

He walks away.

My mouth opens, closes.

Colored kids.

What year is this?

Where are we?

A murmur ripples through the courtroom, the bailiff instructs everyone to return to their seats, and then he says, "All rise," as the judge enters through her tiny, magic door. She takes her seat and peers at me and Dimitri.

She asks us to stand.

"I've carefully considered your sentences. Initially, I decided to give you each twenty years."

She looks at Dimitri.

"I'm giving you twenty years."

She looks at me.

"Mr. Adams, I overheard a conversation you had after the verdict. When given the opportunity to express remorse, you showed none. Since you feel no remorse, I'm giving you an additional eight years."

Her gavel slams like a gunshot.

Twenty-eight years.

I drop my head into my hands.

Officers surround me.

Handcuffs, rings of ice, bite my wrists.

Behind me, I hear my aunts and my godfather wailing. I hear my father screaming. I don't turn, but in my mind's eye I see my mother's face, stricken. Her pain fills my field of vision. I fear suddenly that I will pass out. Then somebody grabs my elbow, lifts me to my feet. My entire body trembles. I'm so cold. I want to cry. I refuse. I will not *cry*. Someone nudges me. I take a step. My eyesight blurs. Filmy faces swim before me—the young woman, Dimitri, Rovaughn, Sugar, Honey, my godfather, my mother—

Another nudge. Another step—

Twenty-eight *years*.

Colored kids.

It's Miller Time.

I'm so cold.

Metal doors clang, jolting me, the sound burrowing into my brain.

Everything goes dark.

7.

Pawns

We walk, Dimitri and I, handcuffed, chained, and silent, through a passageway below the courthouse to Jefferson County Jail. We have been convicted. We have been sentenced. We will soon learn where we will be sent to prison.

Guards lead us inside County and inmates greet us. They know we have gone to court. They, too, have ridden in the van from County to courthouse and back again, waiting now to be transferred to their next stop, their institution. Prison purgatory. They question us like gossipy neighbors thirsting for news.

"What happened? What'd y'all get?"

"I got twenty. He got twenty-eight."

"What? No way. Y'all said you didn't have no record before."

"We don't."

A solemn silence, then a disembodied voice—

"Wisconsin prisons, man."

Less than human.

That's how they make you feel.

How they made folks feel on slave ships, in cotton fields, in camps. We have no names. Guards identify us by our numbers. We are faceless. Ciphers.

"You!" a woman guard shrieks at me during booking. "Move it. You're not moving fast enough."

I sneak a look at her, confused, frightened. She glares back at me.

"Is that reckless eyeballing? Are you reckless *eyeballing* me?"

"No, ma'am."

"I will write you *up*."

In Wisconsin prisons, you can be charged with reckless eyeballing. That is a real infraction. You can go down for that. You can go down for anything.

I call my mother. She hears my voice and begins sobbing.

"You knew, Mom," I say. "You knew what would happen. You were right."

"I couldn't go up there," she says. "I couldn't watch that happen to you."

"Mom," I say, her crying ripping at my heart.

I want so desperately to calm her, but I don't know how. All I know is that I did this to her.

She catches her breath and whispers through her tears, "I don't know what to do now. What do I do?"

"I—I don't know. I'm sorry."

My mother exhales. She pauses. She speaks now and her words explode.

"When they get their hands on our boys, we never get them back."

Her voice splinters and she starts wailing. I remove the phone from my ear and press it against my forehead. I need to say something— anything—to calm her. But I have no words. My mind has gone empty. Finally, I speak into the phone. I manage only to say, "Mom."

We stumble through our goodbyes, her crying never letting up.

I hang up and come to a terrible, inevitable conclusion. In order to survive, I will submerge myself into life in prison, and I won't call her again. I cannot face the heartbreak of what I have done to her.

I call my aunt Sugar. She says she knows I will be spending my days soul-searching, looking for answers, especially to the question, why?

"You have to pray," she says. "Keep praying. Just keep praying."

"Pray for *what*?" I ask.

She gasps in shock.

"You don't think He's watching?" I say. "If you say He's all knowing, the way He is in all those songs you sing in church, then tell Him to stop this."

My breathing comes so hard I start to pant. I feel ashamed for yelling at my aunt.

"He knows what's going on. If you tell me He's got everything under control, then I don't need to pray. I'm just gonna wait on Him. Wait on Him to get me out of this."

"It doesn't work like that," Sugar says quietly.

"Auntie, I'm sorry. I can't think about praying right now. I just can't."

"I understand," she says. "I get that."

"If God is so powerful, then why would He allow racism to exist? We're at the end of the twentieth century, and we still have inequality and unfairness and injustice. Why is that? I can't figure that out, Auntie."

"I know, baby. I know you're hurting."

"I'm eighteen years old, Auntie. *Why am I in here?*"

"We're not gonna let you go. *He's* not gonna let you go. You hear me?"

I don't say anything. Her words sail by me, then evaporate. Words, I think. Meaningless words.

"Think about going to church," she says. "I can't tell you why. Just think about going. That's all."

"Can't make no promises," I say, my voice breaking.

———

Three weeks in Jefferson County Jail. Waiting.

Dimitri and I may be the only Black guys in County. I befriend a ridiculously tall white biker dude named Knapp who's fighting a murder charge. Knapp has been locked up in County longer than I have. He's a fixture here. He's so tall they can't find pants that fit him. The ones he wears come up to the middle of his calf. I find nothing remotely funny in here—except the first time I see Knapp walking across the pod, wearing his ridiculously short pants. We make eye contact, shake our heads simultaneously, laugh. That breaks the ice. We begin to talk.

"You from Milwaukee?"

"No, man. Chicago."

"You're quiet."

"Don't have much to say. What *is* there to say?"

"I hear you."

Knapp and I bond over books. When the book cart comes to our cells, Knapp and I pounce on it. When we both read the same book, we talk about it. One time, he grabs a volume and reads the title aloud.

"You know *The Art of War* by Sun Tzu?"

"Oh, I want to read that. Maybe pick up some pointers. I'll read it after you."

"You take it," he says. "You read faster."

"You sure?"

"Yeah. I got the next one."

We share books, talk books, and Knapp, who knows Wisconsin, schools me on the prisons.

"You'll go to Dodge next. You'll do intake for a week, ten days; then they decide which prison to send you to after that. They might keep Dimitri there. Medium maximum. You could go to Waupun, that's maximum, hard time. Or maybe Green Bay, supermax. You don't want Green Bay. Out of control. Violent. Have to watch yourself. They call it Gladiator School."

He pauses, then yanks up his ridiculous pants.

"The thing is, they're all bad."

I nod, feel my throat dry up.

"How come Dimitri got twenty years and you got twenty-eight?"

"Lady judge said I wasn't remorseful. She tacked on eight more years because I didn't apologize for a rape that never happened."

"Make sure you appeal that. I don't think what she did is even legal."

"Yeah, I should appeal that," I say. "I will."

"Definitely," he says.

"Which institution did you say is the worst?"

Knapp snorts. "All of them."

Knapp's time estimate turns out to be low. Dimitri and I both get sent to Dodge, but I sit in a cell by myself for almost six weeks before my transfer. I lose myself in prison life. I read, book after book, and I play basketball every day, every chance I get. I lose myself in games. Basketball becomes my therapy. I'm small, but I'm among the best on the court. "Court," I think. That word. Maybe the most important word in my life. I do a lot better on this court than I did in the other court. I play point guard, hit mid-range jumpers, dish off to teammates, set them up for layups. Once again, I go from the last guy picked to the guy everyone wants on their team. Someone gives me a nickname—Li'l Chi-Town. The name sticks.

Usually my team wins, so we hold court. Prison ball reminds me of street ball, only rougher. Still, I don't alter my game. I dare to drive the lane, bulldoze my way into the paint, take my chances, mix it up with big guys inside. I get clobbered on the back of the head, punched, scratched, gouged, mauled, even tackled. I rarely say anything. Unless you're bleeding, nobody calls a foul.

On the prison court, I see violence beyond what I ever saw in my old alley games. One day, a player on our team goes up for a layup, and the guy guarding him punches him in the mouth, knocking out a tooth. Our guy mops up the blood with his shirtsleeve, picks his tooth up off the ground, stuffs it in his pocket, and keeps playing. I don't remember him calling a foul.

On occasion, I witness something unexpected during these daily prison games. I witness humanity. Sportsmanship. Even kindness. A guy gets mugged going up for a shot, and someone on the other team helps him up. With a point of a finger, some players acknowledge a good shot, a defensive stop, an accurate pass.

Every day, for these forty-five minutes, I see men escaping. With a basketball in their hands, they transport themselves outside the prison walls to another place in their minds, in their memories. They are seeking normalcy. At these moments, I don't see inmates playing hoop on the rec yard. I see men playing a game. Basketball players. They are not prisoners. They are free.

"I stand silently before the Lord, waiting for Him to rescue me. For salvation comes from Him alone."

I pause in the doorway of the chapel and listen to a group of inmates reading from the Bible. Malik, a thin, older Black man with a long gray beard that covers his neck and flows onto his chest, leads the service.

"Yes, He alone is my Rock, my rescuer, defense, and fortress."

Psalm 62, I recall, as I find myself walking into the chapel and moving toward a chair. I pick up a book lying on the seat and sit down. An inmate points to the page they're on. I nod, find my place, and begin to read aloud with the others.

"Why then should I be tense with fear when troubles come?"

Malik stops and says a few words about the line we've read. I close my eyes and try to lose myself in the words of the psalm and in his smooth, soft baritone.

But instead, I lose myself in the memory of two other voices—Honey's and Sugar's. Every Sunday, when I call my aunts, they ask if I've gone to church. Every Sunday, I admit that I haven't.

"Will you at least think about going?" Honey asks.

"Yes."

"You promise?"

Filled with guilt, knowing that I probably won't be going to church, I don't make that promise. Until last Sunday.

I don't know why, but last Sunday, I said, "I promise."

I go first because I look for any reason to get out of my cell. Then I realize I'm going to church because I feel emotionally and physically safe. The familiarity of the prayers comforts me, especially the psalms. And I go for my mother and for my aunts, for Honey, Sugar, and Peaches.

Now, after only a few minutes, as I sit in the chapel with my eyes closed and my head bent, something unexpected happens. We begin reading Psalm 62 again aloud, in unison, and I start to disappear into the words.

"My protection and success come from God alone. He is my refuge, a Rock where no enemy can reach me. O my people, trust Him all the time. Pour out your longings before Him, for He can help."

He can help, I think.

"God is loving and kind and rewards each one of us according to the work we do for Him."

I read these words aloud, with the group, and then I read them again to myself. For this moment, I feel that I am actually in church. I forget that I am in prison.

A few days later, on the yard, a group gathers on the basketball court. One of the players calls, "Hey, Li'l Chi-Town, you in?"

I wave, start to jog onto the court, and something stops me. An uneasy vibe. I can almost sense danger. I wave back, yell, "I got next," and drift away from the court toward the free weights. I usually lift between games, but I don't see any available barbells. I keep walking toward a guy who has just finished setting up a chessboard. I recognize him—Malik, from church, the guy who leads the services. Hard not to recognize him. With that long gray beard, he looks like a prophet. I heard he's serving a couple of life sentences. I don't know for what. You never ask.

Malik nods at the chessboard.

"You looking to get yourself into some trouble?"

"Nah. I don't know how to play."

"Sit down. I'll show you."

I ease onto the concrete bench across from him.

"Okay, take off your back row," he says.

I hold my hand over the two tallest pieces, both with crowns.

"What are these?"

"The strongest pieces on the board."

I push all the pieces away, leave the row of the smallest pieces in place. To me, they look like gnomes. Or upside-down mushrooms.

"What are these pieces?"

"Pawns," Malik says. "They're like soldiers. But they're deceptive."

"Deceptive?"

"You'll see. Come on. Let's play a game with just those. Pawns only. They move one square at a time."

He shows me. We begin a game with only the pawns. Malik's manner is easy, but his concentration is intense. My hand moves easily, finger to pawn.

"Okay," Malik says, "once a pawn makes it all the way to the other side of the board, it can become whatever you want it to be. Any of the other pieces. You can make this little soldier a king, a queen, a knight, anything you want."

"Pawns are powerful," I say.

Malik looks at me.

"A lot of people don't see that. They disregard the pawns. They overlook them. They don't get that pawns haven't reached their potential yet."

I know Malik is trying to teach me more than chess. He strokes his beard and eyes the inmates playing hoop and lifting.

"Lot of pawns around here," he says. "Lot of pawns in this prison."

Malik shows me where to place the rest of the pieces on the chessboard. He demonstrates how they each move, and then we play a game. I pick it up right away. I love the strategy—thinking three, four moves ahead, imagining contingency plans should my first attack fail. The game ends when Malik surprises me and takes my last remaining pawn.

"Didn't expect that," I say. "Good move."

"A man's character will be displayed in every decision he makes," Malik says.

"Sun Tzu," I say, "*The Art of War.*"

Malik grins. We set up the chessboard and play with all the pieces this time.

I stick with chess the rest of that day, avoiding the basketball court, where, as I sensed, a brutal fight breaks out. The next day, I find Malik.

"Looking for more trouble?" he says.

We set up the board and play a couple of fast games. Malik schools me, but I don't care because I'm hooked. I empty all the cash in my account and buy my own chess set through the canteen. I practice for hours in my cell. At night, I lie awake and envision the chessboard. I work out moves, play games in my head.

When the chessboard dissolves, my usual prison fever dreams return. Images of my mother appear: the shattered look on her face, her uncontrollable sobs. I fight off wave after wave of shame. Why did I put myself in that position? What did I do?

How do you keep yourself from going crazy in this place? I think. You let the daylight seep in, wherever you can find a sliver of light, you embrace that and let it warm you. And you push yourself forward, one step at a time. Compartmentalize—books, basketball, chess, church. Look left, look right, behind you, in front of you, side to side. Think four moves ahead. Stay safe.

The word comes down. I'm being sent to Waupun.

"Watch yourself," Dimitri warns.

"You, too."

"We're gonna appeal this, right?"

"Definitely. We're gonna win, too."

I want to believe that. But I find myself adjusting to life inside.

I still can't bring myself to call my mother, but I write her long letters, expressing how I feel, not holding anything back.

Hello, Mother,

How are you doing? I hope you are in good health when this letter reaches you. I'm attending church services here and taking it one day at a time, but I still have lack of sleep. Just thinking how it really is not fair the way that lady gave me 28 years for speaking the truth. I pray that the Lord removes this anger out of my heart . . . but what was said in that court was a bunch of lies! This is a huge embarrassment to me, you, and the rest of my family. I'd rather be a killer than to be looked at as a sexual predator.

Mom, I love you, and take care. Tell Sugar I'll be writing her next week. Tell Honey I love her also.

I end the letter the way I end all the letters I write her:

Sincerely, White Folk's Property

P.S. I love you, Mom.

My mother and my family are giving me everything they have, every ounce of their love, and all of their support. If they could, they would pay for the kind of attorney who would use every legal means available to prove my innocence. They would do that for me.

But they don't have that kind of money.

8.
Pops

Chained and handcuffed, I come by prison bus to Waupun Correctional Institution, labeled maximum security, a castle-like fortress built in 1851 in a remote part of the state. An officer hustles me off the bus and takes me directly to intake. I walk slowly, my head down, my hands cuffed in front of me. The officer urges me to pick up my pace. I don't. What's my hurry? I've got twenty-eight years.

I slouch down a narrow hallway, passing cells on either side. Medieval and mammoth looking from the outside, Waupun on the inside seems small, out of scale, built for tinier human beings born centuries ago. The prison smells and looks old. It feels as if it has never been updated.

Intake, I discover, will last a week.

And intake, I learn, means segregation.

I spend the week in a minuscule cell, a closet with bars, a bed, a toilet, a slit in the wall that passes for a window. I spend the first days going through the litany of indignities I've become accustomed to—medical exam, cavity search, a visit from the dick doctor. Then I go through a series of meetings with a prison counselor. She creates a file, fills in my religious affiliation and dietary restrictions, completes a psychological evaluation, lists any gang association. By her questions, I gather that she tries to make sure a cell doesn't house two vicious murderers or members from rival gangs. Before I receive my cell assignment and enter into the general prison population, she hands me a file containing all my paperwork, including police and court transcripts and a letter from the appellate attorney who has been assigned to my case. Finally, she informs me that I am required to enroll in a program for sexual predators.

"I'm not going to do that," I say.

"You refuse?"

"Yes."

I look her in the face.

"I don't need that program. I am not a sexual predator."

She clicks her pen several times, shrugs. "Your choice. Your record."

I get placed in the very first cell at the front of the north wing, on the bottom of six tiers, close to the guard who lets people in and out through an automatic door. I walk into the tiny five-by-nine space, holding everything I own against my chest. My roommate, a tatted-up, scowling hulk twice my size, studies me. We don't speak. I climb to the empty top bunk. I know immediately that I can't stay in here twenty-three hours and fifteen minutes a day. I need to get a job. I have to keep myself busy, or I will go insane.

It takes a little time, but I get placed working in the kitchen as a waiter, an ironically fancy title meaning that I stand behind a counter and put milk cartons and juice boxes onto trays. I must be good at this because whoever's in charge promotes me to food server. Three or four times a week, I sling lumpy hash, runny eggs, and unidentifiable globs of gruel onto plates. On mornings when I work breakfast, I get up at five. I don't mind. Having a work pass gets me out of my cell. I soon move even further up the food chain. One day the guy running the kitchen tells me I'm being wasted as a server. He promotes me to *chef.* I think about how I used to help my grandmother cook our meals in the Big House. I'm back in another Big House, the one where you walk in and don't leave for twenty-eight years. I would die of shame if my grandmother ever saw me inside these walls.

Stay safe and stay sane.

My mantra. My life's goal.

I work as a cook four times a week and alternate my rec time playing basketball with the younger guys, most with gang tattoos on their necks and faces, and playing chess with the older guys, most with long beards. I like that look, and because the razors the guards give us couldn't cut paper, I decide to grow a beard of my own. My aunties continue sending letters and copies of Bible verses. One of them buys me a subscription to the *Chicago Sun-Times,* my hometown paper. Each issue arrives a day late, but I don't care. I devour the paper, front to back, linger over the sports, following the Cubs, Bears, and Bulls, the only way I can tell when the seasons change. And I write my mother often. I don't call. I can't.

The prison rotates cellmates. One day, the scowling, tatted-up hulk packs up his stuff and leaves. I sleep alone in the cell for one night, and the following morning my new cellmate painfully lumbers in. He's tall, thick-bodied, and older, at least sixty, a white guy with thinning gray hair and a flabby paunch. He arrives with a companion, a portable oxygen tank. He breathes hard and coughs often. We nod to each other. We don't speak. People call him Pops. Because my previous cellmate left, I'm entitled to the bottom bunk. But I look at Pops, his oxygen tank with its tubes, oxygen mask, and accompanying tray filled with medications, and I don't see how he could make it up to the top bunk.

"I got the top," I say.

"Thanks," he says.

Those five words constitute our entire verbal communication for the first two weeks.

Partly, we don't speak because we rarely see each other. I get up before five for my job in the kitchen. Pops runs the law library. While I'm celled up in the afternoons, he's out. On the yard, during rec time, while I'm playing basketball, Pops, if he's there, sits by himself and reads. At night, we both read on our bunks, or if I'm not reading, I listen on my headphones to the only radio station on my radio that plays rap. I love everything by 2Pac, especially his album *Me Against the World*. I identify with 2Pac—young, Black, disposable, and sent to prison on a rape allegation. Songs like "Me Against the World" and "Dear Mama" rip me up. He could have written them about me. After lights out, I see 2Pac's lyrics before my eyes and I memorize every line. Then I try, desperately, to will myself to sleep. But between my anxiety and anger at being in here and Pops's violent snoring, I seldom manage more than three hours of sleep and never in a row.

One night, around ten, I sit up on my bunk, lost in a book. Suddenly the outside door buzzes. A cell door clanks open. Loud voices fill the hall. Footsteps thump toward us. I jump down and find Pops, reading on his bunk.

"What's going on? You got a visitor?"

"No. They're doing a cell search. Looking for weapons."

I panic.

"They must've heard something," he says.

I have a weapon. Pops knows it. He's seen it. I've stuffed two locks into a sock, a common weapon in here. I've never used it. I pray I never will. If the guards find my weapon, we will both go into the hole.

I reach up to my bunk, shove my hand under my pillow, and grab the sock.

"Give it here," Pops says.

"What?"

"Give it to me."

I hesitate.

"Come *on*."

I hand it to him just as two guards appear outside our cell door.

Pops starts coughing, a sudden roaring death rattle of hacking. He makes his face flush red.

A guard unlocks our cell door, flings it open with a clang.

"What—what's going on?" Pops says between coughs. "I was just getting ready to take my medication."

"We'll make this quick," the guard says.

"You're searching *our* cell? Are you serious? Why are you doing that? You know we don't have anything in here. I'm an old man and he's a kid."

The guards ignore him. They start rooting through our stuff, our sheets, our books, everything. Pops revs up his coughing, holds on to the cell bars for effect.

"At least can I get some water?" He hacks up some fake phlegm. "I'm dying."

"Yeah, yeah," a guard says, looking disgusted. "Go."

Pops clutches his oxygen tank, steers it out of our cell, and heads down the hall toward the nurse's station. I realize then that he has hidden my weapon on the food tray he's taken with him, stashed it among a balled-up paper bag and his medications. A moment later, I see him standing hunched over the nurse's station, sipping water from a plastic cup.

"Spread your arms," a guard says to me.

I do. He pats me down.

"Do you speak?" the other guard says.

I shrug.

"He's clean," the first guard says. "Let's move on."

"You know what'll happen if you get caught with a weapon?" the second guard says up in my face.

I shrug.

"You don't want to know."

August. Dog days. The heat stifles me. Pops, a large man, a sick man, suffers in the heat. He breathes abnormally. He pants. At night, his coughing jags increase.

One day, while I'm playing hoop, the siren sounds, bleating a stac-cato, head-banging alarm. An order screams through the loud-speaker. *Everyone, go back to your cell.* Nobody hesitates. We go. The older guys scatter, abandoning their chessboards, leaving kings and castles in mid-battle. I return to my cell, find Pops hyperventilating in the brutal heat. He presses a plastic Hannibal Lecter mask over his face, sucking down oxygen.

"Suffocating in here," I say, splashing water from our sink on my face, under my arms. I start to climb up to my bunk. I look at Pops, in obvious discomfort, his chest heaving, and I say to myself, "Breathe, Pops, breathe."

We go on lockdown. Rumors fly. We hear that a guy slipped in a puddle of blood, running to his cell. We hear somebody got shanked up on the yard, took a knife between the ribs. We hear a rival gang selected a hit man to settle a score. Then we hear the truth. Some treacherous dude doing life, who was mopping the floor, got into a beef with a tier runner, a guy who passes out phones when you get a call. The dude with the mop went crazy on the tier runner, used the mop like a baseball bat, bludgeoned the tier runner, beating him over and over, knocking out his eye.

The lockdown stays in place for three straight days, all of us going stir-crazy in the heat. The prison rocks with complaints, shouts, cups banging on bars. Then, gradually, a day at a time, guards let out those of us with jobs. One night, I hear that I have a phone call, and a tier runner passes me the phone through our trap in the bottom of the door. I answer the phone, hear my aunties' voices patched to-gether.

They ask first about my health. I mumble something vague, then ask about my mother.

"Why don't you call her and ask her yourself?"

"I know. I should. I will. I—"

I stop.

"What?"

"It's hard. I'm so ashamed. I feel like I hurt her so much."

"She's strong," Honey says.

We both know that's not true.

"She just wants to know you're all right," Sugar says.

Honey changes the subject. "What's going on with your case?"

"I'm waiting on appeal," I say, and then I go into the best description of the case that I can, which sounds flimsy because I really don't know much myself. As I speak, the frustration starts to grip me, and I blurt, "I got railroaded, you know that. I'm innocent. I would never . . . rape . . . anyone. Ever. That didn't happen. If I had a lawyer like Rovaughn has, maybe things would be different. But this is so hard. Because it's *wrong*."

I take a breath, then speak in a near whisper, my voice barely eking out. "I've been inside close to a year. I shouldn't be in here at all."

"You can't lose faith," Honey says. "You have to keep praying."

"Read those scriptures I send you," Sugar says. "They'll help."

"I will. And thank you again for sending me the paper. That helps, too."

"We love you."

"I love you, too," I say, and, trembling, I hang up.

I turn toward the bunk and catch Pops looking at me. The nights have cooled, and his breathing has become more regular. I turn away. I climb up to my bunk and stare at the ceiling. I don't feel like reading or listening to rap. I just want to sleep. No—I want more than that. I want to disappear.

"You asleep?"

Pops. Speaking to me. For the first time since he saved me during the cell search.

"Nah. I'm awake."

"Come down off that bunk for a second."

I lean on my elbow, sit up, and then hop down. Pops moves to the far side of his bunk and pats the mattress next to him.

"Sit down."

I do.

"I couldn't help overhearing the conversation you had with your family, and I have to tell you I'm confused."

"About what?"

"I'm confused because I hear you on the phone talking about your innocence. Everybody in here says they're innocent. But you plead your innocence. You shout it. You demand it."

He pauses.

"I believe you," he says.

I stare at the floor.

"You have a good family. They check on you. They send you mail. The paper. They care about you. You can tell."

I swallow.

"And yet," Pops says.

He stops. I peek over at him, wanting him to keep going.

"I see you out there playing basketball, playing chess, lifting weights. You act like you're at some kind of *camp*. You don't act innocent, like you want to do something about it. You act like you gave up. People who are innocent, they don't wave a white flag. They don't give up. They keep fighting. Especially if they have a case."

"I got a lawyer doing my appeal," I say.

"You had a lawyer who did your trial, didn't you?"

"Fair enough."

"Let me see your stuff."

At first, I'm not sure what he means.

"Your file," he says. "Let me look at your paperwork. Let me see what's going on in your case."

"Okay," I say. I get my file and hand it to him. Pops takes it, turns the file over, and then squints at me.

"This is untouched. You never opened it. You never looked at it."

I sniff. "Nah. I haven't."

"Why not? I know you can read. You read all the time."

"Why do I need to read that for? It's useless. I sat in that courtroom while they railroaded me. I don't need to relive that."

"Let me read it," Pops says quietly. "Maybe I can see something in there that might help you. Would that be okay?"

"Yeah," I say. "That would be okay." Then I swallow again and say, "Thank you."

————

Two days later, they lift the lockdown for the entire prison population. I go to my job working in the kitchen, come back, and find Pops sitting on his bunk, reading my file. I'm surprised to see him. He normally spends all day in the law library, returning to the cell late. Sometimes he doesn't get back to our cell until everyone else has been locked away for the night.

"Why you here?" I say. "What happened? You get fired or something?"

He knows I'm messing with him and allows himself a brief smile.

"Sit down, Jarrett," he says.

I sit next to him on his bunk. "Listen," he says. "I'm going to be in here for the rest of my life for something I did. But you—"

He slaps my file, startling me.

"You're in here for some racist crap. Period. No evidence at all. Guy out there, playing basketball with you, is serving ten years for murder. You pulled twenty-eight for *this*?"

He slaps my folder again. I wince.

"You are not taking this seriously. You have a case. Listen to me—"

He pauses. He speaks so quietly I can barely hear him. A whisper. Hitting me harder than a scream.

"*Listen* to me, son. Those guys out there. You don't talk like them. You're not like them. They're lifers. They're comfortable here. Their life is coming in, getting out, and coming back in. You keep staying out there with them it's only a matter of time before you're walking around with a teardrop tattoo under your eye and another tattoo crawling up your neck. You're going to either end up like them, or you won't make it in here.

"Here," Pops says. "Take this."

He hands me a pen insert and a notepad.

"There are so many inconsistencies and holes and lies in your case. You need to start researching it yourself because nobody can tell your story the way you can. That's what a case is. A story."

I've never heard that before. It seems real. It seems right.

"Write this down," he says. "I want you to go to the law library and look up a Supreme Court case, *Strickland v. Washington*. You got that? Write it down."

I scribble the name of the case on the notepad.

"What is that case about?"

"Ineffectiveness. Your lawyer failed to do his job. It's ineffectiveness alone for him to make the decision to proceed to trial without giving you the option of joining in on the double-jeopardy motion."

He flips through my paperwork, stops at a page, waves his hand over a list of names.

"See this?"

I peer over his shoulder.

"Yeah."

"That's the witness list. Your lawyer didn't call any witnesses. Why didn't he call any witnesses?"

I can only shrug.

Pops jabs his finger at a name on the list. "Who's this?"

"Shawn Demain," I say. "We hung around with him in his room. When the guys went upstairs, I stayed back with him and played video games. We all hung around with him later, too, you know, after—"

"You hung around with him *afterward*?"

"Yeah."

"The accuser, too? The girl?"

"Yeah."

His eyes widen in shock. "Your lawyer needed to call *him* as a witness. He could establish that you had a friendly encounter with your accuser after the alleged fact, that you didn't flee, none of that. This whole case has the prosecution painting you guys as these big Black boogeymen."

I say nothing.

"Your lawyer botched this case," Pops says.

He hands me back my file.

"*Strickland v. Washington*. Look up that case."

I fill out a pass for the law library the next day, but prison protocol keeps me from getting permission until two days after that. That day, I enter the library and find a small room, its four walls filled floor to ceiling with shelves bulging under law books. Fortunately, Pops keeps everything organized and alphabetized. I find *Strickland v. Washington* and settle in to read the case. I read it once, then read it again to make sure I've comprehended the basics; then I say aloud, "This is my case."

According to the Sixth Amendment, everyone who goes to trial is entitled to be represented by a competent lawyer. The *Strickland* case, heard before the Supreme Court in 1984, established a two-part test that defined ineffective counsel. It applies when counsel's representation falls below an objective standard of competence or when counsel's inadequate performance would have objectively resulted in a different outcome. In the *Strickland* case, David Washington's lawyer failed to defend him properly. Specifically, he refused to call any witnesses.

I close the law book, return it to its proper place, and practically sprint back to my cell. I find Pops reading on his bunk, cuddled up with his oxygen tank.

"You hit it on the head," I say. "*Strickland v. Washington* is about a lawyer's failure to represent his client effectively. But I have a couple of questions. First of all, this is my case, right?"

"You tell me."

"Yes. It is. I think so."

"I think you're so excited you need to go back, read it again, break it down, take some notes, make sure. You'll need another pass for the law library."

"What do you think I should do after I read it over?"

"Write a letter to the attorney. Not yours. Not the lawyer off the court panel. He's useless. He'll drag that appeal out forever."

"Boyle," I say. "Rovaughn's attorney."

"Yes, him. Tell him what he missed. Tell him about the witness."

"I'm going to do that," I say. "I'm going to get on this."

Except I don't.

I mean to. I really do. But as I lie on my bunk that night, unable to sleep, a thousand thoughts pound in my brain: "How am I going to get through this? I don't want to become a lifer," and "How will I be able to understand this case? I only have a high school education. I'm not a lawyer." I start to feel overwhelmed and exhausted. Not the kind of exhaustion that puts you to sleep. Something heavier, more lethal. A massive fatigue falls onto me. I feel so tired and weighted down that I can't move. I will eventually identify this feeling as depression, but at this moment I feel as if my only outlet were to return to the mindless world that I've created for myself in prison. So I do. I do exactly the opposite of what Pops told me to do. For the next month, I burrow back into my hole, mentally. I shut everything out. I don't go to church. I don't call my family. I go back to the basketball court and run with the guys I don't want to become. I lift weights. I play chess. I work my job as a cook. I don't return to the law library and read *Strickland v. Washington* again. I don't take notes. I don't write a letter. I don't think about my case. I just try to escape.

The trap in the cell door springs open.

"Adams, you got a visit."

I prop myself up on my bunk. "Me?"

I have never had a visit before.

"Yeah. Get your stuff."

"You have it wrong. Can't be me."

"You got a *visit*. Let's go."

I swing down off the bunk. I slip into my shoes, take a step, and shiver. We've hit early October, and the days have turned cold. I exhale and I see my breath. The guard leads me to the visitors' area. I stop dead. My mother sits at a table, her hands folded. I shiver again, this time not from the cold. I step closer and take the chair across from her.

"Mom," I say.

She looks up at me. She has aged ten years. Her hair has gone gray, and the wrinkles on her face and forehead have widened and increased. Her eyes seem small and shriveled above large creases of skin. I blink. She looks like my grandmother. I start to speak. I want to say, "What are you doing here?" but instead I picture her driving all the way from Chicago and I bite my lip. She's come five hours to visit me for thirty minutes.

"Mom," I say again.

Her lips quiver, she shakes her head, and she starts to cry.

I don't know what to say. I want to soothe her. I want her pain to go away.

"I'm sorry," she says.

"Mom, no, you don't have anything to be sorry for."

She just keeps shaking her head.

I take a deep breath. "I can't believe you came all the way up here."

"I needed to see you. I needed to know you're all right."

I realize then, to my shame, that I haven't seen her in over a year.

"I've been so worried," she says. "Every time the phone rings, I jump. I'm afraid to take the call. I think it's the prison calling to tell me something happened to you."

"I'm sorry," I say.

She shakes her head again, then exhales to compose herself. I train my eyes over her face, aged, tired, looking at all those wrinkles, those lines of anguish, and I feel so—responsible. What have I done to her?

She blots the tears rolling down her cheeks with a tissue she's balled up in her fist. She tilts her head, points a finger at me, and attempts a smile.

"You're growing a beard," she says.

"Trying to," I say. "Not succeeding so well."

She forces a laugh, then folds her lip and grimaces. I see then that her lips are cracked and dry. She's dehydrated from constantly crying.

We sit silently for a while, my mother's eyes wandering around this room, this place—this surreal, impossible place with peeling paint and flickering fluorescent lights—and then she turns back to me and sighs.

"I wanted to tell you Rovaughn lost his appeal."

"On the double-jeopardy motion?"

"He got turned down. He has to go to trial again."

I take this in. And then something shakes me, like a tremor pass-ing through my body. I feel as if my soul has been rearranged. I look at my mother and I say, "Mom—"

"I know, Jarrett, I know."

"I will do better, I promise. I will write you, regularly, and I'll call you and—"

I lean in, fighting off my tears, and I say again, "I'll do better."

She nods, and then her tears come again.

We sit across from each other, in this stark, cold visiting area in Waupun Correctional Institution, my mother sobbing softly, my own sobs clenched inside my chest, swearing to myself that I will do bet-ter, that I *have* to do better. I realize then that by escaping into basket-ball, by losing myself playing chess, and by not fighting for my innocence, I am a coward. I vow from this moment on that I will fight for my freedom. I will fight for her.

Our visiting period ends. A guard emerges from his spot in the shadows to bring me back to my cell. I say goodbye to my mother and watch her walk away, her shoulders slumped, her gait slow, a broken figure on the way out to her husband, my stepfather, waiting for her in the car. They will now drive five hours back to Chicago. The math destroys me. She will have driven a total of *ten* hours to see me. I choke back my tears, my throat tightening, and my head down, my eyes on the floor, I make myself a promise. I will go to *work*. I will claw my way out of this hole, this mental hole.

I start with this. I never play basketball again.

The next day, newly motivated, adrenaline roaring through me as if I've guzzled three Red Bulls, I go back to the law library and study *Strickland v. Washington*. I return the next day and read through a couple other Supreme Court cases, trying to get a feel for the lan-guage, the style, the flow of argument that the lawyers use. This library—this small, book-lined haven—starts to feel safe. More than that, surrounded by books, confronted with arguments, with logic, with strategic thinking, I feel that I've found a home inside this prison. I come to a decision. I have to figure out how I can spend as much time in here as possible.

I talk to Pops. He has a way in. He tells me that judges in the state of Wisconsin require all inmates to earn their high school diplomas or the equivalent. He suggests that I take the test and apply to be a GED and HSED tutor. I decide to do that first chance I get.

The next night, both of us in our bunks, Pops says, his voice weak, sputtering, "Did you write that letter?"

"Nah, not yet."

I hear Pops rustling in his bunk, breathing hard, "Don't you understand how important that witness is? You need to have the lawyer talk to him. He puts you with him—and *her*—in the smoking area afterward. He's an eyewitness. He can save you."

"You're right," I say. "I have to get on that."

In the morning, I fill out a pass and return to the law library. I settle in at a table across from an entire wall filled with books, and I begin to craft a letter to Gerald Boyle, Rovaughn's lawyer.

I rough out a first draft, then take several more days to get the letter right, trying to keep it short, without rambling. In the letter, I reintroduce myself to Boyle; then I say that I understand that Rovaughn is being tried again. I tell him there was a witness named Shawn Demain. I explain that we all hung out with Shawn in the smoking area *after* we went up to the young woman's room, all of us, including her. I end by telling Boyle that he needs to call Shawn Demain as a witness. After crafting the letter by hand, I pay an inmate to use his old manual typewriter, peck out the letter with my nervous fingertips, then give the final version to my appellate attorney, who passes it on to Boyle.

After that, time flits by, elusive, blindingly fast, except on certain days, when time seems to stop. My nineteenth birthday comes and goes, feeling like both another regular day and a symbol of something out of reach, a piece of normalcy that has been cut out of my life. I now hate my birthday—I've spent two inside prison—and I dread holidays. Thanksgiving, always my favorite holiday, has become nothing more than a long, endless nothing. Christmas, New Year's Day, are mere red circles on a calendar. My life here, caged, living not day to day but hour to hour, cannot—will not—ever be considered my normal. But I will never allow myself to become complacent again.

I get the job as a tutor. I inform my boss in the kitchen that I will be leaving. He actually seems upset. "Man, you're the best chef we have," he says.

A low bar, but in Waupun Correctional Institution you take any compliment you can get.

One evening, while Pops is working at the law library, a guard rousts me from my bunk. "Moving you out," he says.

He leads me to another wing of the prison, to a single cell.

"Welcome home," he says, slamming the cell door behind me.

They move inmates around all the time, so I have been half expecting this. Pops and I have been celled up for four months, longer than usual. I drop my stuff onto the floor and recall something an inmate told me in passing: "Don't get too attached to your cellmate."

I remember now who said that.

Pops.

I start working with guys in the law library, helping them earn their high school diplomas. I'm struck by how many of them simply cannot read. The ones who can can't comprehend or remember what they've read thirty seconds ago. I've interacted with some of these men, and I know they're not stupid. In our failing educational system, they have simply been neglected and uneducated. I'm first appalled, and then I'm angry. Poor, Black, discarded. That's these men. No wonder they turn to a life of crime. If you possess normal intelligence but come from a poor family in a tough neighborhood, what choice do you have?

I've continued going to church and reading the psalms my aunts send me. I start to think these guys must ask themselves, at least subconsciously, the same thing I asked myself: "Where is God? I don't see Him anywhere around here." They don't feel God. They don't fear God, either.

One night, after working in the law library, I thumb through the pages of scriptures, and I find myself reading and rereading Psalm 12.

"Lord! Help! Godly men are fast disappearing. Where in all the world can dependable men be found? Everyone deceives and flatters and lies. There is no sincerity left."

Then I read a line that seems to speak directly to me.

"The Lord replies, 'I will arise and defend the oppressed, the poor, the needy. I will rescue them as they have longed for me to do.'"

I know, of course, that I can't rescue these men. But I can at least try to help.

Rovaughn's trial begins, and a frenzy of phone calls follows. I speak to my mother, my aunts, my attorney, all giving me updates. I'm desperate to hear how the trial is going. I long for a legal play-by-play. My attorney doesn't attend the trial himself but arranges to have someone in the courtroom take notes and follow the proceedings.

The jury comes back with an 11–1 verdict—to acquit.

One juror short of unanimous, one vote shy of an acquittal.

Close doesn't count. The result means a hung jury. Rovaughn will go to trial a third time. But even from inside here, I feel the momentum shift.

I bombard my attorney with questions.

"Did Boyle talk to Shawn Demain before he called him as a witness?"

"I don't know."

"Did Shawn Demain testify about the young woman's behavior in the smoking area?"

"A little bit. He mainly said that she didn't seem nervous, or scared. He didn't go into a lot of specifics."

"Did Boyle ask why she would socialize—why she would sit around smoking cigarettes with her so-called rapists—*after her so-called rape*?"

"Not in so many words, no."

My frustration heats up. I need to write Boyle another letter. I need to spell out the details and ask Boyle to *talk* to Shawn Demain. Having Demain describe how we behaved with the girl afterward is crucial. I know that questioning Shawn Demain in depth is the key to Rovaughn's acquittal, and by extension Dimitri's and mine.

I write a second letter to Gerald Boyle. I try to keep it short, but I can't avoid certain details. I explain that Shawn was one of the first people we met at the party. I write how we played video games, how we all hung out together in the smoking area after we went up to the young woman's room. I describe how she said we snuck up behind her, grabbed her, and pulled her into her room—all lies. I end by telling Boyle that he needs to talk to Shawn Demain so he can corroborate all these details.

After sending this letter, I remember a few details I left out, specifically the young woman saying to us, "Act like nothing happened," and asking her roommate, "Are you mad at me? Don't be mad at me." I compose and send Boyle a third letter.

As a result, Boyle hires an investigator to talk to Shawn Demain. The gist of their conversation follows.

Investigator: Shawn, did you see the guys in the smoking area at the end of the night, after they all went upstairs?

Shawn: Yeah, I saw them all. Jarrett went upstairs after playing video games with me; then they all came back downstairs. The girl, too.

Investigator: Did she seem scared?

Shawn: No. We were all hanging out, sitting around, smoking.

Investigator: Why didn't you say this on the witness stand?

Shawn: To be honest, I forgot. But I didn't think I had to repeat everything I said before.

Investigator: Repeat everything? What do you mean?

Shawn: I wrote everything down. I gave you a three-page statement that I wrote.

Investigator: We don't have a three-page statement from you. We don't have anything in writing from you.

Shawn: I wrote it. I gave it to the officer who questioned me about that night.

The investigator tells Boyle about Shawn Demain's statement. Boyle then writes a pointed letter to the prosecutor, saying approximately,

> I am asking you, again, to turn over everything from discovery. Most notably, if you have any reports, notes, or statements concerning or written by this witness, Shawn Demain, I want them.

Confused, the prosecutor contacts Sergeant Scout, the police officer who questioned Shawn Demain.

"Why are they sending me this letter? What is this about?"

"Let me check into that," the police officer says.

The next day, the police officer shows up in Boyle's office with Shawn Demain's three-page statement.

"I must have misplaced this," she says. "Guess it fell through the cracks."

Checkmate.

The prosecutor dismisses all the charges against Rovaughn. My friend goes home. He never spends a single night in prison. Boyle's excellent, expensive lawyering—and, I'd like to think, the three letters I write—set Rovaughn free.

I'm jubilant. This case is cut and dried. Rovaughn has walked. Soon, I am sure, so will Dimitri and I.

But we don't.

The prosecutor doesn't dismiss the charges against us.

He says that because our lawyers went for a no-defense strategy and didn't call any witnesses, he doesn't feel that we should be given a new trial.

I'm blind with rage and then physically sick.

"I don't understand," I say to this new court-appointed lawyer. "Why can't they give us a new trial with the opportunity to go in front of a jury with this evidence, with Shawn Demain's written statement?"

"They're saying that your previous no-defense strategy doesn't allow any new evidence. That's it. Can't do anything about it. I'm sorry."

"You're *sorry*? There were three of us. One of us just walked free. How can that be? How can that be close to *justice*?"

"I don't make the rules. Not my decision. We'll keep fighting for the appeal—"

I shoot out of my chair as if I've been ejected. "You do that," I say.

I signal to the guard that my visit has ended.

I whip around and face this man who has spent the past year and a half doing exactly nothing on my behalf.

"I'll fight this myself from in here. I'm not giving up, because this isn't right. This. Is. Not. *Right*."

The guard leads me back to my cell. He closes the door behind me. I stand in the middle of my five-by-nine cage, facing the blank wall. Suddenly the sheer sour emotion of defeat surges through me, pooling like bile in my throat. My legs buckle. It feels as if someone has sneaked up on me and clubbed me behind my knees.

I collapse onto my bunk.

9.

Li'l Johnnie Cochran with the Glasses

I can't eat, I can't sleep, I can barely move. I don't want to talk to anyone. I don't want to help anybody with their GED. I don't want to call my family, talk to my mother, or look at any of the scriptures my aunts have sent me. I can't muster the strength or the focus to pray. I don't even want to play chess. I just want to die.

My mind runs the result of Rovaughn's trial in a never-ending loop. What happened to Shawn Demain's three-page statement? How could that police officer misplace it? She knew about it. She *had* to know about it. She gets Boyle's demand letter, and suddenly the statement magically appears in her file? How could she get away with lying like that?

I have the answer to that question, but the answer destroys me.

Because of who we are.

Disposable young Black men.

That's how I feel. That's what I've seen. That's how it is.

I lie on my bunk, hour after hour, day after day, feeling murdered by the law, by terrible lawyers, by the injustice of the justice system, by *life*.

One day, my bunk blanketed in shadow, a guard rattles my cell door. "Call your family," he yells; then the trap at the bottom of the door drops open and a telephone appears. "Call them now."

"I can't—"

"Call them or you're going in the hole."

They're doing it again, I think. Tag-teaming me. My mother and aunts and everyone must be calling the prison, badgering whoever answers the phone. I can't blame them. I don't know how long it's been since Rovaughn's trial—a week, two weeks, a month, I honestly have lost track of time—but I have regressed, broken my promise, become the walking dead. I haven't called. I have turned inside myself. Guilt pours out of me like perspiration.

I call my mother and she patches in my aunts. They sigh communally in relief. They cry softly, not all at once, taking turns. Mostly, they envelop me with love, with concern, with thanks that I'm alive, and all that makes the guilt soak me even more.

"We thought you died," Sugar says. "I swear we did."

"I'm sorry. I've been feeling very low. Rovaughn got freed, but here I am."

"You got to fight, Jarrett," Honey says. "You have to pull yourself up and fight."

"I'm so tired, Auntie. I'm exhausted from this. Why did they let Rovaughn out and not me?"

Then someone says—I can't make out who—"Because you're stronger."

"What did you say?"

"You're *stronger*."

It hits me like an electric shock reviving a dead man.

My letters, I think. It was my letters. The letters got Rovaughn out. Boyle knew the laws, knew what to say in court, but if he didn't have my letters, he wouldn't have had his case.

I don't know how long or how hard this climb will be, but on the phone with my family I pull myself off the floor.

————

I go back to the law library and pick up where I left off. I tutor inmates and study law books, searching for the laws that apply to my case. I discover a statute in Wisconsin that seems to indicate Shawn Demain's three-page statement would have qualified as new evidence and that my lawyer could have—*should* have—asked for a new trial. I bring this to his attention. He stonewalls me, gives me the run-around in legalese, hitting me with excuse after excuse: I've already begun the appeal; I don't want to ruffle any feathers; this wouldn't apply, because he doubts it would be considered new evidence at this point; it's after the fact; and my least favorite excuse, it's so hard to get a new trial. Unlike Boyle, this guy refuses to take my legal suggestions seriously. I don't pretend to know more than a practicing lawyer. But I no longer feel like a naive nineteen-year-old inmate with no knowledge of the law. I have some knowledge, scant as it may be. I read. I study. I feel energized by the law and what the law can do.

Of all the cases I read, I'm most inspired by *Brown v. Board of Education* and Thurgood Marshall, the attorney who argued the case in front of the Supreme Court. I remember learning about the case in high school but haven't dived into the details until now.

In 1951, Oliver Brown, a Black resident of Topeka, Kansas, joined a class-action lawsuit with twelve other claimants. They stated that the local, all-white public schools had refused to admit their children, forcing the families to send them to segregated schools much farther from their homes. In the suit, the families asserted that the Topeka School Board's action violated the equal protection clause of the Fourteenth Amendment. The suit asserted that the city's Black and white schools were not equal to each other and never would be.

The U.S. District Court for the District of Kansas ruled against them.

Undeterred, the claimants brought their case to the NAACP. The organization's chief counsel, Thurgood Marshall, appealed the district court's decision and ultimately argued the case in front of the

Supreme Court. He won a unanimous, 9–0, decision. This established that racially segregated schools are unconstitutional and set a precedent for future civil rights cases.

For every reason, this case both stirs me and fills me with hope. It validates my feeling that if you have truth and right on your side, you can overturn a decision on appeal—with a good lawyer.

In the weeks that follow, Thurgood Marshall becomes my role model. His approach to taking on cases follows the way I've begun to see the law—a means to an end, a chess match, a series of well-prepared strategies, a competition.

"You do what you think is right and let the law catch up."

That is what Thurgood Marshall said.

That is what I believe.

I sit in the law library, waiting for an inmate named Brick. He's late for his tutoring session, but I don't mind. I use the time to begin strategizing about writing a new letter. Based on the new evidence I've uncovered—Shawn Demain's statement—I want to see if I can find a lawyer who will represent me and fight to get me a new trial. I will request a writ of certiorari, a procedure that asks a court to review a case. I plan to send the letter out to as many lawyers as possible. I've already begun compiling a list of attorneys I've read about in the newspaper, attorneys who win cases. I've also made a deal with the guy who has the typewriter. I'll pay him to type out a template for the letter. That way I can fill in each lawyer's name and address without needing to type out dozens of letters. Because that's what I plan to do. Overwhelm attorneys with my letter, with my argument, with my plea. Send out letters until I find someone who will take my case.

Finally, Brick arrives. He storms into the law library and throws himself onto the chair in front of me.

"This place, man," he says. "They gave me a shot."

A shot means a disciplinary ticket.

"For what?"

"For *nothing*. For a bunch of bull. They saying I made a weapon out of my plastic shaver. I didn't make no weapon."

"Out of a shaver?"

"Yeah."

"Those cheap things they buy in bulk from Walgreens?"

"*Yeah*. Those things are dull, man. They can't even shave us."

"I know," I say, absently rubbing my face. "What did you do?"

"I broke the plastic guard off so I could shave. Otherwise you end up *pulling* out those hairs. You know what happens then?"

"You get ingrown hairs," I say.

"Hello," he says. "Exactly."

I nod in sympathy. Almost every African American guy I know in here breaks off the plastic guard so he can get a closer shave. Nobody worries about cutting his skin without the protective guard. The razors are too dull. Even after you break off the plastic guard, the razor barely works.

"What was the exact complaint?"

"Got it right here," Brick says, sliding the paperwork toward me. He pianos his fingers on the table, squints over at me. "What does it say?"

Brick struggles with reading. We've been working on that.

"Manufacturing a weapon," I read.

"I'm gonna lose good time," he says, miserably.

"You could."

For every year you serve without an official complaint or disciplinary ticket, you receive fifty-four days of good time, meaning time taken off your total sentence. Those fifty-four days add up. Inmates hoard those days, bank them, count on them, live for them.

"This *place*, man. I'm gonna lose my good time because I wanted to *shave*?"

"Fight it," I say.

"How?"

"You can request a hearing. You go in front of a panel from the prison and argue your case."

He sniffs. "I can't do that. I don't know what I would say."

"You can have an advocate. Someone to argue on your behalf."

He stops cold. Stares at me.

"You do it."

I quickly scan the law library, the shelves of books, then think about the time I've put in reading the law, studying the law, thinking about the law. I turn back toward Brick. I can feel that I'm smiling.

"I'll do it," I say.

I sit at a table facing two guards on the other side of the glass, the reporting officer—the one who wrote up Brick's ticket—and the hearing officer, a second guard assigned to the case. Brick sits in a separate room, out of sight. If he loses, a third guard will bring him to the hole. I will never see him leave.

I adjust my glasses and listen to the reporting officer read the complaint alleging that Brick manufactured a weapon. When the hearing officer calls on Brick to rebut the charge, I explain that I'm his advocate.

"Every inmate receives a shaver," I say. "And every inmate I know, at least all the African American inmates, *alters* their shaver. But not for the purpose of creating a weapon—"

I hold for effect.

"For the purpose of *shaving*. We need a sharper blade to shave with. It's because of how we were born. Even so, this altered shaver isn't sharp enough to be used as a weapon. It's barely sharp enough to pierce the skin."

I say Brick's real name; then I press my point.

"This man should not be penalized for wanting to keep himself looking neat. He's doing his best to be clean shaven. He's attempting to maintain a good appearance. He serves as a model to other prisoners. He is not making a weapon. Far from it. The charge is false and unwarranted. I move that his disciplinary ticket be thrown out. Thank you."

The two officers look at each other, exchange a few hushed words, then turn back to me.

"We have ruled," the hearing officer says. "The disciplinary ticket will be thrown out."

That's it. We win. Brick avoids segregation.

All it took was ten minutes.

Word spreads.

After I clear Brick's ticket, inmates start asking me to help them fight their shots. I find I have a knack of explaining legalese in simple terms to inmates. They hand me their paperwork, baffled by terms like "res judicata" and "issue conclusions." One guy, I'll call him Aaron because he has the Green Bay Packers logo tattooed on his face, says, "Man, can you break this down for me? I don't understand any of this. What does this *mean*?"

I read through his paperwork. "Okay, look, I'm not going to be able to help you with this, because all your issues have been issue precluded."

"Huh?"

I look at his Packer tattoo. "Okay, let's say the ref calls pass interference. You're the coach. You think it's a bad call. What do you do? You throw the red flag. The play goes to replay review. That's an *appeal*."

"Oh, I get what you're saying."

"In order to overturn the penalty, you have to have *what*?"

"Clear evidence."

"Right. Can't be a tie. Can't even be close. Has to be clear to overturn it. If it's a tie, the decision stands. That's what happened with your appeal."

Aaron looks up at me, his eyes wide.

"I get it," he says. "That is some bull, but I get it."

Aaron leaves, and on his way out I hear him talking to some other inmates: "Hey, man, talk to him. He'll break it down for you."

At first, I don't accept payment, but then I start asking inmates to pay me in stamps. We get an allotment of stamps, a book of ten, but I know I'll need a lot more if I'm going to send out letters to lawyers.

In one instance, the prison officials have offered an inmate, Major, thirty days in loss of good time. He can accept the thirty days or fight the ticket, but if he loses, they'll give him *a hundred* days in the hole. He weighs his options. Give up good time or spend three months in segregation. Major talks to Brick, and Brick encourages him to see me.

I look over Major's paperwork and tell him that I think I can help him.

"How much will it cost me?"

"Two books of stamps."

"Steep," he says.

I shrug.

"You really think you can beat this ticket?"

"Slam dunk," I say.

In order to survive in here, you need to show that you've got game. When it comes to legal issues, I've got game.

"They're not giving you due process by following their own administrative handbook," I explain.

"I don't know what you talking about."

"I'm saying you can win this."

I write up the case, give him the paperwork, and tell him to file it. He does.

I forget about Major's case, lose myself in tutoring and helping other inmates fight their tickets.

One day, right before dinner, I'm bunked up, reading, and I overhear a conversation outside.

"Major, hey, man, I thought you were in segregation."

"I got out of it, man."

"You did? How?"

"Guy on the first tier, man. He did it for me. You got to see him."

"Who on the first tier?"

"The guy in the single cell. You've seen him. Li'l Johnnie Cochran-looking mofo with the glasses."

———

Everyone inside gets a nickname. I never know anybody's real name, even Pops's. A year and a half in, I graduate from Li'l Chi-Town to Li'l Johnnie Cochran–Looking Mofo with the Glasses. The name sticks. I become everyone's go-to legal guy.

Inmates pull me aside at church, hand me their paperwork. I open their file, catch a book of stamps that falls out. I work on cases, help guys overturn their tickets, start stashing stamps. I don't win every case, but I win way more than my share. I rarely have to appear in front of a panel. I mostly write civil petitions or letters to the prosecutors themselves. I find it so surprising that most people cannot craft even the simplest, most basic one-paragraph letter. In many instances, that's all I do—write an effective, convincing letter. I familiarize myself with legal jargon, making sure I use the proper language, emphasizing key points of the argument. I send off these letters; in return, inmates receive justice.

Months go by. We head into a bitterly cold winter followed by a brief, balmy Wisconsin spring, then another hot summer. Between tutoring and working to overturn disciplinary tickets, I not only stay busy but feel somewhat content. I would never call my time in prison comfortable, but those months in Waupun, spending almost every waking hour in the law library, come close. I settle into a routine. I know how to maneuver Waupun to survive each day, avoiding danger, embracing my nickname—Li'l Johnnie Cochran–Looking Mofo with the Glasses. I like being identified as a savvy, successful lawyer. I receive nods of respect from inmates, stares of recognition from guards.

One stifling summer night, sweating through my thin, scratchy sheet, I finally doze off somewhere after 3:00 A.M. At 4:30, the door to my cell flies open. Two guards rush in, shake me awake, grab my legs, pull me off my bunk, force me to my feet, slam handcuffs on my wrists, and drag me toward the open cell door. I don't resist, but I'm in such shock I barely move.

"Let's go!" a guard screams in my face. "We're moving you out."

"Where?"

"Segregation."

"What? Why—?"

"Let's go. *Now.*"

The guards yank me by my arms. I go slack, then reach out and hold on to the bars of my cell.

"You have to tell me why. What did I do?"

"Conspiracy to start a riot."

"What?"

"Conspiracy to start a *riot,*" the guard repeats haltingly, as if struggling to remember a term he was told to memorize from the prison handbook five minutes ago.

"Do you even know what that means?" I ask.

The guard slams my face into the bars. The other guard catches me before I slump to the floor, then pulls me away from the bars by the handcuffs. I feel the metal slicing into my flesh.

"Don't make this harder. You're already going into the hole."

"You can't do this. You need evidence."

"We have a CI," the guard says.

Confidential informant.

"Sure you do," I say.

He shoves me out of the cell, leads me down a dark, narrow hallway.

The guards walk me over to the segregation unit located in another wing of the prison. I'm going to jail, I think. That's what segregation is—jail—the place where you get sent if you commit a crime inside prison. On the way, I see guards leading several other guys to the segregation unit, many of them inmates I helped with their disciplinary tickets. I wonder if the prison has decided to punish them for getting their disciplinary tickets overturned and if I'm being punished for helping them. As the guard leads me to isolation, I picture certain pages in the handbook and try to calculate how much time I will spend in segregation. Minimal, I decide, because they're charging me for something completely bogus, a made-up charge. Total fiction. Thirty days at most. I'll fight it and win. I am Li'l Johnnie Cochran–Looking Mofo with the Glasses.

I spend the night in segregation, in what's called TLU—"temporary lockup." Two days later, I get the word. The prison has issued me a disciplinary ticket for "group resistance and petition," a fancy term meaning conspiracy to riot. What nonsense. The prison judicial system, joke that it is, has twenty-one days to investigate me. They have to issue a conduct report within that time or release me from segregation.

Three weeks to the day, a guard rousts me from my cell and brings me to my disciplinary hearing in front of the reporting officer and the hearing officer. This hearing will determine the answer to two simple questions: Did I violate the laws of the prison, and if so, how should I be disciplined? The hearing officer hits me with the official charge of group resistance and petition.

"We have confidential informants," he says, an executioner's smile spreading across his face. "They heard you in conversation with other inmates planning to take over the institution."

"I've never had any such conversation," I say.

The two guards glare at me.

This is serious.

The fiction has become true crime. I'm helpless, shackled to a table in this sham of a hearing, this kangaroo court. These two guards want my head. They want to send me to *jail*.

Then I remember an article I read about Boscobel, the brand-new supermax, made up of only isolation cells. A few years ago, an inmate at another institution ambushed and murdered a fellow prisoner, the notorious "Milwaukee Cannibal," Jeffrey Dahmer. As a reaction—or overreaction—the state built "Wisconsin's most secure facility," Boscobel, designed to house 509 of the "worst of the worst" prisoners. The state is in the middle of a prison boom. Maximum-security prisons like Waupun have become overcrowded, while Boscobel, the supermax, sits half-empty, providing unoccupied bed space. When I finished the article about Boscobel, I imagined some state higher-up saying, "We built it. Now we have to fill it."

The hearing officer shouts my name, jarring me.

"Guilty," he says.

They charge me with inciting to riot, with group resistance and petition.

I almost shout, "Bull! This isn't about an infraction. This is about bed space!" but I hold my tongue.

They send me to Boscobel.

They sentence me to 360 days in segregation.

10.
Segregation

Those who decide not to die choose to live.

    I remember reading that somewhere. During the next year of my life, that becomes my mantra, my meditation, my fuel.

In the heat of an endless day, I sit chained to a bench in a bus without windows. The bus groans and rolls over rough roads for a torturous two and a half hours, trudging from Waupun, where I saw my status grow, to Boscobel, the supermax, where I will once again tumble into anonymity, a nobody identified by a six-figure identification number. On this drive, I make that determination, that choice. I refuse to allow the system—this twisted, tainted, elitist criminal justice system—to swallow me, to submerge me, to beat me. I will beat the system. I will use words, language, persistence, guile, faith, and the law. I will use these means because they are all I have.

Segregation.

I used to only associate that word with racism. With my forebearers. With the Mississippi cotton fields where my relatives toiled, broken and beaten, emotionally, mentally, and physically. Today, again—

Segregation.
Where I will live for the next year.
In isolation. Apart from the population.
In the hole.
A hole in hell.

I live in a cell the size of a parking space.

The room feels too tight to roll over.

I have a cardboard-thin mattress on a concrete block, a toilet, a sink, a shower, and a TV that gets five channels, all news. I have a rectangle in the wall the size of a hardcover book they call a window. I live in here twenty-four hours a day. I never leave, except for one hour each week when I can walk around the yard accompanied by a guard. They may call this segregation, but I think of this as quarantine. I feel as if I have contracted some horrifying virus. I wonder if that's how my relatives felt back in Mississippi—quarantined, as if being Black were a deadly disease.

I can't stay still. I pace in my cell. Sometimes I walk in circles. I need to move. I need to walk. I walk for—I don't know how long. Hours, maybe. In segregation, time becomes my cellmate. Time has breath, time has a pulse, time has a soul. I don't lose track of time. I can't. That would be like losing a piece of myself.

I write letters in my head. I scribble notes on a pad. I drop to the floor, rip off twenty push-ups, build up to thirty, fifty, a hundred, flip over, power through a hundred sit-ups, two hundred, five hundred. Then I pace, walk across my cell, drop to the floor, and rip off another set of twenty, thirty, forty, a hundred push-ups. Before long, I'm up to a thousand push-ups a day.

One morning, from the floor, I glance at the TV and see a plane fly into one of the twin towers of the World Trade Center in New York

City. A few minutes later, a second plane flies into the second tower. I watch, paralyzed, as the towers explode, then emulsify, dissolving like pillars of sand. Nothing seems real. Nothing seems right. I change the channel. The towers explode on every one of my five channels. Who did this? Where am I? Caged. Quarantined.

The country is frozen in fear. We go to war in a far-off desert against enemies we don't know, an evil we can't see or imagine. Meanwhile, I pace and do push-ups. I turn twenty-one, alone. I celebrate by jotting notes down on my pad, priming arguments, promising myself and my family that I will stay alive. Twenty-*one*. I am of age. I can vote, I can drink—out there, that is. Not in here. I imagine my friends in bars, drinking, toasting, partying. I pace. Thanksgiving comes, goes, Christmas comes, goes. Happy New Year, 2002. I count down my sentence as I pace. Tick, tock. Approximately twenty years to go. Tick, tock.

I live in a row of ten cells. I see no one, hear a constant chorus of doors slamming. I do learn that we have a celebrity on the row—Christopher Scarver, Jeffrey Dahmer's killer. One day, I look through my tiny book-sized window and lock eyes with the inmate in the cell across from me. He stares back, his face expressionless, his eyes dead. After a moment, he disappears. I wonder if he's in here because of a false conviction as I am or if he's one of the worst of the worst. I wonder if that's Christopher Scarver. I never see him again.

I need to exercise my mind. I am pacing one day when I hear a voice. I stop, freeze. I knock on the wall. I bend down, talk through the vent on the floor by the shower. "Hey, yo, next door. What's up, bro? Where you coming from?"

"I came from Green Bay Correctional."

"Hard time, I hear."

"*Hard* time. Wild West, man. Where you coming from?"

"Waupun Correctional."

"Okay."

"Hey, yo, man, you play chess?"

"Yeah, man. I do."

"Cool. Let's get up a game."

I draw out a chessboard on my pad. Sixty-four squares. I number each square, one to sixty-four. On the back row, I write "rook," "horse," "bishop," "king," "queen," "bishop," "horse," "rook" on squares one through eight; then I write *P* for pawn on the row in front, squares nine through sixteen. I get on the floor, put my face close to the vent. We decide to alternate who will be white and go first and attack and who will be black and defend. I get white first, study my homemade paper chessboard, and announce my opening move by calling out which piece I'm moving to which square. We play two games of chess that day, then try to keep going every day at about the same time. I play chess to survive. And I read.

Once a week, a guard arrives outside my cell pushing a book cart. I notice that the guard always starts at the far end of the cellblock, at the cell farthest from me. He comes to me last, after all the popular books have been taken. A slight, but the guard doesn't know I'll read anything, and I do, books about gardening, cooking, parenting, politics, poetry, even books by Freud. I request two or three books at a time, and the guard shoves them through the trap at the bottom of my cell door. I read voraciously. I'm like a starving man who's stumbled on a buffet. Some days, my chess partner and I discuss books. We communicate this way, through chess and books and ideas, the two of us. Two disembodied voices connecting through a vent below a prison cell shower.

They keep the lights on twenty-four hours a day. Often, I can't tell the time until the guards deliver food, always some disgusting variation of potatoes, like hash browns for breakfast and au gratin for dinner. Hours and days tick away. Weeks whip by. Months pass. I play countless games of chess. I take mental vacations through my books. I read a book about Gansu Province in China and imagine myself traveling there. I visit the Silk Road, the Gobi Desert, the Jade Gate, the temples, the grottoes, the rugged mountains. And as I escape in my books, losing days, weeks, and months to my imagination, I plot my literal escape. I write letters, frantically. As the guards dump books into my trap, they pick up letters I write to my mother, asking her to keep the faith, telling her that I miss her, that I think of her, and that I am surviving. And the guards pick up letters I write to lawyers, law firms, and organizations like the ACLU and the Wisconsin Innocence Project asking them to hear my case. When I receive a return letter turning me down, or I don't hear back for a period of time, I write to them again, trying a different approach, coming at them from a new angle.

There's an image I keep at the forefront of my mind. I see a huge, monstrous tree. I know this tree bears fruit, and I want to taste it. I need to have that fruit. It's my tree, my fruit. I start by kicking the base of the tree, but all I get are leaves falling down on me. I know I can't keep kicking the base of the tree the same way because all I'll get are those useless, fluttering leaves. I have to take a different approach. I go to the back of the tree, try to find a weaker point of impact. But this time, I don't kick the tree. I start rocking it. I see if I can get the fruit to fall by making the branches sway back and forth. I know this tree has fruit. I can see it. If this approach doesn't work, I'll try something else. Maybe I'll climb the tree. I won't give up. I'll keep trying until I cradle that fruit in my arms.

I use this approach with my letters. I know I have to keep them to one page. No lawyer will read past that for free. I write and rewrite, focusing on creating a more compelling opening as I argue for my innocence, explain my wrongful conviction. Having read dozens of books, I'm aware that my vocabulary has widened and become more precise. I take hours crafting these follow-up letters. I'm in a rush, but I won't hurry. I'm in segregation. I've got nothing but time.

Everything happens through the mail.

Slowly.

Through the warden's office, I file an official complaint to the security director of the prison. I explain my grievance, insisting that I have been placed in segregation without proper cause and with insufficient evidence. I refute the decision that put me into segregation on what has been a blatant failure of due process. According to the law, the state must respect my legal rights. Instead, the state has harmed me, put me into segregation without following the law. The state has *violated* my legal rights.

Weeks pass.

One day, I receive a reply from the security director. He upholds my original disciplinary ticket, keeping me in segregation.

I don't give up. I file a writ of certiorari to the outside court that oversees the prison, the Dane County Court. I cite an exhaustion of remedies, meaning that I have run out of choices within the prison system and I need to ask the appropriate outside court to consider my case. I argue that the evidence as presented didn't support—nor did I have the opportunity for—due process. The Waupun Correctional Institution officers based my misconduct ticket on a vague, questionable statement attributed to a confidential informant. I never saw anything explaining or confirming what this alleged informant claimed except for a redacted statement that left only two lines that were not blacked out. This gave me no chance to refute the informant's statement because I couldn't see the statement at all.

Several more weeks pass.

I receive a reply. The attorney general argues that I should be kept in segregation.

I respond to the attorney general. I again cite exhaustion of remedies, insisting my rights have been violated and that I have been put into segregation without evidence.

A week passes, then another, and another. A month passes, then two. I calculate that I have been in segregation for close to a year.

One day, an officer grunts outside my cell, slides open my trapdoor, and shoves through a stack of mail. The letters land with a thud on my floor. I roll off my mattress and open the letters systematically. I rapidly read each one. Form letter from an attorney, rejecting my case. Form letter from a law firm, rejecting my case. Form letter from a legal nonprofit, rejecting my case.

Then I come to two envelopes with state seals. I tear open the first with trembling hands. The court in Wisconsin, after three years, has denied my appeal for a new trial. They report this in a form letter. No explanation. No reason given. No nothing. They didn't answer any of my questions. They didn't consider my request to question Shawn Demain, the eyewitness, the guy whose testimony got Rovaughn's charges dismissed.

I want to rip the letter into a thousand pieces and flush them down the toilet. I want to howl. *Rovaughn's charges get dismissed and I can't even get a new trial?* I stand in the middle of my cell and I shudder, my body quivering, as if I've come down with fever.

I plop down on my bed and slowly pry open the last envelope, expecting another form letter delivering more bad news. I see that it's not a letter at all. It's a court order. I start reading it. I sit up.

Dane County Court has reversed my conduct report.

The state will be removing me from segregation within seven days, during which time they will determine my next placement.

They've given me a "Get Out of Segregation Free" card. But it has been anything but free. It cost a year in isolation.

I grab my pen and pad and furiously write a letter back to the department of corrections.

"My conduct report was reversed by the Dane County Court," I write. "I'm writing to say that I am willing to go anywhere in the state except for Green Bay Correctional. I ask you to please not send me to Green Bay because I have a hardship issue. My mother is a senior with health issues. She lives in Chicago. It would be too far for her to come all the way to Green Bay. She wouldn't be able to visit me and that would be a hardship for both of us. Thank you for considering my request. Sincerely."

I get a letter back two days later.

They've considered my request.

They're sending me to Green Bay.

11.

Born at the Scene of the Crime

Everything about Green Bay Correctional Institution seems unreal, starting with its location: a stone's throw from Lambeau Field, the iconic home of the Green Bay Packers. The front entrance looks like a medieval stone structure. Built in 1898, the prison feels, smells, *is* decrepit. The walls sweat in summer and freeze to ice in winter. Seven hundred men live in this complex, almost all of them young, angry, and violent, the rest of them mentally disturbed. At least that's what I hear through the prison grapevine.

I arrive at Green Bay in the fall of 2002, not yet twenty-two years old. I get celled up with a guy younger than I am, a frenetic, furious, loudmouthed gangbanger who doesn't talk; he screams incoherently and never seems to shut up. I don't know whether he's strung out or simply in a constant state of rage.

By this time, 2002, prisons in general have become overcrowded. Drugs, especially crack, have ripped families apart just as our government has gotten tough on crime. Fear—the same kind of fear that got me convicted, the fear of us, of me, of the *other*—has put nearly

1 million young Black men behind bars. In a couple of years, that number will swell to 2.4 million. And for reasons that I can't understand, in the state of Wisconsin, the courts send the most violent young men, ages eighteen to twenty, here, to Green Bay. I see almost immediately why my chess-playing neighbor at Boscobel called Green Bay Correctional the Wild West and why others call it Gladiator School.

My second week at Green Bay, my cell door breaks open for lunch. I slide out of my cell and find a place in the chow line. I instantly feel a ripple of movement, pushing, shoving; then somebody shouts, "Bitch!" and right behind me I hear the sickening sound of hard metal smashing into a human skull. Then screaming. I stand to the side, crouching, coiled, ready to defend myself, praying I don't have to defend myself. Punches thrown. Fists striking bone, hands slapping flesh. Bodies hitting the floor. The alarm sounds.

Guards run in while inmates continue pounding each other. The guards dive into a pile of humanity, untangling arms, legs, slamming inmates with their fists, nightsticks, pulling them off each other. Then they herd us back into our cells. My cell door slams. My cellmate circles me, stalks me, snarls into my face, spits, "What are you doing up here?"

"I wish I knew," I want to say. But I lock my eyes into his, staring, unblinking, until he backs away, still taking the measure of me, probably thinking a fight with me might not be to his benefit.

After that melee, it seems as if every time the guards open our doors, a fight breaks out. Guys from rival gangs go at it over long-held grudges. Latino guys and Black guys fight in here over territory in neighborhoods they just left. Black guys and the Aryan Nation tear each other up just because. I see revenge hits. Contract hits. Skinhead gangs. Biker gangs. MS-13 gangs. I can't keep track of all the designations. One day on the rec yard, a minute before I head out to find a chess game, two rival gangs go to war. A free-for-all. Heads get cracked open. Blood flows. Guards descend like an army, hurling tear gas, shooting beanbags.

After lockdown lifts four days later, an inmate with a mental disorder approaches the guard at the front desk. The inmate sniffs. Rubs his nose. "I didn't get my medication," he says.

"You didn't come out when we opened your cell," the guard says.

"I was in there. Where do you think I was?"

"You didn't come out, so you missed it."

"I need my medication."

"You have to wait. Next time maybe you'll come out when we tell you."

The guy snaps. He leaps over the desk and starts whaling on the guard, smashing the guard's face, clawing at it, biting him, then choking him. Alarms sounding, guards running, flooding the area near the front desk, pulling the inmate off the guard. The guard slumps to the floor, beaten to a bloody pulp, barely alive. Medical personnel appear, cart him away on a stretcher. It will be nearly a year before I see that guard again.

I try to wrap myself around the anarchy, the violence, that erupts every day. How can this place, this punishment, this system, this *solution*, be beneficial to anyone, in any way? There's no rehabilitation in a place like this. Only blood and survival. Every week a bus arrives with a new group of inmates, many walking into the prison with different versions of the same violent agenda.

I make adjustments. I learn to identify signs of danger whenever I leave my cell. Mostly, I watch faces and hands. Cold eyes and cupped hands indicate that a guy is about to strike, a weapon hidden in his fist. I also pay attention to sound. The prison turning unusually quiet means something heavy is about to go down. I avoid stepping out into silence. As a rule, when my cell breaks open for chow, I hang back, staying as close to the end of the line as possible. I befriend a new guard, a rookie my age, white, nervous, looking like a deer caught in headlights. I engage him by talking sports, a common denominator for most men in any setting, even this. A week or two later, they transfer my cellmate out, replacing him with a giant who takes up three-quarters of the cell and who rarely speaks. An improvement. At least now I can dare close my eyes at night.

And yet, even in this place, I experience occasional hints of goodness, of humanity.

After lights-out, we enjoy a nightly concert. Inmates break into song. They clang cups against cell bars, some harmonize and some with big voices solo. One guy—we call him Urkel because he wears thick Coke-bottle glasses—sings like an R&B star, his voice honey soaked and filled with pain. I lie on my cot, thinking, "What a waste." He should be making music. The world should hear that voice. The world should feel that pain.

In this system, your reputation—your "jacket"—follows you from prison to prison. A guy with connections stays connected inside. A snitch stays labeled a snitch. You are who you have been before, what you have earned, or how you have been perceived. For better or worse, your jacket sticks.

Two months in, I learn that at Green Bay, I arrive with my reputation intact. A young man, early twenties, heavily muscled, tatted up to his neck and face, scarred, and sinister looking, tracks me down at the edge of the basketball court.

"Hey, man, how long you been down?"

I do some quick math, realize I can't calculate the exact number. My time in has become fuzzy.

"About three or four years," I say.

"You been up here the whole time?"

"Nah. I got to Waupun in 2000; then I left."

"Did you know my man Carlyle? He was in Waupun."

"I don't think so—"

"He said if I see you, talk to you. He say you be good with legal work. That right?"

"Well—"

"Li'l Johnnie Cochran–Looking Mofo with the Glasses," he says.

I crack a slit of a smile. "Yeah, okay, that's me."

The sinister guy squeezes out a smile to match mine, thin, tentative.

"Need your help," he says and hesitates. "You look over my legal work?"

"I could."

We pause.

"How much? How many stamps?"

"Depends. I have to see. At least one book."

He nods. I nod. I'm back in business.

I again get a job as a tutor, and I spend so much time in the law library that I might as well sleep there. I jump in, taking on as many inmates as possible, writing dozens of letters on their behalf. I want to help people because I see how badly the criminal justice system has victimized them. I can relate to that. As I write my own letters to lawyers across the country trying to find a way to appeal my case with new evidence, I get a sense of validation helping other people win their appeals, overturn tickets, or even reverse unfair court decisions. We win the majority of these cases, and if I'm winning for them, I feel even surer that I can win for me.

Plus, I know that every hour I work for an inmate in the law library or meet someone at chapel to go over his legal work is an hour I avoid danger. I don't want to become collateral damage between two gangs attacking each other on the yard. I don't want some deranged inmate to stab me between the ribs or drill me in the head with his metal lock on the chow line because he doesn't like my glasses. Random, brutal violence occurs every day. It happens instantly, without warning. A sense of paranoia buzzes through me, through the general population. Inmates murmur that they would prefer being put into segregation. I want to say, "That's because you've never been in segregation," but I hold my tongue. I keep my head down, plot my escape, my legal escape, holding my breath every time the van arrives with another group of inmates.

Word travels. *Cost you some, but he good with the legal work.* Guys seek me out in the law library, in church, on the yard, even in the chow line. They hand me their paperwork, books of stamps tucked inside their folders. At one point, the amount of cash in my canteen account dips, diving toward a zero balance. I move away from using stamps as payment and ask for cash to be put in my account. As my canteen grows and I remain flush with stamps, I start to notice something. I'm getting into a groove. The more I send out letters and deal with attorneys, the more I feel I fit with them. I speak their language. I understand their game. I learn to play it. I learn to play it well.

I can't spend every waking moment working on legal cases—mine and others'. I read books, study the psalms, go to church, trying to maintain my faith and keep my energy and spirit up. Even so, I struggle with moments of malaise. Sometimes I scan this place, this unholy place, and I have to fight to stay sane. I try to smother my feelings of depression, despair, abandonment. The same questions nag me: How did I ever end up here? How can our country accept punishing people in this inhumane way? I call my mother as often as I can. I read the scriptures my aunts send. Ritual saves me. Work. Read. Survive. Write to attorneys about my case. Have faith. Read. Survive. Pray. *Pray.*

I think of the story of Joseph, famous for the Technicolor dream coat his beloved father gave him. His half brothers hated him, threw him in a pit, and sold him into slavery. I especially relate to what happened to Joseph after some slave traders pulled him out of the pit and a rich man took him into his house. Like me, he got falsely accused of rape, convicted, and sent to prison. In prison, he found his way and thrived. He helped the other prisoners—they went to him for counsel—and eventually the warden put him in charge of overseeing the entire prison population. When he got out, he became one of the most powerful leaders in the world. His story inspires me. He fought for his innocence. He won. He received justice. I will, too. Somehow.

One day, I see three inmates on a visit: a guy everyone here calls Pops; his son, Old Man; and *his* son, G-son. Three generations incarcerated—grandfather, father, and grandson. They're being visited by three well-dressed women. One of them holds a squirmy toddler on her lap. The great-granddaughter, I think. Nobody says much. The little girl, no older than three, snuggles with her Barbie doll as the adults talk quietly. Soon, an alarm sounds, ending the visit, and the family says their goodbyes. The little girl springs off her mother's lap and, clutching her Barbie, walks over to a guard. The little girl automatically spreads her arms, allowing the guard to pat-search her. She doesn't flinch, doesn't blink, doesn't move a muscle. To her, going in and out of a maximum-security prison to visit her great-grandfather, grandfather, and father is as routine as going in and out of a playground or school.

I watch her stand stock-still as the guard pats her down. I feel heartsick. She's *three years old.* The guard continues to pat her down as if she were thirty, searching her to see if she's concealing a weapon or contraband. I quickly scan the little girl's face, hoping I see innocence. I don't know if I see that from where I stand, but at least I don't see hardness or anger. I lower my head and pray that this little girl will find a different life. I can't avoid seeing a cycle of violence, of pain. How can we prevent her from following her father, grandfather, and great-grandfather into prison?

The family leaves, the little girl holding her mother's hand with one hand, clutching her Barbie with the other. She'll be back because this is her life, the only life she knows. I glance at Pops, Old Man, and G-son, and I shake my head.

"Keep that little girl safe," I whisper. "Keep her away from this life. Allow her to break this cycle."

A few days later, a guy approaches me on the yard. Not my usual "client." They call him Fish. White dude. Shaved head. Tall, wiry, his face craggy and pockmarked. Fish walks with a swagger as if he knows nobody can touch him, his eyes lasered straight ahead. I recognize him as one of the leaders of the prison's Aryan Brotherhood and the instigator of the prison brawl that broke out when I first got here. Not someone I would ever associate with nor anyone I would do business with. But I wonder if I could put my bias aside, set aside his jacket long enough to hear what he wants. I'd rather take my chances with him in the law library than on the rec yard.

I decide I will hear him out. I also decide to charge him triple my usual fee.

"I'm having an issue," he says, sitting down in front of me.

"Which is?"

"Well, two things. First, my lawyer got my sentence structured all wrong. I have to get that redone."

"Okay," I say. "We can petition the court."

"And—"

He looks away, passes his hand over his face, and pauses, giving me time to stare at the impressive array of tattoos that covers his entire body.

"I'm not allowed to see my kids," he says.

"How many kids do you have?"

"Two."

He dips his head, speaks to the floor.

"I haven't seen them in a long time," he says.

"How long?"

"Fifteen years."

"Fifteen *years*?"

"They're teenagers now."

Fish looks up and stares at me. His blue eyes, the color of a sky, flutter and fill up.

"I just want to have a visit," he says.

I probe a little and find out that Fish has been given a life sentence for committing some heinous crime on more than one of his family members. He gives me a sketchy outline. Something to do with a meth lab. A murderous takeover. He doesn't give me all the details. I don't want to know all the details. Fish says that time has healed wounds. The family member who survived supports him having a visitation with his kids.

"Can you do this?"

"Maybe," I say. "I'll need three letters. One from your family member saying that he supports your having visitations with your kids. And one from each of your kids saying how much they want to visit you."

"Then what?"

"I'll write a letter to the prosecutor and a letter to the judge. I'll plead your case, attaching the three letters you're going to get for me."

"Will that work?"

"Can't promise anything."

Fish sniffs, swipes his nose, flicks a bony finger at the tears that have begun to trickle down his cheek. He clears his throat, stands abruptly, and leaves. I jump right in. Over the next thirty days, the more I work on his case, the more I learn about him, more than I want to know. Fish runs a whole sector of the prison. If something bad ever happens to him, this place will explode.

I get pushback. Black dudes I know and some I don't know glower at me. Big George, an inmate I'm helping, calls me out directly in the law library.

"You know he don't like Black people."

"I know."

"Then why you helping him?"

"Two reasons. One. It's not about him. I don't care about him. I care about the *law*."

"And two?"

"I'm charging him three times what I'm charging you."

Big George raises an eyebrow and nods with respect.

Fish wins. The court changes its ruling. Fish arranges for his first visitation with his kids in fifteen years. I hear all this through the prison grapevine. I don't hear from Fish. Predictable. Understandable. We don't travel in the same circles. The win alone validates me.

———

My mother and stepfather come all the way from Chicago for another visit. I sit across from them in the visiting area, our voices quiet, subdued, my emotions raw. I explain how I have been working with inmates while at the same time trying to stir up legal interest in my own case. I've written dozens of letters but so far have received only rejections in return or no response at all. Each time I open a rejection letter, I scream silently; then I take a deep breath and write a second letter—a better letter, tighter, stronger, more forceful, more insistent. If I get rejected a second time, I'll write a third letter. A fourth. A fifth. I won't give up. I'm trusting my life to letters.

"It will happen," my mother says. "Someone will respond."

"You're right. Somebody will."

I say that with a pasted-on smile. I don't want to allow any of the frustration or desperation I feel to darken our visit.

Just behind her, I see a guard leading in an inmate. Fish. He sits down a few tables away from me, and after a while another guard leads in two teenagers, a girl and a boy. I keep my focus on my mother, but in my peripheral vision I see Fish's shoulders shake as his kids sit down across from him. He smiles, and I hear him and his kids laugh. The normal sounds you hear during a visit. Lowered voices, occasional laughter, muffled sniffles. Two teenagers visiting their father in prison.

At one point, as if choreographed, my family and Fish's family get up at the same time to purchase snacks. By rule, inmates can't move from our seats. I track my family walking to the snack machine, and then I turn and look toward Fish. He's looking at me, staring, his blue laser eyes cutting into me, and then he nods. His thank-you. All I'll get from him. All I need. A moment of humanity.

I nod back.

The calendar flips.

Happy New Year, 2004.

I work my case, write my letters.

I work other inmates' cases. We lose some; we win more.

By March, I'm flush with stamps.

I send out my letters.

Nothing happens.

When will it be my turn?

Will it ever be my turn?

I ask my aunties on the phone, "How come God doesn't come when I call?"

"He's coming. He doesn't work on your clock."

"My clock is ticking," I say.

"Have you been going to church?"

"Yes."

"Have you been praying?"

"I have."

"Pray harder."

"Okay," I say, slowly shaking my head. "Sure."

When I hang up the phone, I settle back onto my cot and slowly scan my cell. I realize as I sit here, in this cage, that through all my time in Green Bay Correctional, the roughest, wildest, most violent prison in the state, I have never been attacked.

Maybe God is already here.

I get a letter.

I open the envelope, skim the letter, then stare at it. I read it slowly, methodically; then I read it again, and *again*. I have to make sure I'm not hallucinating. No. This is real.

After five years, someone has replied to me about my case.

12.

Competence

Dear Mother,

How are you feeling? I am blessed . . .

Enclosed is a case where a guy had his case overturned by filing with the Feds. As you'll see, the other courts denied him as is in my case, but he stuck at it and filed a habeas corpus. He was denied but appealed and that won! His issues are so much like mine it's scary . . .

Mother, it took me a couple years to study this law, but I've gotten the handle on this case, and by the grace of God, I'll prove my case very shortly. Mother, these people have the same evidence but they chose to ignore it because of the obvious . . . the color of our skin, which I'm very proud of . . .

Love, Jarrett

Three months after writing that letter to my mother, I sit in my cell and reread the letter from Rob Henak, an attorney I contacted in Milwaukee.

It begins,

> Dear Mr. Adams,
>
> This letter is to inform you that I will be able to assist you in editing your pro se filing to the federal district court . . .

I exhale slowly, my breath fluttering the paper in my hand.

I remember Rob Henak well.

Every day in the law library, I scour the local newspapers—the *Milwaukee Journal Sentinel,* the *Wisconsin State Journal* from Madison, and the *Green Bay Press-Gazette.* Most inmates look at the funnies or the sports, but I go right to the crime report, noting which lawyers are mentioned the most when it comes to winning appeals. The name Rob Henak appears more times than almost any other. I write him an impassioned letter, one of my best. I lead by telling him how much I admire his work. I point out that he is fighting battles and winning wars that few attorneys even attempt. I describe my case. I argue its validity, point by point, using *Strickland v. Washington* as a reference. My hope is that I have grabbed his attention and his interest. I close by saying I have been writing my habeas petition from the law library in prison and I hope he'll consider helping me with my pro se filing in federal district court.

"Pro se."

A legal term meaning that I am arguing the case on behalf of myself. At this point, I have no attorney. I am on my own.

I'm stunned when Rob replies. But as I think about it, I'm not surprised. I wrote a strong letter. I have a valid case. I just need help. Rob has mailed me a lifeline.

To this point, I've jumped through the legal hoops available to me.

First, state appellate court.

Two years ago, my court-appointed lawyer presented the reasons for appealing the verdict, listing everything that went wrong at the original trial. This became what's called a de novo review—asking for a new trial. *But.* I can only appeal based on what has previously been introduced into the court record. If I have new evidence, I have to essentially start all over, beginning at the trial court.

I have no new evidence.

At least in the eyes of the court.

I believe that Shawn Demain's written statement should be considered new evidence.

The court doesn't agree.

The court calls his statement derivative evidence.

They claim that because they have his *testimony* on the record, they don't need the full, three-page statement that he wrote.

But they do need the statement. I've argued this, vehemently—in the confines of my cell, inside the dirty, peeling walls of the law library, in my head, and in my letters.

"You don't have Shawn's full statement," I argue. "You have a meager, partial response to questions the lawyers asked him. That's not enough. You don't have the details. You don't have his narrative. You never got the eyewitness's full story of what happened that night. The prosecution never brought that statement forward. The police officer buried Shawn Demain's statement, claimed she'd misplaced it. The prosecutor dismissed Rovaughn's case because he knew that Shawn Demain's full written statement would blow his case out of the water—so he dropped the charges."

His name is in the record, the appellate court rules. *His name is already known. We're not going to consider his statement, or a new trial, because your lawyer chose a no-defense trial strategy.*

Not sufficient new evidence.

The court defers to the original ruling.

I lose.

How can I go on?

I have to go on.

The next step. A formality. My lawyer presented my case to the

Wisconsin Supreme Court. As expected, the supreme court refused to hear my case and rubber-stamped the appellate court's decision. That formality—from filing to hearing the decision—takes a year. Now I have one year to file my final appeal in federal district court—without an attorney. At this point in the appeals process, the state will no longer provide me with an attorney, and I can't afford to hire one. I will have to file pro se. I look up how often pro se litigants win their cases. I stare at the number. *Two* percent of the time. Two out of a hundred cases.

If you can't afford a lawyer, you lose. That's not hyperbole. That's math.

Every day I wake up, stare at the bars of my cell, and play a trick on myself.

I tell myself, "Today, I will work all day on my case because I am getting out of prison tomorrow."

I put myself into a sort of mind warp. I repeat this notion to myself so often that I believe it: "Working this case to the bone. Killing this case. You're working it so hard, so convincingly, you're getting out tomorrow."

I know how impossible and insane this sounds. I don't care. In prison, you have to live in a fantasy world because the real world can kill you physically and destroy you mentally. I find hope in my fantasy. I know how close to the precipice I creep. I know I'm dancing on the edge. And I know that some people would say that hope is a fantasy. Especially in here.

I don't care.

I live by a code, a code I create. I am locked in a cage, my body symbolically, if not literally, in shackles. But I refuse to allow my mind or spirit to be locked up in the same way. "Never tell yourself no," I repeat. "Let someone else do it." In other words, don't fear failure. Try. Don't give up. *Try.*

———

My mother buys me a typewriter, a small, compact Brother electric. I have told her what I need, according to prison rules. The typewriter has to be quiet so as not to cause other inmates or guards to complain, especially because I type my letters late into the night. The prison cuts the lights at ten, so I type by the light of my small television. Even when the day's programming ends, I continue to type in the shadowing glow of the TV's blue light. I never learned to type, so I peck, furiously, and with surprising accuracy. If I do mess up, my Brother comes with erasing tape. I can back up a maximum of three spaces, place the eraser over the letter I want to correct, type, watch as a white blotch covers the mistake, then type the correct letter. I type so many letters, I nearly deplete my canteen account buying correcting tape and replacement cylinders.

Five years in, I come to a near dead end. I have exhausted all of my state court remedies. I have one more tool I can use. Habeas petition. I can assert, in writing, that my constitutional rights have been violated and, as a result, I have the right to petition a federal court to review my case. I lean into *Strickland v. Washington*. The gold standard. As a citizen, I have been given the constitutional right to effective assistance of counsel. I have the right to a competent attorney, and this right has been violated.

Now, by law, how do you define "competent"?

Strickland v. Washington presents a two-pronged definition of ineffective counsel. Both prongs have to apply.

Prong one. The tricky prong.

Was your lawyer ineffective?

Prong two. The trickier prong.

Did that ineffectiveness affect the outcome of your case?

As for prong one, I have heard astounding, upsetting stories. Beyond your typical run-of-the-mill lazy, unprepared, ignorant, overall awful lawyering, I've heard about lawyers who have fallen asleep in the courtroom while defending their clients. I've heard of lawyers who have been high on cocaine. I've heard of lawyers who had several drinks during the lunch recess and returned completely hammered. Incredibly, lawyers in these conditions don't necessarily meet the standard deemed ineffective. You have to prove that second prong as well—that these egregious actions affected the outcome of your case.

In Rovaughn's case, when his attorney discovered Shawn Demain's written statement and brought it to the prosecutor's attention prior to a potential third trial, the prosecutor saw that he would lose and dropped all the charges.

My attorney never called Shawn Demain as a witness. That proves prong one.

Prong two should be a slam dunk: same defendants, different attorneys, two completely different outcomes.

Rovaughn's attorney got all his charges dismissed, while my attorney got me twenty-eight years. What can you call that but blatant ineffectiveness, which resulted in a completely different outcome?

But I face two obstacles.

The first is protocol, the fact that the state will no longer provide me with a lawyer. I have to either go it alone—pro se—or hire an attorney. Not only do I not have the money to hire a private attorney, but I can't find an attorney to hire. Nobody wants to take my case. Dozens of letters returned or unanswered continue to prove that to me, day after day after day.

My second obstacle is time.

I have a drop-dead deadline—one year to appeal for a new trial. One year to exhaust all remedies. One year. And the clock is ticking. I consult my calendar and see that three months have blown by.

Then—I get the letter.

I write Rob Henak back the same day I receive his reply. I know I can't afford to retain his services for the entire case. To go the distance, to defend me all the way through trial, a lawyer like him would likely cost in the neighborhood of fifty thousand dollars. I tell Rob the truth. I tell him that I value his time and I know he's worth every penny he charges his clients. But the five years I have been incarcerated have obliterated my family's finances, driven us to the brink of bankruptcy. I ask if he'd be willing to accept payment for just helping me structure an airtight habeas petition. I mail this letter and hold my breath.

Rob writes back. He explains his hourly rate. He says he will charge me half that and cap his hours. I feel so excited I nearly sprint around my cell. I call my mother. I can feel her heart skip over the phone. She'll find the money somehow, she says. I'm not sure how she pulls it off, but she does. She sends Rob a check.

I didn't want to scare off Rob before he agreed to work with me, so I waited until we had an agreement to reveal that we're facing a ticking clock. After our initial back-and-forth, we now have seven months to put together my habeas and file my final, last-chance appeal. Given that we will do all of our work by mail, I know we'll be cutting it close. I tell him in my next letter that I've been working on my habeas myself for weeks and I think I have it in pretty good shape. I don't tell him what I really feel—that I've in fact been working on it for *months*, and considering I'm not a lawyer, I've written, in my opinion, a professional, nearly flawless habeas. I have the same feeling I got back in high school after I'd studied hours for an exam. "I aced it," I think. "I destroyed this habeas."

Another couple of weeks go by. Rob sends me back the habeas petition I've written. I pull it out of the envelope, and I see a blotch of indecipherable black words drowning in a sea of red. The page looks blood spattered. Rob has gutted my habeas, torn it apart, shredded it, red lined every word. The only two words he hasn't red lined are "Jarrett Adams."

I thought I got an A on this test. This guy gave me a D. Maybe an F.

Rob's reaction throws me—for about five minutes. I come to feel, in the strangest way, that I have begun my own private law school and Rob Henak is my professor. I need to rewrite my habeas and fast. I lock myself in my cell. I go over Rob's changes. I go to chow hall at 5:30 A.M., wolf down breakfast, then return to my cell and rework the draft. I skip lunch, don't make it to dinner. My stomach growling, I stay up until three in the morning, working by the blue light of my tiny television, writing, rewriting, thinking, rethinking. I don't know how long I hole up redoing my habeas—days, weeks—but finally I finish incorporating all of Rob's changes and send the new version off to him. I breathe a sigh of relief, of satisfaction, of completion.

A few weeks later, Rob sends back this version—red lined. Another river of red, though not quite as bloody as my first version. I look at it and laugh. We're getting there, I think.

I rewrite the habeas again, send it back to Rob, wait, pace, bleary-eyed, staring wide awake at the ceiling all night. Rob sends that one back. Red lined. Blood soaked. Though noticeably less. I write another version, send it to Rob. We go back and forth for weeks, our relationship conducted completely through our letters. Meanwhile, I keep my eye on the ticking clock. The deadline terrifies me, looming like an ax over my head. Five months away . . . four months. I lose track of time and revisions. I wait for Rob's next revision—his revised version of my revision of his previously revised version of my third or fourth or is it *fifth* red-lined version of my original habeas petition? I wait. I turn to my enemy, the calendar, tear off another week.

Three and a half months left.

One day, I receive an envelope from Rob. I open it weakly. I can barely tear the paper. A letter flutters to the floor. I pick it up and read two words from Rob.

"We're good."

While working with Rob on the habeas petition, I've continued to write letters to individual lawyers and to organizations who might be willing to represent my appeal pro bono at the federal district court. I write to the ACLU, to the NAACP, to any group that seems appropriate and even some who seem like long shots. One night, I pause, check off the places I've written to, and remember that more than a year earlier I wrote to the Wisconsin Innocence Project. I've been intrigued by the WIP, located on the campus of the University of Wisconsin–Madison, ever since I saw a segment on the news about how they reversed the conviction of Christopher Ochoa, a man serving life in prison after being falsely convicted of murder. The organization exonerates innocent people by using DNA evidence. My case doesn't involve using DNA, so I've considered the Innocence Project one of my longest long shots. I'd forgotten in the flurry of working on my habeas revisions and in the blur of time passing that someone from the Wisconsin Innocence Project had written me back and requested a copy of my transcripts. I made copies and sent them off but never received a response. As usual, I moved on.

Now, getting the go-ahead from Rob, I mail out a new wave of letters, this time containing a punchy, very streamlined two-paragraph cover letter and attaching my habeas petition.

I hear keys jangling, clicking into locks.

The sound of guards delivering mail.

I sit up, a Pavlovian response.

Inmates don't look forward to the mail. We *live* for the mail. Now there's a key clinking outside my cell door. And then a letter.

I tear into the envelope.

I read the letter hungrily.

The Wisconsin Innocence Project has sent me a confirmation. They have received my submission.

My mouth goes dry.

We have received your submission.

That's it. Nothing else.

I squint at my calendar. My birthday approaches. Christmas and New Year's loom. We are crawling toward 2005.

I have one month left.

I hold my breath.

We don't have enough time. Thirty days until the deadline drops onto my neck like a guillotine. I will be out of chances. Out of luck. I pace in my cell. I want to climb these bars. I make a fist and pound it into my forehead. Think, Jarrett. *Think.* What should I do? I'll call them. I have to tell them we're running out of time. I'll call them, first thing tomorrow—

Another clinking of keys.

Another envelope.

I tear it open.

I have a legal visit the next day—tomorrow.

It doesn't say with whom.

But—a *legal* visit?

I have to be ready.

Before going to sleep, I gather all my paperwork—letters, correspondences, memos to others, to myself, notes I've jotted down on pads, and my habeas petition. I crawl onto my cot, my body one buzzing nerve ending. I drum my fingers on the side of my cot, trying to force myself into unconsciousness by batting out a slow, easy rhythm. No dice. I don't sleep at all. I practically hop out of bed at first light. I tear another day off my calendar. And then, late in the morning, or early in the afternoon, I can't tell, my cell door pops open and a guard mutters, "Legal visit."

I come into the visitors' area and see three people sitting at a table— a young Black woman and a young white man, college age, both dressed conservatively, and an older man, a professorial type, his blue eyes eager, focused as beacons. He offers up a smile inside a neatly trimmed goatee. I blink as I approach.

"Jarrett?" the professor says.

"Yes." I want to be gracious, but I'm cautious. I have no idea who they are or what this is about.

"Keith Findley," the professor says, extending his hand. We shake and his smile broadens. I sit at the insistence of the guard, who backs away. Keith waits for him to settle into the shadows and then introduces the others, his students, Courtney Reed and Jim Miller.

"We're from the Wisconsin Innocence Project," Keith says.

I exhale so loudly, everyone in the room probably hears me.

"From the University of Wisconsin," I say.

"Yes," Keith says. "Jarrett, I know we're facing a deadline so we need to work fast."

He looks at Jim. Jim leans in and says, "We're going to begin by doing a quick intake."

"Right now?" I say.

"Yes, all your information," Courtney says. "All the details of the case."

"We're on a fast track," Keith says. "We really have no time to waste."

I look at him, then at Jim, then at Courtney. I swallow, hold for a count of three, and then I say, my voice cracking, "So, I mean, do you—"

"We want to take your case," Keith says, grins, nods at his students. "I wasn't sure at first. They convinced me."

For a moment, I cannot decipher or comprehend a single word.

That sentence—"we want to take your case"—crashes in my head like a crack of thunder. The words echo. The words drown out all other sound.

Finally, I'm able to focus. Keith says he needs all my documentation. I hand him my paperwork. He shuffles through it and shakes his head.

"I've never seen anything like this," he says, still shaking his head. "You're so *prepared*."

"I spend a lot of time in the law library," I say.

"Unbelievably impressive."

"Thank you."

"We get an overwhelming amount of submissions," Keith says. "We're a nonprofit. We rely on our students. We try to look at every one, but given our situation—"

He pauses.

"We only take on the cases we're confident we can win."

I nod, feeling myself biting my lip.

"Okay," Keith says. "You'll need to sign an agreement, allowing us to represent you, assuming that's what you—"

"I do," I say.

Jim slides the agreement across the table toward me.

I do.

That's what two people say when they get married.

In the visiting area of the Green Bay Correctional maximum-security prison, I'm marrying the Wisconsin Innocence Project.

For better, for worse . . . I pledge myself to you . . .

Till death do us part.

Fourteen days until the deadline.

I get on a conference call with Courtney and Jim, the two students from the Innocence Project. They have gone over the habeas petition I worked on with Rob Henak and begun preparing the adjusted, official habeas petition, the one they will submit. They compliment me on how well I've presented my argument of ineffective assistance of counsel. I'm grateful to Rob, who got me to this point. Courtney and Jim explain the next step. I will have another meeting with them and Keith to go over their argument and give me a copy of the final draft, the certificate of appealability. No one mentions the loud ticking of the clock we all hear.

Six days before the deadline.

Keith, Courtney, Jim, and I meet again in the visiting area. Keith absently strokes his goatee.

"Jarrett, you have a very strong argument here," he says. "We are absolutely going to include the ineffective assistance of counsel. But that is one of the hardest burdens to meet. We want to lead with another argument."

"What would that be?"

"Insufficient evidence," Jim says.

"Your case reeks of obvious racism," Courtney says.

"The young woman testified that nobody threatened her, nobody forced her," Keith says. "She said that over and over."

I see their argument. I hear their outrage.

Keith leans in, raises his voice. "For the court to uphold this guilty verdict, they would have to say that the mere presence of three Black kids in a room with a white girl was enough to equal force, or threat of force. That is egregious."

I look past them, at the guard who gazes at me vacantly, and try to decide what I think.

I've known all along that racism lived at the core of my conviction. Other than the three of us and our families, the only black you saw in that courtroom was the judge's robe.

But I never considered leading with that. I have spent literally *years* agonizing over how to present a succinct, clear, powerful argument of ineffective assistance of counsel, and now Keith, not only a lawyer, but a law professor, wants to lead with insufficiency of the evidence. It makes total sense. And it feels overwhelming.

I spread my arms on the table and feel my eyes starting to close. I have never felt so wasted, so completely—depleted.

"Man, I'm tired," I say.

"What do you think?" Keith says. "About leading with that argument."

I don't care what you lead with as long as you lead me out of here.

That's what I think. I don't say that.

I say, "Look, when you put your name on my case, when you say this is coming from the Wisconsin Innocence Project, people will take notice. I defer to you. I believe in my argument. But I am comfortable with whatever makes you comfortable."

"We think it's the way to go," Courtney says. "At least that's how we should lead."

I lift my head.

"I need to say one thing. This is my opinion, based on my observation, from my experience and from working with inmates for years. I don't think any court in Wisconsin will acknowledge that race is a problem in criminal cases."

"This—?" Keith says, gesturing across the room. "I mean, come on. You got twenty-eight years? What happened to you is beyond egregious. It's criminal."

I don't know if I agree. I've been filing cases for inmates, going with my gut, but always making sure my arguments were sound, and I've been winning. I realize now that I have to give up control. I have to trust Keith and the Wisconsin Innocence Project with my future.

"Okay," I say. "Let's lead with insufficient evidence."

I go back to my cell, my mind racing, my body burning.

Six days.

I pace. I speak quietly, but aloud, to myself, to God. I pace, then stop and press myself against the bars. Since when are Black people treated fairly in this country? Especially in the state of Wisconsin?

I pace some more, wear out the cell floor; then I collapse onto my cot.

I don't want to be defeatist, but I feel beaten up.

A question haunts me: Am I about to enter a fight that has been fixed?

Do I already know the outcome?

Five days to go.

Four.

Three.

When I don't hear from anyone, I start obsessing.

What if they don't file on time?

What if something happens to the paperwork?

What if they get into an accident?

Maybe I should bypass them and send in the submission myself.

I can't miss this deadline.

Two days to go.

Nothing. Not a word.

I feel sick. My nerves turn in on me. My body aches. I get stabbing pains in my stomach. I feel so impotent, so out of control. I pray. I list every sin I've ever done, every action that comes close to a sin, and I beg for forgiveness. I drop to my knees in my cell and I pray: "Please let them make this submission on time, please. Whatever I did, I'll never do it again. Please, oh, Lord. Please."

The deadline comes. The deadline goes. Silence closes in on me. I hear nothing, not a sound. It's as if I've suddenly gone deaf. I can't eat. Forget sleep. I can't concentrate on anything.

A day passes. Another.

Then the clanging of keys.

I get mail.

I receive a packet from the Wisconsin Innocence Project. They have filed on time, a day *before* the deadline, and they have sent me a copy of the filing. Then I get a phone call—Keith, Courtney, and Jim on a conference call.

"We just wanted to let you know we filed," Keith says.

"I got the copy. Thank you."

"Here's what happens next," Keith says. "We wait."

I laugh.

"This could take a minute," Keith says.

It will take a lot more than a minute, I think. I lost in the appellate court two years ago. It took another year for the Wisconsin Supreme Court to refuse to hear my case. This will likely take another year. Each stage in the process has taken a year of my life.

"Now, you could be denied by the federal district court and prevail in the U.S. Court of Appeals for the Seventh Circuit," Keith says. "That could happen."

"That will happen," I say.

I blurt that because I believe it.

"I'm going to win on ineffective assistance of counsel. I feel it."

"Well, we think the other argument is so strong—"

"It is strong. It's a good argument."

I take a breath before I speak.

"I sit up here and all I do is read cases. If the court rules that way on race, it will open the floodgates. Everyone will start using that argument—that race was used to meet an element of force or threat."

I raise my voice, raw with emotion—rage and frustration and exhaustion rushing out in one massive exhale.

"The Supreme Court and all the courts have never been sympathetic to Black people making arguments based on color. That is a fact. Look at how the courts treat us. The Supreme Court in *Dred Scott v. Sandford* ruled that we were not even *human*. Do you remember that? Look, I appreciate everything you're doing and I am hoping against hope, but how can you expect me to have confidence that justice will prevail based on *race*?"

Silence.

For a moment, I think they have hung up the phone.

I whisper, the emotion congealed like a rock in my chest. "No justice is going to happen for me in a Wisconsin court. I've got to get out of there, out of the district court. I will win in the Seventh Circuit. Again, I sit up here all day long, day after day, reading these rulings on other people's cases. They didn't touch the importance of my eyewitness. They never acknowledged that. All they say is your lawyer had a trial strategy. That is utter nonsense. They didn't even address Rovaughn's 11–1 verdict to acquit. It's outrageous."

No one speaks. I sigh and whisper even lower. "I'm sorry. I'm so—"

"I know," Keith says.

"I'm sorry," I say again.

"I wish I could speed this along somehow," Keith says, "but it's out of my control."

"I know how that feels." I sigh again. "Okay, so we wait."

After a pause, I say to reassure them, to reassure myself, and because I believe it, "One way or another, we *will* win."

I thank them, hang up the phone, and return to my cell.

I pace, I pray, I wait.

———

A week passes. Happy New Year, 2005. Two more weeks pass. Then three weeks. I keep working my cases. Busloads of fresh inmates arrive, some guys I remember from Waupun. They huddle in the bullpen, waiting intake. "Li'l Johnnie Cochran," I hear more than a few times. "What you doing up here? Hey, man, you take a look at my legal work?"

Time passes. Weeks, months. Buses of prisoners arrive continually. Green Bay Correctional bulges at the seams. Every second I spend away from the law library, I fear that some newbie who's either drugged or deranged will lose his mind and come at me. Meanwhile, nothing from the district court. I'm so antsy I can't sit still in my cell. I pace like a maniac. I'm in constant motion. I bet I've logged a thousand miles walking five feet by nine feet and back again. Then, one night, two guards barge into my cell—one the size of a nose tackle with a mean streak, and the formerly friendly guard who used to talk sports with me. That was before. He's since turned cold and hard. They roust me out of my cot, yanking my legs.

"Hey, what—?"

"Pack up your stuff."

"Why?"

"You're going to segregation."

"**G**roup resistance," they say. "Smuggling drugs into the prison."

Another trumped-up charge. The same confidential informant nonsense.

They tie me to a crazy scheme involving a program where inmates make teddy bears for kids. Inmates have been sending the bears to a wrong address, where someone on the outside stuffs them with cigarettes and weed and mails them back, return to sender. Guys call this program the Teddy Bear Mafia. I don't take part, but an alleged confidential informant has tied me to the smuggling ring. The reporting officer calls me an instigator, a direct threat to prison society.

As punishment, they give me another 360 days in segregation.

I'll fight this. I'll litigate my way out as I did before. I'll file a writ of certiorari the way I did before. It's a ridiculous replay of previous events. Déjà vu all over again.

I tell myself I'm ready for segregation this time. I know how to do it. I'll read, I'll write, I'll read my Bible verses, I'll pray, I'll enjoy my weekly shower. I'll play chess through the vents. I'll talk to the walls. I'll sit and stare at the TV, flipping through my five channels. All while I wait in agony for the ruling to come down from the district court.

It sounds insane. But to stay sane in segregation, you have to do insane things.

I tell myself that I can do segregation again.

That's what I tell myself.

I have to.

But no one can do segregation. Segregation does you.

Two months in, while reading the Bible, I suddenly find myself filling up with rage. "I'm sick of this crap!" I shout.

But maybe I shouted in my mind.

I pace furiously, drop down to the floor, rip off a hundred push-ups, pause, rip off another hundred, then *another* hundred. I keep going until I collapse, drained, exhausted. I feel numb, and then I feel gutted. Nine more months of this? When will I hear about my writ? When will I hear from the court about my petition?

I stare into space, the world appearing foggy, murky. When did I start thinking only in questions?

Then, as if God has a pager, He finds me. He sends me a message.

An angel.

That night, I gaze at my TV, listlessly flipping through my five channels, ABC, NBC, CBS, CNN, PBS. I stop at a program on PBS about the death penalty. I stare transfixed at a face that fills the screen. A white man. Stephen Bright, a director of the Southern Center for

Human Rights in Atlanta. A frenetic bundle of nerves, his eyes blazing behind horn-rimmed glasses, his face thin, almost gaunt.

The interviewer asks Stephen a question about his work and his views on the death penalty. Stephen goes off. A lawyer, he represents mostly poor people and people of color who have been given the death penalty. He talks about how he finds this population to be the most vulnerable and the most underrepresented. Poor people, Black people, and brown people facing the highest stakes are the ones most often put to death because they don't have good lawyers.

That is fundamentally unconstitutional.

I don't know whether Stephen Bright says that to me on PBS or I say that to myself in my cell. Either way, he speaks to me. We have a broken system, he says and I parrot back, nodding emphatically at the TV. I watch this man, this fiery, seemingly inexhaustible attorney fighting to right a wrong and defend people who need competent representation, and I say to myself, I have to get out of here and I have to join that fight.

I'm not sure if I determine that I will become a lawyer at that exact moment, but I know that Stephen Bright's passion motivates me.

Pick yourself up off the floor, I tell myself. Literally. Figuratively.

You got work to do.

13.
Innocence

Two months into isolation, I lie on my cot, reading. A guard rattles my cell. "You have a phone call." I slowly roll up to a sitting position. I lower my feet to the floor, moving even slower. I lick my lips. I feel a sense of doom. The guard grunts impatiently as he shackles my legs. I shuffle in front of him, walking slowly, painfully, my leg irons clanging.

I take the phone and murmur a muted hello.

Keith greets me and introduces me to two other voices on the line, the students who have joined him this semester, Carl Williams and Andy Twitmeyer, replacing Courtney and Jim. After a formal, even stiff set of hellos, Keith, Carl, and Andy halt and seemingly share a single breath. Then Keith speaks, breaking the clumsy silence.

"We got the ruling from the federal district court," he says. "They denied your petition."

"We're shocked," Carl says.

"We're going to appeal it to the Seventh Circuit," Andy says.

"I know we've just met," Carl says, "but I—we all—feel very frustrated. As a Black man myself, I feel you have been wronged."

These students, I think. Brimming with optimism, idealism. They mean so well.

I look at the line of cells, try to shut out the sounds of the night: inhuman cackling, a cappella singing, men screaming for no reason at all. I peer at my handcuffs as if seeing them for the first time. Are these my wrists? I float away mentally for a moment. Where am I? Who am I? Segregation messes with your head. Then I come back to earth, to this place. I eye the guard snarling at me, ten yards away, looking for any excuse to rough me up. He clears his throat as if announcing his presence, and I think, *These students, their world out there, is some sort of fantasy world.*

"Listen," I say. "Keith, Carl, Andy. I don't want you to feel bad. You did your best. But I am not at all surprised. I fully expected us not to get any justice from this court."

"I know you said that," Keith says.

"I just don't understand it," Carl says. "How can they gloss over this?"

"We're going to win the appeal at the Seventh Circuit," I say. "That's our best shot. We'll finally get out of Wisconsin. I see going to the district court as a formality."

"Jarrett," Keith says, "you really are something. How do you stay so positive? I want to bottle that."

"I've just seen a lot," I say. Then I add, quietly, "I've seen too much."

Months later, a guard leads me out of temporary lockup at Green Bay and into a van. I am driven back to Boscobel, the all-segregation supermax where I previously spent nearly a year in isolation. The prison feels as foreboding and as ominous as ever. Banished to Boscobel. A guard brings me down a narrow corridor and deposits me in my segregated cell. I take one step in and feel as if I've walked into a coffin.

Time drips like a slow leak. I crave news. Then, one day, a sliver of light knifes across the floor. The Wisconsin Innocence Project notifies me that they have officially filed the appeal to the Seventh Circuit, located in Chicago. My birthplace. My home. The city that now holds my fate in its hands. I try not to obsess. I try to distract myself from waiting. I write. I read. I play chess through the walls. I pray. I pace. Repeat. Each day hollows me out a little. Each day takes a nick out of my soul.

Two months evaporate. Then news comes. The Seventh Circuit has granted my certificate of appealability. Keith asks for an oral argument. Not a given. But a good sign for us if the court grants it. I believe in the strength of our argument, its solid, legal foundation. Keith will argue the case in front of a panel of three judges. Good, I think. I have the law on my side. *Strickland v. Washington* alive, in living color.

Time drips . . . drips . . . drips . . .

My birthday comes, goes, then Merry Christmas, and the calendar reads 2006. With the New Year comes an unseasonably sticky heat in the air that signals a premature spring. My cell turns into a sweatbox. I pace, my head pounding, my pores gushing. The heat suffocates me. My body feels on fire. Then, one day, I get the word. The Seventh Circuit will hear the oral argument.

On the day of the hearing, a guard opens my cell, handcuffs me, shackles my legs, and leads me the length of a city block to a pay phone. Because I'm in segregation, the state won't allow me to attend the hearing, but I know my mother and aunts are there. The guard hands me the phone and stands to the side. Keith has arranged to patch me into the courtroom. I grip the phone tightly, squeezing the receiver. My mouth goes dry as I hear Keith start his defense—the ineffective assistance of counsel. He explains that my lawyer used "no defense" as his strategy, failing to investigate and call Shawn Demain as a witness.

The presiding judge, Diane Wood, interrupts him. "Why would he do that?"

"He didn't get it," Keith says. "He simply didn't get it. I guess he thought it was a valid strategic defense."

Keith proceeds with his defense. After his allotted ten minutes, he concludes his argument and thanks the judges. The judge calls the prosecutor, who begins by offering a definition of ineffective assistance of counsel.

Judge Wood cuts her off.

"We know the standard of review for ineffective assistance of counsel. We can repeat that in our sleep. I want to know why counsel didn't call Shawn Demain as a witness. It would seem extremely pertinent."

"Well, Your Honor—"

"When you don't have much, you need to call witnesses, and this *strategy* of calling no one bothers me."

"It was a strategic decision," the prosecutor says.

"But why? Not going with a witness is a little . . . *odd.*"

The judge pauses. I feel my palms sweat. I move the phone to my other ear.

"Why didn't he try to find the witness?" Judge Wood asks.

"I think he made an effort."

"What was that effort?"

"I—I assume he called the campus—"

The judge dismisses this. "The co-defendant's counsel found him."

Rovaughn's attorney, I think. Boyle.

"It couldn't have been all that hard," the judge says.

She asks the prosecutor a few more questions, and then the judge raises her voice in what sounds like either frustration or irritation.

"It's really hard to see force in her account of what happened."

"Well, the *threat* of force," the prosecutor says, and adds in a small, thin voice, "I admit it's a close case."

"Did she ever explain why she didn't leave another way . . . when she's being *threatened*?"

"She doesn't fully explain that."

The prosecutor then offers what sounds like a halfhearted summation. She ends by saying, "I ask that you deny Mr. Adams his petition."

Judge Wood thanks the prosecution, thanks Keith, and says they will take the case under advisement.

The hearing ends. It has lasted a total of twenty minutes.

The line goes dead.

They will take my case under advisement?

They are taking my *life* under advisement.

My hand starts shaking.

The guard steps forward and asks for the phone.

I try to hand it to him, but I can't pry my fingers off the receiver.

June 30, 2006.

I pace in my cell, my body slick with sweat. Since the hearing, I have done almost nothing else. I try reading the Bible verses my aunties send, but I can't focus. Words prance across the page, the letters scrambled. So I pace. I trek another million miles in my cell, waiting.

Then, one day, I hear keys jangling in the distance. Coming closer. The jangling abruptly stops. My trapdoor slides open with a boom. I jump. I blink furiously. I know it's too early for mail. I stare at the open trap, and then the guard says, "You have a legal call."

"All right," I say. "All right."

I retreat a few steps, allowing the guard to come into my cell.

He chains me up. He puts me in shackles.

I want to say, "I'm going to a phone call, not my execution."

But I don't speak. I can't speak. I shuffle out of my cell, hunched over. I feel like a condemned man.

The guard leads me on that long walk to the phone. He hands me the receiver and backs away. I expect to hear silence as I wait to be patched into the call, but I pick up the phone and I hear laughter over a speakerphone. It's as if I've broken into someone's celebration, a private party. The voices speak happily over each other, and after a moment I make out Keith's voice, and Carl's, and Andy's, and I swallow and say, "Hey, it's Jarrett."

"Jarrett," Andy says, drawing my name out, almost as if he were singing or shouting at me across a room.

"Carl," Keith says. "Why don't you tell him?"

"Wow, sure." Carl pauses. "Jarrett, we've got some good news."

"Okay."

"We won. You won the habeas appeal."

I cannot speak.

My mind snaps shut.

"Did you hear me?" Carl says. "YOU WON."

Click.

The line goes dead.

They've hung up.

Or—someone has hung up.

The guard bull-rushes me from the shadows, grips me by both biceps, pulls me away from the phone. "Let's go. Call's over."

He shoves me back toward my cell.

"Wait," I say. "That was a legal call. Attorney-client. That's privileged."

I speak to silence. To air. The guard grunts and practically drags me back into my cell. He slams the door and storms off.

They were listening, I think. I've been filing complaints against being in segregation, trying to litigate my way out, complaining against the guards' treatment—especially this guard—and *they were listening.*

I hit my emergency call button. I punch it with my fist. No one comes. I lean on it, slam my palm over it, hold it down. Finally, the same guard returns.

"I was on a *legal* call," I say. "The phone hung up."

The guard stands outside my cell, folds his thick tattooed arms, and stares at me. He pretends he hasn't heard what I said.

"You got a legal call," he says.

Back on the phone, I wait for Keith, Carl, and Andy. After what feels like ten minutes, I hear a hum, some static, and then their voices come on, overlapping.

"That was strange," Carl says. "The line went dead. Like someone hung up."

"Like someone was *listening* and hung up," I say.

"That's never happened," Keith says. "In all my years as a lawyer. They can't do that. Breaks every protocol, every rule of law."

"They wouldn't do that," Carl says.

"Well, I didn't hang up," I say.

"Neither did we," Andy says.

"So," Carl says. "Did you hear what we said? You *won.*"

"I heard," I say.

Yes. The court has vacated my conviction. My record will now appear as if the first trial and conviction never happened. The court has ordered the state to either retry me or dismiss all the charges.

"It's *amazing,*" Carl says. "We're thrilled for you. Aren't you happy?"

I don't feel happy.

I feel numb and terrified. This feels so fragile. I "won" at my first trial, too. Yet here I sit not just in prison for nearly eight years but in segregation.

"We won this round," I say.

"Well, we know, but—"

"There are two more parts."

"Two more possible parts," Keith says.

"Two more levels," I say. "The Seventh Circuit reversed the district court. But they still have an opportunity to petition for a rehearing en banc."

En banc.

"We won in front of a three-judge panel. The prosecution could say they felt something was missing at the hearing and request a rehearing in front of all the judges in the Seventh Circuit."

"It was unanimous, Jarrett," Keith says. "All three judges agreed that your conviction should be reversed. Based on evidence. *Strickland v. Washington.* You were right."

"They could appeal," I say in a hushed voice. "And if the Seventh Circuit denies it, they could request that the Supreme Court look at it. There are two more possible steps."

"It won't happen," Keith says. Then, after a moment, he adds, "I can't believe you even knew about en banc. You're more knowledgeable than some lawyers."

"Keith," I say, my voice shaking. "I'm very glad we got where we are. I am. But I'm in here locked up for no reason. You have to excuse me for being cautious."

Then I lower my voice again. "They could still be listening."

"Who?" Keith says. "The guard?"

"I have to be careful," I whisper. "I have to think two steps ahead. I can't disappoint my mother again. It'll kill her."

"We understand," Keith says. "Still, I believe this decision will hold."

"What happens next?" I say.

"They have 120 days to either release you or retry you. If we hear nothing in that time, then your case has been overturned."

"So, I wait some more," I say. "Plus, I'm still a ward of the state, still have to do segregation, unless I litigate out."

"Unfortunately," Keith says.

"A hundred and twenty days," I say.

Are you listening? I want to shout into the phone. I'm in segregation and they still want to take away any shred of privacy I have left.

"One hundred and twenty days until I walk out of prison," I say.

"Yes," Keith says.

"Not like in the movies, is it? I won. But I don't walk."

"No. Not like the movies."

"Four more months," I say. "A lifetime."

"Jarrett," Keith says, "this is going to happen."

One hundred and twenty days.

Each morning feels like a week. Each afternoon, another week. The nights don't exist. They seem like shadowy versions of the day. Lying in bed, I replay the first phone call: Carl telling me we won, the phone line going dead, then the second call with Keith explaining the time I have left. A hundred and twenty days . . . 119 . . . 118 . . .

One day at a time.

If I don't take that approach, I'll go crazy.

Too late, I tell myself.

A hundred and *sixteen* . . .

———

Two and a half months after the Seventh Circuit's decision, I get word that my writ of certiorari has been granted. The legal department sends me a notice. I will be released from segregation. I'm going back to general population.

Where?

Waupun.

Where I first went, a lifetime ago. The prison where I started.

"When?" I ask.

As soon as a bed opens up.

How long will—

As soon as a bed opens up.

Thirty-two days to go . . . thirty-one . . . thirty . . .

A bed opens up.

I check with Keith.

"We've heard nothing," he says. "Not a thing. You have to think—"

"We still have thirty days," I say.

"I know, but—"

"Thirty days," I say. "Forever."

On the bus from Boscobel back to Waupun, I start sensing a different vibe all around me, a new aura surrounding me. *His case is being overturned.* The chatter vibrates through the prison underground. Inmates look at me differently. *He's getting out.* I begin wearing that truth like a layer of clothes. But then I start to feel antsy. My body shivers involuntarily from nerves. I see the finish line. I see it, but it suddenly moves farther away, a tiny line in the distance. I can't rush the days. I can't force time to speed up. I slowly tear away the days in my mind.

Twenty-two days to go.

The officer at the desk greets me as I reenter Waupun. Captain Belinsky. I know him. Old white dude. Fat fingers stained yellow from cigarettes. His breath reeks of cigarettes and beer. He wears a handlebar mustache that he subconsciously twirls like a cartoon villain. He hates me. I'm not crazy about him either.

"What's your number?"

He coughs, doesn't cover his mouth.

I recite my number, etched in my brain for forever—"385073."

"I'm not gonna have no trouble with you this time, am I?"

"What do you mean?"

"You know what I mean."

"If you mean the constitutional work I do, helping people with their due process, then, yeah, you might have some trouble with me."

He hacks up some spit, wipes his mouth with his sleeve.

"I hear you're getting out."

"Ugly rumor."

"Ain't that *nice*. I'll see you when you come back, telling me your number all over again. Because you will be back. Don't worry. We'll keep your bed warm for you in segregation."

"I'm never coming back. At least not as an inmate."

Twenty days to go.

I don't go out to the rec yard. I don't go out to the chow hall. I take quick showers. I read my psalms. I go to church. I hardly speak. I don't want to say the wrong thing, so I don't say anything.

Nineteen . . . eighteen . . . seventeen . . .

Then single digits. I count down as if I were about to be sent off into space. Five . . . four . . . three . . . two . . . one.

Day 120 comes.

I call Keith.

"We haven't heard a word," he says. "Not a single word."

"So—"

"Technically, they have until the end of the day. If we don't hear anything, they have to let you out."

"Midnight," I say.

I pace. I sense it now. They're not going to call. I know we have won. I decide to get rid of everything, all my belongings. A purge. A cleanse. I can't have a yard sale, so I have a cell sale. I give away my TV, my thermal underwear, my flip-flops, my chess set, my typewriter, everything that's not nailed down.

Midnight passes.

The Innocence Project doesn't call.

I panic.

I call Keith an hour after dawn.

"A sheriff is on his way to bring you to Jefferson County Jail," Keith says. "They haven't authorized you to go home yet. But you're leaving prison."

"Are you sure?"

"He has a court order," Keith says.

The sheriff, court order in hand, waits for me at the threshold of a doorway inside Waupun Correctional Institution. By law, the prison has to deliver me to him. He can't cross the threshold. As the sheriff waits, a guard comes into my cell, chains me up, puts me in shackles. Another nonsensical protocol.

"Is this really necessary?" I say.

The guard grunts, pushes me out of the cell.

I don't look back. I'm not sure if I want to take this walk slowly, savor every second, or if I want to sprint down the corridor and shriek goodbye to this place.

I come to Captain Belinsky at the front desk. He twirls his mustache with his cigarette-stained fingers. He coughs, snaps at me. "What's your number?"

I stand as straight as I can, the shackles biting into me.

"370583."

"That's not your number. You trying to be a smart guy?"

"Oh, no, *sir*. I'm giving you my number backward because I'm giving it *back* to you. I don't need it anymore."

He curses under his breath.

The sheriff looks at me, gestures at my shackles. "What is this? Why is he all chained up?"

"That's how we do it," Belinsky says.

"Take all that off. Handcuffs will do."

Belinsky sniffs. "He could make a run for it."

"I kind of doubt that a guy who's about to get out is going to try to *break* out," the sheriff says.

As the guard undoes the shackles on my legs, I think about how I came in here as a convicted nineteen-year-old rapist. That's how they all saw me. Now, for the first time, someone—this man, this sheriff—sees me as a human being.

"Thank you," I say.

November 2006.

A week before my twenty-sixth birthday.

I sit across from my new court-appointed attorney, John Rhiel, in a small stuffy room in Jefferson County Jail. John, more knowledge-able, focused, and passionate than the other court-appointed attorneys I've encountered, has just delivered bad news.

"It looks like the state might be planning to retry you," John says. "I want us to be prepared. We're going to be proactive. Let's put everything together. If they want to take you to trial, we'll overwhelm them with evidence. Again, that's the worst case."

"This has been nearly ten years of my life," I say. "I've already gone through the worst case."

"I just want to be ready," John says.

My birthday feels different this year. I'm no longer in prison, I'm in jail. In prison, inmates have reached their end. They are often men who are spending years without hope. In this jail, I still sense hope from these inmates, men believing that they will be found not guilty and released. The atmosphere feels less tense, less dangerous.

I also have more access to the phone, so I speak to my mother and my aunts regularly, and the Man upstairs has decided to give me a special birthday present this year: a Chicago Bears dream team. The linebackers Lance Briggs and Brian Urlacher anchor a vicious defense. The quarterback Rex Grossman leads an explosive offense, and Devin Hester, a thrilling rookie speed merchant, returns six kickoffs for touchdowns, a record, I'm sure. I devour the sports pages and stay glued to every game. My Bears demolish opponent after opponent, running their record to 13–3. I have no doubt that this team, led by Lovie Smith, an African American coach, will make the Super Bowl. This force of a team, my Bears, becomes the symbol of my fight. I am the Bears. The Bears are me.

In early December, John and I go to my bond hearing. Simply put, my case now reverts to its beginning stages. Everything starts over. Until all charges have been dropped, the court can look at me as if I have just been accused of the same crime.

To that end, at the hearing, the prosecutor argues that the court should set my bond at a thousand dollars for each year of my original sentence—twenty-eight thousand dollars.

My lawyer grabs my sleeve to keep me from leaping up and shouting.

"Don't respond," John says. "I got this."

"Your Honor," he says, standing. "My client and his family have gone through an ordeal in every way, including financially. The family doesn't have that kind of money. They're drained. We're asking that you set the bond at a reasonable amount so he can be let out and go home. I'm asking for five thousand dollars."

The judge splits the difference, sets the bond at fifteen thousand dollars. To him, it's a compromise.

To me, a punch in the gut. There's no way my family can afford it.

After the hearing, John and I huddle in the hallway before I return to my cell at Jefferson County Jail.

"This is all a ploy," John says. "They want you to plead. If you plead, nobody on the state side will be held liable. Prosecutor's not liable

and the judge is not liable for what was clearly a wrongful conviction."

"Plead to a lesser charge," I say.

"Right. You do that, you go home. Probably today."

"Why do prosecutors go after the innocent?" I ask.

"Because they can," John says.

"I know. They figure, set an astronomical bond, an amount he can't
possibly pay. He's desperate to go home. He's this close. He'll accept
the deal. He'll plead."

"That's exactly right," John says.

"Well, two things. First, I've spent more time in the law library
than anyone I know, probably more than some lawyers. I know how
this works. If I plead guilty to some lesser charge and go back to court
and the breaks don't go my way—which they won't because of who I
am and who my lawyer will be—I'll end up back in prison finishing
up my twenty-eight years. Am I right?"

"What's the second thing?" John says.

"I'm innocent. I'm not pleading guilty to *anything*. Ask for a new
bond motion."

"You have to wait thirty days."

"At this point, what's another thirty days? I want all the charges
dropped. I'm *innocent*."

Happy New Year, 2007.

John files for a new bond motion. The court sets the hearing date
for late January. The weekend before the bond hearing, on a brutally
cold day at Soldier Field in Chicago, the Bears destroy the New Or-
leans Saints 39–14 to win the NFC Championship. They will face the
Indianapolis Colts in the Super Bowl on February 4 in Miami. The
game will be historic. Both the Bears and the Colts have African
American head coaches. Even if the Bears lose, I will take some sol-
ace that for the first time in history the Super Bowl winner will be
coached by a Black man. A milestone for the sport.

Friday, January 26, 2007. John and I attend the bond hearing. We take our seats and Judge William Hue, the same professorial-looking judge who presided at my arraignment nearly a decade ago, walks in. His hair has gone completely white and he wears it shorter, but otherwise he doesn't seem to have aged. I don't expect him to remember me, but when he looks up, I see a flicker of recognition in his eyes.

John asks the court to reduce my bond to five thousand dollars, from fifteen thousand. Judge Hue takes a moment, considers the circumstances, and splits the difference again, lowering the bond to ten thousand dollars. I heave a huge sigh. I spoke to my mother two days before the hearing. She told me if we could get the bond down to ten thousand dollars, the family will somehow, some way, find the money to get me home. John and I agree to the bond. That will do it. My mother will pay it, pick me up, and I will walk out of Jefferson County Jail and the State of Wisconsin prison system.

"Okay," Judge Hue says, "bond is set at ten thousand dollars." Then he leans forward at the bench and speaks directly to me.

"Best of luck, young man," he says. "I'm sorry that this had to happen to you."

"Thank you, Your Honor."

Two days later—Sunday, January 28, 2007—I am released.

That morning, I can't stop thinking about *time.*

Time served. Time spent. Keeping time. Time flies. Time's up. Wasting time.

Doing time. Hard time.

I did my time.

And mostly, I have lost so much time.

As I prepare to leave a five-by-nine-foot cell forever, time stops, time blurs. Years later, my memory will fog over when I try to recall what comes next.

I remember telling my mother on the phone, "Mom, I'll be home for Valentine's Day."

I remember seeing my mother in the waiting area of Jefferson County Jail, her hair thinned and white, her face drawn, wrinkled, ravaged. I have been behind bars for almost ten years. She has aged twenty.

I remember walking out of Jefferson County Jail, a nondescript boxy white building in the middle of nowhere.

I remember stepping into a shaft of frigid air, stopping for one second, and squinting up at the sky as I leave the building, even though the day is gray and cloudy. The bitter cold air snips my face, and my eyes burn.

I remember my stepfather holding my mother, holding her up.

I remember my mother crying softly and wanting to hug me, to cling to me. I hug her briefly and say, "Mom, please, I have to get out of here. Please. I need to get into the car."

I remember getting into the backseat of the car and my stepfather driving us away from Jefferson County Jail. I curl forward, watching the building filling up the rearview mirror, then becoming smaller and smaller until I can no longer see it; I only feel it.

I remember music playing quietly and only occasional conversation. I want to answer all of my mother's questions. I want to soothe her. But I know nothing I say will soothe her.

I remember her crying on the way home, asking, "What will you do?"

And my answer.

"I'm going to be a lawyer."

I remember saying that.

I don't explain how I will achieve that, because I have no idea. I just know that I will.

I remember stopping at a Red Lobster. I remember watching all the diners, then looking in front of me, to the sides, behind me, trying to process that I am in a restaurant and not in a prison chow hall. I remember eating as if I haven't eaten in ten years, which, in some sense, is true.

I remember returning to Chicago, skirting and passing downtown, arriving in an unfamiliar suburb, pulling in to the driveway of a house I don't know.

I remember my stepfather stopping the car and turning back to me. "We're home, Jarrett."

Home.

I don't remember what that is.

II.
Rise

14.

Home

"Jarrett."

My mother, leaning against the passenger door, speaks softly.

I look at her, standing outside, her frail body trembling, her breath forming cloud circles. I feel glued to the backseat, immobilized.

"Come in the house, baby," she says. "It's cold out here."

I exhale my own cloud, haul myself out of the car, and drag myself up the driveway. As I walk toward the door, I hear imaginary voices in my head.

You must be so happy to be home. You must feel so relieved.

I don't feel happy or relieved. I feel deeply—anxious.

My stepfather opens the door and I walk inside. I stop suddenly in the living room, as if I have slammed into an invisible wall. The house feels comfortable, lived in, and foreign. I don't know this place. I see no bars, but I feel closed in. Trapped. Then I look around and I can feel my mother in here. Her presence. I recognize a few of her things: a piece of furniture, a decorative pillow, a photo album on the coffee table, my framed high school graduation picture. I take a couple of steps farther in, and I hear something behind me. I whip around, my hands balled into fists. My stepfather nods and quietly closes the door. I unclench my hands and take a few more steps into the room. I make a show of looking around. I feel so displaced. I find my mother's eyes, and I smile at her clumsily.

"Nice," I say.

"We like it," she says.

I swallow, trying to dislodge the knot in my throat.

"Do I—where do I—?"

"Oh, your room. Let me show you," my mother says.

My room, I think. Leaving prison, I never thought about having a room of my own that wasn't a cell. I never considered where I would sleep, where I would live when I got out. I think now, first with irony, then with building anger, that by leaving prison, I have become a man with nothing. I have no money, no clothes, no possessions. The company line—*you leave with a clean slate; you'll start all over, from scratch*—is meant to sound hopeful. Now it feels like an admission that when you get out of prison, you not only have nothing; you *are* nothing. You are no one.

My mother opens the door to the guest bedroom. I take in the single bed, end table, curtains. My room. I skirt the room, walk along the perimeter. My mother watches me. I stop at the foot of the bed.

"Habit," I say. "I'm used to checking for someone who might attack me. I have to adjust to—"

I can't finish the sentence, because I know the word I'm searching for is "everything."

"Take all the time you need," she says.

"Time."

That word again.

I point at some clothes folded neatly on the bed. A few undershirts. Pajamas. Socks.

"What's all this?"

"We didn't know if you had any clothes," my mother says. "Those are James's. Until you can get your own."

She's right. I have no clothes. I came home with a tracksuit I bought at the canteen, a pair of socks, and prison-issue work boots they force you to pay for and wear on your way out of jail.

"Thank you," I say.

My mother lowers her head, bites her lip. I hug her and she loses it, tears rolling down her cheeks, her breath choking with sobs.

"I'm back, Mom," I say.

"It's unreal."

"It is," I say. "Completely unreal."

"You must want to make up for lost time," she says.

"I didn't lose time," I say. "They stole it."

A few people come over to see me and to support my mother. My childhood friends Deshaun and Shaunte stop by, along with their parents and grandmother, and then my brother and his wife arrive with their two kids. I haven't had much contact with my brother since I went to prison. He's made a life for himself, raising a family and working a full-time job. At first, I feel a strain when we speak, as if I were talking with a stranger, someone I've just met. Those basketball games we played in back alleys by hanging a crate off a telephone pole seem like something I read in a book, not part of my actual life. I try to engage with my niece and nephew, but they seem shy, not sure who I am, how I fit in their world. I haven't seen my nephew since he was a baby, and he's not sure what to make of me now. He's nine, almost ten. I have never met my niece.

"I missed all this," I say.

"We missed you," my mother says.

"I mean, I missed those years, that time. It's been cut out of my life. I never had those years."

I look at my brother. "Think back at your life," I say. "Picture each decade. You're ten years old, twenty, thirty. You can see events from those years. Birthday parties, graduation, marriage, jobs, the birth of your kids. Now imagine looking back at your life and there's a ten-year gap where you see nothing. There are no memories. It's blank. That's what I mean when I say I missed all this. I never had it. I missed an entire decade."

We visit a while longer until the kids and I both start to get tired.

My brother scoops up my niece. She grins, twists toward me, and allows me to kiss her cheek. My nephew shyly ducks his head and extends his hand.

"You know what?" I say. "I think I'm gonna have to give you a hug."

I lift him up and hug him. He doesn't mind.

After my brother and his family leave, I sit at the kitchen table with my mother. We talk about the house, the neighborhood, this relative, that cousin, my aunts, her sisters. She asks about my plans. I tell her I want to pick up where I left off ten years ago, when I graduated from high school—finding a job, getting my car up and running, saving some money, going back to school, and moving into my own place. In other words, doing all the things you normally do when you turn eighteen. Except I'm going on twenty-seven.

"You'll do all that. I know you will," my mother says.

I suddenly feel hollowed out. The adrenaline coursing through me all day has fizzled, leaving me drained. I yawn, fidget, and adjust my position in my chair. I look past my mother, at the refrigerator.

"What's the matter?" my mother asks.

"I was wondering—"

I hesitate.

"What?"

"Could I get a glass of milk?"

"Of course. You don't have to ask for anything. This is your house. You get whatever you want from the fridge, anything."

You don't have to ask for anything. It seems so obvious. Normal. How do I explain to her that for ten years I have had to ask for everything? A pen. A pass to go to the law library. Permission to make a phone call. How do I explain how hard *normal* feels, how strange, how surreal, how unsettling?

"Thank you," I say.

I open the refrigerator, and for a moment I just stare inside. My eyes travel over the contents—milk, juice, soda, beer, cheese, cold cuts, a jar of pickles, fruits, vegetables—I gawk at it all. I ease out the carton of milk, close the refrigerator door, go to the cabinet, and pull down a glass. My hands shake as I pour the milk.

"I'm sorry, I'm just . . . I'm so used to, you know—"

"I know," my mother says.

But you don't know, I think. You can't know.

Wearing my stepfather's pajamas, I cruise the perimeter of the bed-room. I check the locks on the door and the windows, and then I look under the bed. Clear. I crawl into bed, try to find a comfortable position. The mattress feels soft, cushy. My back sags. I need a harder mattress.

The bed is in the middle of the room. I have spent ten years sleep-ing on alert, my back against the wall, facing the door. Lying in this position—on my back—away from the door causes a jolt of anxiety. I try to breathe it away. I eye the ceiling, inhale, exhale slowly, take an even slower breath, and then my breathing amps up, and I fear I may hyperventilate. I sit up, grab my pillow, and walk to the living room, trailing the blanket behind me.

In the living room, I go through the same routine. I walk the perim-eter of the room. I check the locks on the windows, check the lock on the front door, look through the curtains, scan the yard, the street, look as far as I can in every direction. Clear. I turn back and realize, thankfully, that the couch rests against the wall. I press the seat cush-ions, find them firm, harder than the bed in the guest bedroom. I lie down and push myself against the back of the couch, replicating the position I grew accustomed to in prison—back against the wall, fac-ing the front of my cell. After a while, my head slumps, my eyes flut-ter, and I drift off to a semi-sleep. Then I jerk awake. I hear something outside. Someone screaming on the second tier. No. A cat howling. I start to close my eyes again. A car backfires. Or is that a gunshot? I curl up against the couch again, fly back up when I hear a siren.

Before I know it, the first light of day sneaks across the living room floor. I extricate myself from the couch, gather up my pillow and blanket, and return to the guest bedroom. I don't want my mother to know that I can't sleep here. I can't abide her worrying about me. I've put her through enough. I lower myself onto the edge of the bed and look at my hands. I turn them over and study my wrists. I see invisible handcuffs. I feel the cold metal. I look up at the ceiling. I have left prison but prison has not left me.

The second day I'm home, I visit my aunts who live in the city. Honey and Sugar have aged, but being older hasn't diminished their physical strength. They take turns crushing me in a series of hugs. They cry; then we sit at the table, sipping coffee, and talk about faith and the power of prayer. I admit that when I first got incarcerated, I didn't have much use for God.

"I couldn't see Him," I say. "I couldn't feel Him."

"He could see you," Honey says.

"I found that out. Going to church saved me. The verses you sent saved me. Believing saved me."

"Now you have to find out what He has in mind for you," Sugar says.

"I will," I say. "I promise."

I offer to go to the grocery store for my mother. She writes out a list, gives me some cash, and slips an extra twenty-dollar bill into my hand.

"Get something for yourself," she says.

"Thank you," I say, and I do feel thankful.

I also feel humiliated. I should be buying her groceries out of my own money. But I have no money, no job, no bank account. I will start looking for work this evening. Now I walk into the grocery store, a casual, everyday errand nobody thinks twice about. I open the door and take a few steps in, and I freeze. Paranoia lunges at me, grips me.

Face and hands, I think, surveying the store, the shoppers, the clerks, the cashiers.

I walk farther into the store and keep my eyes fixed on faces and hands.

I blink and see myself back at Green Bay Correctional. Gladiator School. Every week a hundred new inmates infiltrate the population. I don't know where they stand, how violent or crazy they are, what message they may want to send. I don't know when something will happen, but I know something will.

"Sir?"

I see a man wearing a green apron standing behind a glass case. I'm at the meat department.

"Oh. I'm sorry."

"You're next."

My hands shake as I look over my mother's list. I can't decipher her writing, can't make out the words.

"Chicken," I say.

"How do you want it? Pieces? Thighs? Legs? A whole chicken?"

"I, uh—"

I stare at the man at the meat counter. He taps his fingers impatiently on the top of the glass case. I swivel my head and see a woman behind me, shaking her head. She must think there's something wrong with me. I want to explain to her and to the man at the meat counter that I just got out of prison. I spent a decade locked up for a crime I didn't commit. Being thrown back into normal society isn't as easy as you think. They don't prepare you for going in, and they prepare you even less for getting out.

But I don't say any of that.

"Thighs," I say.

My mother's ancient computer wheezes and whirs when I boot it up. I log on to Yahoo, a popular search engine, and look for jobs. I don't find much, and the computer's sluggish dial-up connection drives me crazy. My mind shouldn't move quicker than the computer. After an hour of poking around the Yahoo classifieds, I hit nothing but dead ends. I come away feeling inadequate, realizing that in order to get hired, I need a driver's license, a state ID, and a strong résumé.

Strange, I think. At seventeen, being interrogated by the police, I wanted only to go home. Now that I've come home, I feel this burning urge to leave. I want to be on my own, to stop being a burden to my mother, to be my own man. In prison, I was a lawyer. On the outside, I feel helpless.

My third day home, I take the train downtown to get my driver's license. Before heading to the DMV, I walk through my old neighborhood. The whole time I feel as if I've taken a wrong turn and entered an entirely different city. Businesses I remember have been replaced by stores I don't know. The corner grocery store has been torn down, a twenty-four-hour convenience store put up in its place. Houses have been demolished, leaving an alarming number of empty lots. I remember there being a pay phone on every corner. Now I see none.

I decide to go by my grandparents' old house, the Big House, where I spent so much of my childhood. I find the Big House sitting regally on its oversized corner lot. But the two big trees that used to be in front have been cut down. The new owners have also removed the garage. That is the house, I think, but it's not the house I knew, the house where I learned to cook, to read, and to love the Cubs and the Bears. It's a big house, not *the* Big House. I slowly move away.

A crowd of loud, impatient, unhappy people waits inside the DMV, all of them wanting to be somewhere else. I pause at the door to catch my breath and find my bearings. I have to be here. I have no choice. To find a job—to move ahead with my life—I need to get a state ID card and renew my driver's license.

I have come prepared. I've brought a copy of my birth certificate that my mother keeps in an envelope in her desk drawer; my old, expired license; my prison ID, which I hope I won't have to show; my mother's old cell phone that I'm still figuring out how to use; and some extra cash she thrust into my hand before I left and I guiltily folded and stuffed into my pocket.

I move away from the door and see that the crowd has been directed into several lines—a line to take the written test for a driver's license, a line for an eye exam, a line to take a road test, a line to obtain a state ID. I step into that line, shifting my weight anxiously. I count fifteen people ahead of me. I look behind me, check out everyone within ten feet of me. I settle in and wait.

An hour and fifteen minutes later, I come to the head of the line.

"Next," a woman's voice calls, loud, bored, annoyed.

I step up to an older woman framed in a window below the words "State ID." She reminds me of my aunt Honey but without her sunny personality.

"Hi," I say, smiling. "How are you?"

"State ID?" she says.

"Yes. And I'd also like to renew my driver's license."

I hand her my expired license. She types my information into her computer, then speaks without looking at me. "You have a car that's been impounded because of unpaid parking tickets. The vehicle was considered abandoned."

She scowls at her computer screen.

"Eight *years* of parking tickets."

I start to explain. "See, it was this old Chevy. I completely forgot about it—"

"You will have to pay the fines and all the fees to a collection agency before you can renew your license."

"How much would that be?"

She types in some more numbers.

"Twelve hundred dollars."

"What? Seriously?"

"Seriously."

"I'm going to have to deal with that later. I'll just take the state ID."

"Birth certificate, please."

I hand the document to her.

She looks it over, scowls again, continues to speak without looking at me, hostility dripping off her like perspiration.

"This is a copy," she says.

"Yes. It's a copy of my birth certificate."

"You need the original."

"I don't have the original."

"Then you have to *get* the original. You fill out a form. Send it in. Takes about a month, six weeks."

"I don't have that kind of time—"

"You also need a second form of ID."

"I need two forms of ID to get my ID?"

"Yes."

"Like what?"

"Social Security card. You have that?"

"No."

"Go to Line C and *get* a Social Security card."

"Line C," I say. "Social Security card."

"*Next.*"

I turn away from the window and walk to the end of Line C. I count thirteen people ahead of me. After ten minutes, I move two feet forward. Suddenly the cell phone pings. I hold it away from me. I bring the phone closer and see some words on the screen. "Got your VM. At work. Talk later. D."

I stare at the words.

I turn the phone over, bring the face closer to me.

I reflexively press a key.

Nothing happens.

I reread the typewritten message and determine that somehow my friend Deshaun has typed a message to me on this phone in response to the voice mail I left on his phone last night. I'm not sure how he was able—

"Text message," I say aloud. "He told me about this."

The guy ahead of me in line turns and looks at me.

"Got a text message," I say, trying not to sound too proud or too ignorant.

"Wow," he says, inching away from me.

An hour later, I arrive at the window to get my Social Security card. A woman about my age leans on her elbows and smiles. "How you doing?"

"Well, it's been a long morning."

She laughs. "I hear you. Okay, let's get you a replacement Social Security card. I'll need two forms of ID."

My stomach flips.

"Two forms?"

"Yes, like a birth certificate, a driver's license, a state ID."

I say quietly, "I waited over an hour in that other line to get a state ID. The lady there told me I couldn't get one without a Social Security card. She sent me to this line to *get* my Social Security card, but now you're telling me that I need a state ID to get *that*."

"Do you have your birth certificate?"

I hand her the copy of my birth certificate.

The young woman looks it over. "This is a copy."

"And you need an original."

"I'm sorry," she says.

"Please tell me—what do I need?"

"Any two forms of ID. A piece of mail that establishes your address, a utility bill, a phone bill, a library card."

"A library card," I say.

"Yes."

"I'll get a library card."

Once again, I will be saved by going to the library.

"To be clear," I say to the woman at the window, "I'm about to leave here with nothing."

"Welcome to the DMV," she says.

————

Sunday, February 4, 2007.

I watch the Super Bowl with my mother, stepfather, some family members, and a couple of friends. During the pregame show, I say, "This is unreal. I'm home, and the Bears are in the Super Bowl."

"Life is *good*," someone shouts, and everyone laughs.

The Colts kick off and Devin Hester runs it back for a touchdown. Takes exactly fourteen seconds. We score again and take a 14–6 lead at the end of the first quarter. Then the wheels come off. We can't stop Peyton Manning, and the Colts' defense buries us. In miserable Miami weather, the rain pouring all game, the Colts win 29–17. That Super Bowl sticks with me, though. The Bears come close, a Black coach holds the Vince Lombardi Trophy aloft, and for the halftime show Prince kills. But my most memorable moment? At halftime, I pad into the kitchen, open the refrigerator, pause at the choices I have, all for free, all for me. I say a silent prayer of thanks, slide out a soda, and close the refrigerator door. At least for this one moment, I catch a glimpse of what *normal* feels like.

I apply to a reentry program at a nonprofit to learn basic job-seeking skills—using the computer, writing emails, crafting an effective résumé, maneuvering through online job searches. I walk into a nondescript building downtown, sign in, sit close to the front, and take a ton of notes. The instructor, a soft-spoken woman in her forties, begins by explaining the basic steps of writing a résumé. At one point, I swivel my head and assess the room. Some of the ex-convicts have fallen asleep, some stare blankly at the instructor, a few, like me, eagerly take down every word the instructor says. At the end of the day, the instructor tells us that tomorrow we'll be taking a deep dive into the Internet.

The next day, I arrive early, notebook in hand, bringing two pens this time—just in case. I say hi to the instructor as I take a seat in the front row.

"Oh, Mr. Adams," the instructor says. "I need to speak to you. Let's go into the office."

I follow her to a tiny room with just a desk and a chair.

"Mr. Adams," the instructor says. "I checked your status, which I have to do with everyone. It's routine."

"Okay . . ."

"We can't offer our services to you. We have to stick to the rules and guidelines."

"I don't understand."

"We can only offer this program to people who are previously incarcerated convicts."

"I was incarcerated," I say.

"You were *exonerated*. You don't have a record. You're not an ex-convict. Our grant money is committed to convicted felons only."

"I spent ten years in prison."

"I don't know what to say. I feel terrible. You can't stay in the program. I have to ask you to leave."

"I did ten years," I repeat, helplessly. "I was wrongfully convicted."

I wave at the door leading to the classroom.

"I need this program as much as anyone out there. I have to get my life back. I *need* this program—"

"I'm sorry."

"I don't mean to offend you, but I am so sick of people saying that to me."

I leave her small office and charge out of the classroom. Outside, the cold air ambushes me. I put my head down and walk. I need to calm down. I walk a couple of blocks, finally surrender to the frigid wind that slices my face. I climb the platform to the El and take the train back to my mother's house in the suburbs. My heart pounds as I barge inside. I find my mother at her desk.

"You're home early," she says. "Did they cancel the program today?"

"No. They canceled *me*."

"What?"

"They kicked me out. I don't qualify for the program."

"I don't understand."

"You have to be an ex-convict. Can you believe that? Being a convict gets you into the program. If you're not a convict—if you're wrongfully convicted like me—then what? Where are the programs for us? We did the same time. We went through the same hell. We're in the same situation now. You commit a crime, you get found guilty, you get paroled out, you get some money, you get to stay in a halfway house, you go into a job-training program. That's part of your parole. But there's nothing for us. The state doesn't provide any reentry programs, or any money, no benefits at all, and we didn't do anything. All we did was *time*. We got screwed and ended up in prison. Then we get out and we're still screwed."

"Jarrett, I'm—"

"Mom, please, don't say you're sorry."

I storm into my room, grab my notebook, and tear out every page of notes I took in the reentry class. Then I grip the notebook with both hands, howl, and rip the notebook in half. Panting, spent, I throw myself onto my too-soft, too-comfortable bed and slam a pillow over my head.

My poor mother, I think, as my breath backs up on me under the pillow. I destroyed her when I went to prison. I can't keep destroying her now. I have to pick myself up. But I don't know how.

I fall asleep in my clothes, lying prone on my back, falling unconscious on my bed at eleven thirty in the morning, gone to the world until darkness falls.

The next morning, I get up and smile at my mother in the kitchen, trying to appear casual, holding in the anguish that churns in my stomach. I don't want her to see me this way. I know she does, though. She knows me too well. I battle my way through breakfast, acting as cordially as I can.

I leave for the day and I make progress. I get my library card and, braving the herd of impatient, unhappy people, return to the DMV. This time a kind employee takes my library card, miraculously accepts the copy of my birth certificate, and allows me to get a replacement Social Security card, which enables me to move into another line and get my state ID. I come home buoyed, upbeat. I'm not helping inmates with their legal work, but I have accomplished something, taken one small step forward.

Then I take another step. A few days later, a friend puts me up for a job installing equipment for a cable company. I have to go through a three-step application process, but my friend knows someone at the company, and she's almost certain I'll get the job. I fly through step one, the written application. I proceed to step two, the personal interview, feeling confident, prepared. I hit it off so well with the interviewer that I believe she's about to ask me to babysit her kids. She calls after the interview and informs me I have reached step three, the background check and drug test. I whiz through the drug test. Two days later, I get a call from the interviewer telling me that I've made it to the finish line. All that remains is for corporate to sign off, a formality. She wants to give me a head start and tells me my hours and my probable location. For the first time since I walked out of Jefferson County Jail more than a month ago, I feel as if I can breathe.

A day goes by. I pace the house, try to read, get distracted. I don't do well with idle time. I go for a long walk, come home, fix dinner, take in the Bulls game.

Another day goes by. The cable company doesn't call. I take another long walk, come home, frantically sift through the mail.

"Nothing came for you, baby," my mother says.

"Nothing from the cable company," I say. A statement, not a question.

"No. When are you supposed to hear?"

"Two days ago. A formality they said. Just paperwork for me to fill out, my W-2, that kind of stuff, lock in my location, my start date."

Later, I pick at my dinner, my nerves crackling. That night, I don't sleep.

Day three, and the weather turns nasty. Blustery winds, sleet, the sky dark all day. The mail comes late. I flip through it. I stop at a letter from the cable company. I tear it open and read—a form letter.

"After further review, we regret to inform you that due to an inconsistency in your credit history, we are unable to offer you a position at this time."

"Unable to offer you a position," I say.

I thrust the letter at my mother. As she reads, the phone rings. I answer and hear the voice of the woman who interviewed me.

"Did you get the letter?" she says.

"Just now."

"I wanted to explain. Corporate turned you down. They found something in your background."

"What would be in my background? I don't have a record. I've been exonerated."

"It was the credit check," she says. "They do it by the book. No room for interpretation or explanation. The credit check listed your last known address as a supermax prison in Wisconsin."

"But I've been *exonerated*."

"They flagged you. They've made their decision."

"And that's final?"

"It is. I'm so—"

"Sorry," I say, finishing her sentence. "I know you did your best. I appreciate that."

I hang up the phone without even considering that I might have hung up on her. I sit down heavily on the chair across the table from my mother. She doesn't speak. She places the letter from the cable company on the table in front of her. She smooths it out once, then again. I want to grab it from her and ball it up. I look over at my mother, and she slowly shakes her head, her eyes filled with love, with worry, with exhaustion, and I lose it. My chest contracts, and for the first time in ten years, since my first days in Cook County Jail, I sob. My entire body quakes. I cry so deeply that I can't catch my breath. A torrent of tears surges down my cheeks. I'm blinded by my tears. Finally, my body still quavering, my tear ducts dried out, I see that my mother has left her seat at the kitchen table and has moved over to the stove. She stands, swaying slightly, her eyes closed, her arms around her torso, hugging herself.

"It's going to be okay," she says. "I know now it's going to be okay. Oh, Jarrett, I'm so happy."

I manage to lift my head. "You're *happy*?"

"I've been so concerned about you. You keep everything inside. Today is the first time you've let it out. That's why I'm happy. You have to let it out."

"I don't—I don't want to make you cry," I say, and my tears come again.

"It's okay. This is good. You need to do this."

I can't speak through my sobs.

Then my mother comes over to me, wraps her arms around me, and slowly, gently, begins to rock me.

"Let it out, baby," she says. "Let it out."

15.
The Door

I feel stuck between two worlds: prison, where I didn't belong but learned to survive, and a world outside that seems more challenging, disruptive, and despairing than prison itself. Everywhere I turn, someone seems to slam a door in my face. I feel alternately frustrated, angry, beaten down, and stuck in neutral.

And so, I walk—to clear my head, to let off steam, to try to devise a plan, to figure out where I belong. As I walk, I try to understand the world.

How do I figure this world out, this world of cell phones, text messages, social media, and the Internet? I have missed the entire online revolution. I am analog man trying to dig my way out in a digital world. I feel left behind. As I reconnect with friends now in their mid- to late-twenties, most with good jobs, spacious apartments, new cars or trucks, girlfriends or wives, some starting families, I feel happy for them, but I am ten years behind. I'm living with my mother, drowning in debt; I have no money, no insurance, no car; I can't get a job, a credit card—*I can barely figure out the internet.*

And so I walk. I feel oblivious to the cold, the icy wind, the mostly grim gray days. Unless a blizzard hits, I walk every day for hours, exploring the neighborhood, venturing into other neighborhoods, and then I take an alternate route back, come into the house, and either stay in my room and read or sit at my mother's old humpbacked computer and try to find a job. I make lists, I make calls, I receive nothing but silence and turndowns.

One day, I walk in a completely different direction. I need to clear my head. I'd love to find a park, a playground, maybe shoot some hoop, find a game to blow off steam, even in this cold weather. I have just finished a frustrating hour or so going nowhere on the Internet. The sun has come out, but the temperature has plummeted into the teens. *What am I doing wrong?* I think as I slap my gloved hands together. It can't be that complicated. I know it's like learning the basics of a new language. I just need someone to help me for an hour, or maybe I should take a class.

And then right in front of me, I see a sign.

South Suburban College.

I approach a cluster of modern white buildings that could easily be mistaken for an office or industrial complex. I face what appears to be the main building. I don't remember walking in the front door. I just find myself inside, standing in the doorway. The warm air fogs my glasses. I wipe them on the bottom of my shirt and see another sign that reads "Guidance Counselor." I definitely need guidance. Maybe I can find someone who can guide me to figuring out the Internet.

I walk farther into the building until I come into a kind of waiting room with a dozen people, probably students, some seated, some milling around. I scan the room. Faces, hands. I must look confused or lost, because someone says, "There's a sign-up sheet over there." I see a clipboard and a pen. I sign my name and take a seat.

After a short wait, a woman calls my name. I follow her into an office, a cluttered, cozy space filled with sunlight and books. A computer that looks sleeker and trimmer than my mother's sits on the corner of her desk. The woman gestures at the chair across from her.

"I'm Linda Bathgate," she says as I sit. "I'm a guidance counselor here. How are you today, Mr. Adams?"

This woman—white, forties maybe, wide smile, a flow of reddish-brown hair that brushes her shoulders—exudes a quality that at first I can't define. Then I recognize what I see in her.

Warmth. A mother's warmth.

"Not bad," I answer. "Been worse."

Linda Bathgate smiles. "What can I do for you?"

For two months, I have wandered aimlessly, I think. I have tried to be *normal*. I have tried to fit in. I have not relaxed at all. I have not tried to be myself. Now, sitting in front of Linda Bathgate—I know it sounds crazy, or strange, or even eerie—I feel the presence of God. And in the moment that Linda asks that simple question—*what can I do for you?*—I feel that she needs to hear my story. I feel compelled to tell her.

"I have a pretty interesting story," I say.

"Oh?"

"I should have been sitting across from you ten years ago. But our criminal justice system stole those ten years from me."

"What happened?"

"I went to prison for a crime I didn't commit. I am here because I am desperate to pick up where I left off. I had just graduated high school, about to start college. I was at the very beginning of my education. That doesn't adequately explain it. I was at the beginning of my *life*."

"You are so articulate, Mr. Adams."

"I read a lot," I say. "Had a lot of time to read where I was. And, please, call me Jarrett."

"Linda," she says. "Jarrett, I'd like to hear your whole story."

"Really?"

She opens her palms toward me in a gesture that feels so welcoming and encouraging that I actually *want* to tell her my story. I've never felt this way before. I've never told my story to anyone. I never expected to confess it all to a stranger. That's what this feels like. A confession. A purging. An emotional cleansing.

I tell Linda Bathgate all of it: the night of the party, my arrest, the trials, prison, becoming Li'l Johnnie Cochran with the Glasses, being put into segregation, writing letters constantly, working with the

Wisconsin Innocence Project, and finally getting out. When I finish, I see tears in her eyes.

"I don't know how you survived," she says.

"I'm not sure I have."

"That sounds like another story."

"Still working on that one."

She reaches for a tissue from a box on her desk. "How do you think it ends?"

I move to the edge of my chair.

"With me becoming an attorney," I say.

She smiles. "A happy ending."

"Linda, I want to enroll here, get my associate's degree, go on for my bachelor's, then go on to law school."

"You've thought this through," she says.

"Not really," I say, and she bursts out laughing.

"But at least I have an ending in mind," I say.

"I'm going to help you," she says. "Full disclosure. Once you're a student here, I wouldn't be assigned to you as a counselor. I work with students who have special needs. I just happened to be here today helping to get students enrolled for summer classes. That's actually a good place for you to start. Summer school."

"What courses should I take?"

She flips through a course catalog, stops at a particular page. "I think you should take one course. See how it goes. Warm up first, then start running. If it goes well, take a full load in the fall. At that point, I suggest you concentrate on General Studies. It's the quickest way to get your associate's degree. That will set you up well for law school. Call this step one."

"I'm glad you said one course. Right now, I can't even afford that."

She goes quiet.

"I'll figure that out," I say. "I'll get a job."

"Once you're enrolled full-time, I may be able to help with financial aid."

"Thank you."

"A pleasure. Honestly."

I bite my lip, smile, and say, "So, what course should I take? Please don't say math. I'm really rusty in math. I love to read. I could do an English course. Or philosophy—"

"Speech," she says.

"Speech?"

"Speech 108. Oral Communication. Public speaking. You have a ten-year gap in your résumé. I think you are going to have to tell your story. A lot. You need to get comfortable talking about it."

"Step one," I say.

"Yes, step one," Linda says. "Three credits."

"Are you sure you can't be my counselor?"

"Not officially."

"Can I check in with you unofficially?"

"Absolutely," Linda says. "I have to see how the story ends."

16.
Loose Ends

Twenty-six years old and I'm starting college. Insane. Yet it feels necessary and right. If I'm going to make up for lost time, I have to start now.

First, I need my driver's license. To get it, I have to pay off the fines, fees, and parking tickets my piece-of-junk car has accumulated. To me, it's an unreal amount of money. Twelve hundred dollars? I don't have twelve dollars.

I can't ask my mother or my aunts. I feel so in debt to them already. I refuse to ask them for more money. But I need my license. I need to be able to drive to school and to a job. I have to get the money somewhere.

I make calls. I swallow my pride and ask everyone I know to lend me a few dollars. In a couple of weeks, I raise the cash, promising to pay people back with interest. I return to the DMV and settle up.

The woman at the driver's license window doesn't smile. She sneers at the amount of money I owe for my tickets.

"I know your kind," her look says. "Deadbeats. Guys who can't stay out of trouble. Losers."

"Wrongfully convicted," I want to shout at her sneer.

"Here's the address of the impound garage," she says. "I assume you'll want to take possession of your vehicle—"

"Keep it," I say. "Sell it. Junk it. I don't care. I don't want it."

"You no longer lay claim to your vehicle?"

"No," I repeat. "Now, please, I would like to take my driver's test."

She points me to a different line, one that snakes almost out the door. I thank her. Later, finally, I walk out of the DMV with my driver's license. Only takes me three hours.

I call my attorney John Rhiel to check on the status of my case.

"No word," he says. "They still have not officially dismissed the charges."

"My conviction has been reversed. This should've been done already. What are they waiting for?"

"I don't know. They could opt for another trial. I seriously doubt they will, but—"

"Anything's possible. I've learned that."

"If you want to speed it up, you could still plead guilty to a lesser charge."

"Never," I say. "I'll wait them out. Let's see who blinks first."

"Meanwhile," John says, "you have to tie up that other loose end."

"I'm on it."

Sex offender.

That's how the State of Wisconsin has labeled me.

A lie. An outrage.

After you have been convicted of a sexual crime, your name immediately goes on a sex registry. Nobody tells you that once the conviction has been reversed, you have to notify the state and request to remove your name. You go through a *process*, filling out paperwork, showing documentation. The state puts you on the sex registry instantaneously. They take forever taking your name off. This infuriates me.

Sex offender.

Two words that enrage me, offend me. Two words that describe the opposite of me.

I want this stain obliterated from my record, erased from my name *now*. It means everything to me.

My cousin Craig buys a new car and gifts me his old one, a temperamental clunker that guzzles gas and runs on a prayer. A godsend. I just need something on four wheels that will transport me the few miles back and forth to a job and in two months to school.

After getting the car, I register with a temp agency specializing in factory work. They don't run background checks. They work with the state and don't care who you are, ex-con or wrongfully convicted. I quickly find out why. They offer two types of jobs: dehumanizing and dangerous.

My first day with the temp agency, I arrive at a boxy building located in the rear of a parking lot. I exit my car, add my name to a long list, and stand in the parking lot milling with a mass of people, most of whom have spent time in prison. I wait anxiously, making small talk, keeping vigilant, watching faces and hands, keeping clear of shadows, my head on a swivel. After about twenty minutes, someone calls my name. I sign a form, and the guy holding the sign-up list hands me an index card that I will give to the foreperson at the factory I've been assigned to. I get back inside my beater and drive to my first job in almost ten years outside a prison—stuffing K-Cups of coffee into cardboard containers. The job pays minimum wage, $7.50 an hour.

I work fast and efficiently, and soon I find a rhythm and shut off my mind. After thirty minutes, I start to sweat from the stifling heat in the factory. In another few minutes, the heat feels so suffocating I think I might pass out. I glance at the workers around me, almost all of them recently released from prison, and I see that we're all dripping with perspiration. I realize then that I have been breathing through my mouth because the smell finally hits me full force—a tear-inducing blast of sour coffee. I start to gag. I try to void my mind of all thought, and then, before I know it, a horn bleats and my six-hour shift ends. I calculate my day's pay—forty-five dollars less taxes. I stagger out of the factory, the stench of coffee and dried perspiration draped over me like a blanket. I can't wait to shower.

I come back the next day, and the next. After my Friday shift, the foreman stops me on my way out the door.

"You work hard," he says. "We want to put you on permanently."

I'm stunned, flattered, and disgusted.

"I can't do that," I say. "I can't keep doing this."

"I'll raise you to eight dollars—"

"No, thank you." I'm desperate for the money, but I can't walk through life reeking of French roast.

Monday, I return to the temp agency and ask that they assign me anywhere other than the K-Cup factory. An hour later, I receive my next job—working at a company that makes brass fittings for pipes and pays a lofty ten dollars an hour. I arrive at this place, hand the floor manager my index card, and follow him to my station.

"Here," he says, pointing me to a spot between two burly guys standing at an assembly line, neither of whom speaks English.

"What do I do?" I ask.

"What they do. Run the machine. Watch them. He's Oscar; he's Luis. You have any questions, holler, 'Luis.' He speaks better English."

"But I haven't had any training. Maybe somebody should train me how to work the—"

"Training?" Baffled, the manager looks at me and walks away.

I squeeze between Oscar and Luis, smile, say hi. They grunt in unison.

I watch what they do, a series of lightning-fast, orchestrated movements that culminate in yanking back and slamming down hard on a piece of machinery resembling a rudder. Luis works two machines at once and pays absolutely no attention to me. I follow his moves, and after a while I have some idea of what I'm supposed to do. But how do I turn this thing on? I catch Luis's eye and shout above the din and rumble of the machinery, "Turn on?" He looks at me as if I were hopeless, leans over, and flicks an ignition switch right in front of me. The machine groans into motion.

I spend the day copying whatever Oscar and Luis do, rarely exchanging a word with them, my goal during the eight-hour shift being to keep my fingers from being crushed under some erratic, boomeranging piece of metal. Mercifully, my shift ends with both my hands intact. I spend the next two days working the machine, yanking up and slamming down on the rudder, dumping finished brass fittings onto a tray, then starting all over, occasionally yelling at Luis for clarification, advice, help, and even companionship. Meanwhile, on my own, I've studied the company manual and determined that this place makes every kind of brass fitting imaginable. I quietly chant the names of the fittings to pass the time—elbow, tee, reducer, union, coupling, cross, cap, swage nipple, plug, bush, expansion joint, adapter, steam trap, long radius bend, flange, valve, and—repeat. One day, as I prepare to leave the floor, the floor manager pulls me aside.

"Hearing good things," he says.

"From who?"

"Luis. He says you know all the fittings, and you picked up the machine real fast. We can use a reliable full-time guy. I can kick you up to eleven an hour. Let me know by end of the day tomorrow."

I hate this job. But I'm swimming in debt, and I need to start putting money aside for my own apartment. Every day I stay at my mother's, I feel I'm stunting my independence. She and my stepfather have done so much, but I need my own place. I decide to accept the manager's offer. I find the work mind-numbing, but I have survived worse.

The next morning, I arrive at my station and smile at Luis and Oscar, who grunt a hello. I flick on my machine and prepare to settle in for the long day, thinking about how I will feel accepting the floor manager's offer. I pull back on my mechanical rudder, and a severed piece of a tool flies back and hits me in the mouth. I howl. Blood gushes. I collapse to the floor, Luis shouts, and before I know it, I'm sitting in a hospital emergency room, receiving seven stitches. Waiting to be discharged, pressing an ice pack to my throbbing mouth, I make a decision.

I'm never going back to that place.

I decide to take a chance on myself.

I start my own company.

I will do odd jobs, handyman stuff, putting up shelves, hanging TVs, minor carpentry, easy electrical, painting, and my specialty, masonry, building garden walls out of bricks and stones. I print business cards and hand them out to family and friends, while my mother floods the neighborhood with my cards and calls everyone she knows. The card identifies me as a mason, or bricklayer, which is true. I took a masonry class in prison and received a certificate.

I start with one client—my mother. I hang her new flat-screen TV over the fireplace. She invites friends over to see my handiwork. She's proud and persuasive, bordering on pushy, assuming her role as my vice president of public relations. Within a week, I get a call to hang her friend's TV, then a call from another friend to put stones around her garden. Word spreads. Before long, I'm hanging TVs, building bookcases, and creating backyard gardens, my fledgling business starting to bring in some cash.

The speech class at South Suburban begins. I arrive early, take a seat in the classroom, and feel my leg pumping from nerves and excitement. I cannot believe this day has come. I hope I blend in. I hope I don't look too old. And I hope that when I get up to speak, I don't stumble and stammer and make a fool of myself. I like reading, but I'm not sure how I'll feel speaking in front of a bunch of strangers.

Two other students come in, women who look my age or a few years younger. They sit near me, and we all begin making small talk.

Then another student comes in, a guy at least my age or older. He sits across from us and joins the conversation. Before I know it, all twelve students taking the class and the teacher have arrived and we're all engaged with each other, chatting, laughing, getting acclimated. I not only blend in; I *fit* in. I feel wired, energized by this casual conversation. Simply being in this setting and interacting with students stimulates me.

The teacher takes over and asks each of us to introduce ourselves and reveal something about us, a surprising fact, or a goal. We go clockwise around the room. When it's my turn, I give my name, admit that I'm a little nervous, and say, simply, "My name is Jarrett Adams and I am going to be a lawyer."

I fall into a comfortable rhythm. I spend my days working, usually hanging TVs or lugging heavy stones in a wheelbarrow and landscaping gardens. The weather turns warm, then hot. On good days, I book back-to-back jobs, then rush home, shower, drive to school, and settle in to class. I give speeches, ace the midterm, prepare for the final, which will be a speech utilizing a prop, a demonstration speech. I get to know the other students in the class, become friendly with most, friendlier with others. I even go out on a date. It's pretty much of a disaster. I'm anxious the whole time, looking all around me for faces, hands, my attention everywhere but on the young woman who sits across from me in the casual restaurant I've chosen. Too soon, I think. I love being in school, but, yeah, I'm not ready for *this.*

For my final exam, the demonstration speech, I raid my mother's kitchen. I grab a bottle of water, a wire strainer, and a bowl of cherries. I've rehearsed the speech in my mind, but I'm so confident now speaking in front of others that I know I can speak off the cuff and kill it. When the teacher calls on me, I explain that I'm going to demonstrate a concept called straining. I tell the class that I learned about this in a psychology book I read a few years ago, when I had a lot of time to read.

"Life," I say, cradling the bowl of cherries, "can feel overwhelming.

Sometimes you feel as if you're flailing, even drowning. You feel so overwhelmed that you can lose your way."

I dump the cherries from the bowl into the strainer. Then I hold the bowl under the strainer and take out the bottle of water.

"In order to find your way, to figure out what's truly important, to identify what you enjoy, what turns you on, what turns you off, you have to go through a process of straining. Take a look at everything in your life and decide what really matters. Keep those things. Remove the rest."

I pour the water over the cherries. The water trickles through the strainer, flows into the bowl, leaving the cherries, glistening with droplets of water.

"The cherries? That delicious fruit? Those are what matter. The essentials. The core parts of your life." I slosh the water around in its bowl. "This is the excess. You can dump this out. Identify what matters in your life and strain out everything else."

The class applauds.

One of the guys says, "That was really unique."

"Yes, it was," one of the women says. "Now you better bring those dishes back before your mother finds out."

I come home after the class feeling exhilarated. When I walk into the kitchen, my mother says, "I was wondering where my cherries went."

"I took them to school," I say. "They were my final exam."

Two days letter, I receive my grade for the course—A.

In midsummer, while I'm painting a woman's garage in blistering heat, John Rhiel, my lawyer, calls my cell phone.

"You sitting down?"

"No. I'm scraping old paint off a garage. Then I have to put on two coats. Gonna die in this heat. What's up?"

"It's over."

Time stops. The ground pulsates from the heat, or my pulse

pounds all the way from my heart to my feet. I burn, and then I literally go mute.

"Are you there?"

I nod.

"Jarrett?"

"I'm—yeah."

Then I do sit down—on the driveway. I feel light-headed, as if I might faint.

"You mean—?"

"Yes. The prosecutor agreed to dismiss the charges. Officially."

"*All* the charges?"

"Everything. Your record will be totally expunged. Your conviction is being reversed."

"This is final."

"Final. The court will send you a letter   "

I leap to my feet.

"No."

"What do you mean?"

"I want to be there. I want them to look me in the eye. I'm going to be at that hearing when they dismiss the charges."

"You sure you want to drive all the way up to Wisconsin?"

"Without a doubt."

My lawyer and I sit at a table in the courtroom, facing the bench. The prosecutor sits to my left. The court reporter sits to my right. The only other people in attendance, my mother and my stepfather, sit in the row behind me, or as I still think of it, the first pew. We have driven five hours from Chicago to attend this hearing. As we wait for the judge, I think about the number of times I've sat in courtrooms like this, churches of law, feeling intimidated, helpless, and afraid, awaiting my fate, the temperature always turned way down, a bitter chill slicing through the room. *Icing the defendant.* Looking for any way to intimidate you. Not today. Not ever again.

I close my eyes and exhale slowly. Then the sound of fabric rustling. The judge enters. I recognize her. I will never forget her. She is the same judge who sentenced me nearly ten years ago. She looks older but still seems as severe as a high school vice-principal. She doesn't look at me. She addresses the prosecutor, beginning the hearing. They have a shockingly brief exchange. "Yes," the prosecutor says, "I agree to drop all the charges." "Fine," the judge says, "that will be done." The judge then proclaims that my conviction has been completely reversed. She slams down her gavel and ends the hearing. She stands, turns her back on me, and exits the courtroom.

I can't believe it. The proceeding takes less than five minutes.

The judge never acknowledges me or my mother, doesn't apologize to me, doesn't wish me luck, says not a word. The one time in my life I want to hear someone say, "I'm sorry," I hear nothing. Silence screams through the courtroom.

"They wasted our time," I say to my mother in the car as we drive back to Chicago. She sniffs, dabs at her eyes. She has cried so much in her life.

"They didn't even *acknowledge* us," I say. "They acted like they didn't see us, like we didn't exist. It was like those ten years behind bars never happened. They made me feel invisible."

I squint at the rolling hills of Wisconsin through the back window of my stepfather's car.

"I'm going to come back here as a lawyer," I say. "They're going to remember who I am. If it takes the rest of my life."

17.
Safe

With Linda Bathgate's help, I choose my courses for the fall, everything at night so I can continue working days. Linda helps me fill out the forms for financial aid. The financial aid office responds quickly. They'll cover all my expenses for one semester.

"What about after that?" I ask Linda.

"Working on it," she says.

School can't start soon enough. I walk through campus the first week of fall semester, trying not to appear too eager, but I can't help it. I have found my place. I feel fired up going to classes, interacting with students, engaging with professors, even studying. I struggle when I'm not on campus.

When I am most alone, in bed at night, staring into the darkness, unable to sleep, I feel my body jerk with sense memory. I don't dream, but moments of terror pump through me. I sit up, suddenly not sure where I am, thinking I'm in segregation. I get up, wander through the house, my body feeling hot, flush as if with fever. I open the refrigerator to cool me down; then I stare inside, inventory the contents, still amazed at everything available to me on the shelves. One sleepless night, around 4:00 A.M., as I close the refrigerator door, I feel someone's eyes on me. I turn quickly and see my mother's shadow disappearing down the hallway.

"I've been wanting to talk to you," she says one morning as she stands at the sink, drying dishes.

I wait for my mother to continue.

"I see how hard this has been for you—"

She stops, curls her lip, and looks at me, her eyes full.

"I think you should talk to someone."

"You mean a shrink?"

"Yes. A therapist."

"I don't need that."

"You're going through a lot. It could help to talk it through—"

"I can handle it."

"I know you're strong. But this is different. You may need some help."

I go quiet. I think about her watching me the other night as I looked inside the refrigerator. I see myself awake all night, staring at the ceiling. Walking the perimeter of every room I enter. Checking the locks on doors, windows. Watching strangers' faces, hands, shadows.

Thinking about *time*.

The time I lost, doing time. How long have I been out? How long have I been home? Time blurring by at warp speed.

In my experience, in the Black community, young men experience PTSD, which we say stands not for post-traumatic stress disorder but for *persistent* traumatic stress disorder—a condition brought on by exposure to constant violence. We normalize violence and live with its aftermaths—depression and anxiety. When we feel unsettled or desperate or depressed, we tough it out. We don't talk it out. We don't do therapy. We look away from therapy. We look down at therapy.

"Will you at least think about it?" my mother says.

I don't answer.

But I don't say no.

———

During the days, I book as many jobs as I can, but work comes inconsistently, and my bank account balance continues to hover precipitously close to zero. I face a pile of bills every month, paying off the loan on my old car while accruing new ones—school books, supplies, gas for my car. I think about asking out a girl in my English class, but what do I have to offer? Dinner at McDonald's? A drive through the neighborhood in my clunker? A stroll through the mall, my head on a swivel, checking frantically for faces and hands? I don't think so. I abandon the idea.

One day, a woman who owns several houses in the area calls me for a job. She asks me to redo the flower bed in the front of her house with garden stones. She wants to plant shrubbery, put in an attractive garden, her goal being to sell the house. She wants to create curb appeal and believes a plush garden surrounded by stones will do the trick.

When she gives me the address, I hesitate. The house sits on a street in a neighborhood known for one of the highest murder rates in Chicago. Then she tells me how much she'll pay me—the most I've ever gotten for a job. If I work nonstop, I can do the job in one day. Get to the house at dawn, get out before dusk. I don't have school that evening, so I'll have the whole day to complete the work. "I'll take it," I tell her.

Driving to the house, I know that the job requires two men, especially given the late August heat and my determination to finish the work before dark. But I refuse to bring on a helper. I need the money, and I doubt that anyone else can work at my pace, maniacal. I arrive at the house, and I see that we're talking about grunt work, moving a large stack of heavy stones from the back of the house to the front, laying them down carefully, and then hustling to the back for the next load. At my request, the woman leaves a wheelbarrow in the garage.

The day breaks even hotter than the forecast. By 10:00 A.M. I'm doused in sweat. By eleven, I'm stopping every fifteen minutes to sip water. By noon, I'm guzzling water from the garden hose, the heat slithering up from the pavement, causing me to feel slightly delirious. Gradually, the pile of stones in the back diminishes, the garden in the front takes shape, but then darkness starts to fall. I look at the amount of stones that remains, and I don't know if I'm going to make it. I have at least two more loads, and I'm beat. Maybe I should come back tomorrow.

Then, from the next street over, I hear a shout, some running, and a round of automatic weapon fire. Then screams. More running. More gunshots. It sounds like a war zone.

I don't want to get caught in the middle of a firefight. I make a decision. I'm finishing right now and getting out of here.

I'll pack everything into one load, stick the wheelbarrow into the garage, lock up, and *book*.

I load all the remaining stones in the wheelbarrow, forming a small stone mountain. I can hardly see over the pile. I lean in, lift, groan, and slowly push the wheelbarrow toward the front of the house. The wheelbarrow sways, wobbles, but I push my weight into the handles to steady the load. The wheelbarrow slides off the concrete, tips onto the grass, and a stone sails off the top of the pile and lands on my foot. I wail. I hop with pain. I limp in a circle, my hands on my hips, the pain scorching through my foot. My eyes water.

The automatic weapon fire begins again. Definitely a machine gun. And it sounds even closer.

In a haze, I somehow move the pile of stones to the front of the house, unload the wheelbarrow, finish the job, return the wheelbarrow to the garage, lock up, and roll into my car. As I drive away, the pain rips into my foot, burns through my boot. My head pounds. I get home, limp into the house, and slowly shimmy off my boot. My foot has swollen to twice its normal size. I locate a bucket, fill it with water and Epsom salt, and soak my foot, the pain moving through varying levels of excruciating. I will not consider that I have broken my foot, will not accept that, because I can't have broken it. I have no insurance, I have no time, I have school, studying, and I have to work. I cannot take time off. I have already taken ten years off. I am twenty-six years old. I'm young. I'm strong. I can fight through it. This pain is minor compared with the types of pain I've fought through in my life.

I spend the next day soaking my foot. That evening, I stretch an Icy Hot pack over my foot, wrap an Ace bandage around that, and somehow limp to my first class of the week. I drop onto my seat and moan, my foot searing in pain. The Icy Hot pack has done nothing to alleviate the pain but has caused a strong medicinal odor around me, a nostril-buckling funnel cloud rising from my boot. As class starts, a young woman sitting behind me blurts, "Whoa, someone smells like an old man."

The class laughs. I don't. I want to whirl around and glare at her until she slinks away. Instead, I slump into my seat, trying to concentrate through the pain. The class ends and I limp through the rest of the evening. I limp through the next week, through the next month. As the semester goes on, the pain changes in intensity from feeling as if someone has driven a hot stake through my foot to a persistently dull ache that I manage to tolerate, even ignore—except in cold weather when my foot tightens up and cramps.

Even with my aching foot, I continue my handyman business, taking any job I can. I desperately need the money. When I factor in my expenses—driving my iffy car back and forth to a distant suburb or downtown to a job—I barely break even. In November, as I approach my twenty-seventh birthday, I stare at a suddenly uncertain future. My financial aid package will max out after this semester, and I have no idea how I will be able to afford my courses. I make my usual appointment with Linda Bathgate to talk about what classes I should take next. I want to tell her that I may not be able to take any more. I consider canceling the meeting, but I find myself in her office, my eyes fixed on the floor, trying not to appear as morose as I feel.

"Let's see," she says, smiling at my midterm transcript. "I don't see any Bs on here."

"Yeah," I say.

"All As."

"I know."

She places my transcript on her desk and looks at me. "What's wrong?"

"My financial aid has run out. I don't have any way to pay for spring semester."

I look past her, unable to meet her eyes.

"I'm going to have to drop out," I say.

She frowns in a way I've come to learn means she's considering options.

"Life can sometimes be a chain," she says.

"I don't follow," I say.

"I contact someone who gets in touch with someone else who contacts another person who finally gets to the person who can make a decision."

"In other words," I say, catching up to her, "twenty people say no. Only one person can say yes."

"Exactly," she says. "Jarrett, I think it's time."

"Time?"

"For you to tell your story."

Linda tells me about an organization called One Million Degrees (OMD) that supports community college students from low-income families. We put together an information packet that Linda and the financial office submit to OMD.

"OMD wants to interview you," Linda says one day. "Sort of a big deal. They pick a total of five scholars."

"From the school?"

"From the *district*."

I move up the chain.

I meet Michael Golden, one of the founders of the organization. Mike and I talk way past the time allotted for our interview, relating like a couple of friends who haven't seen each other in years.

"Tell me what you want to do," Mike says.

"I want to become an attorney," and then I tell him my story.

When I finish, Mike goes mute.

"I don't know how you made it through that," he finally says.

He walks me out of his office. We exchange our contact information and vow to get together as friends. Not your generic goodbye. We both mean it.

The next day, I get word that One Million Degrees has chosen me as one of their five scholars.

Later that week, I receive a letter from the financial aid office informing me they have awarded me enough money to cover most of my tuition and expenses for the spring semester, renewable if I maintain a certain grade point average. One Million Degrees will pick up every dime after that. When Mike and I get together a few weeks later, I tell him how I'm struggling to make ends meet. My handyman business doesn't bring in nearly enough to live on, especially because I desperately want to get my own apartment. Then I tell him about the stone falling on my foot.

"You need a job with medical insurance," he says.

He tells me to contact Robert Blackwell, who runs a company called Electronic Knowledge Interchange. I explain that I have no electronic knowledge at all. I've only recently gotten comfortable using a computer.

Mike laughs. "Be sure to tell Robert your story."

I shake hands with Robert Blackwell, a tall, rangy man, crackling with energy and intelligence. Robert has created a technology consulting firm from scratch and has since become one of the tech industry's leaders. I'm not sure how I fit in here. When it comes to technology, I have no skills.

"What do you want to do with your life?" Robert asks.

"I want to be an attorney."

"Are you in prelaw?"

"No, but I know all about the law," I say and then launch into my story.

I have it down now, thanks to Linda Bathgate and that speech class. I hit the key moments of that night, my arrest, the two trials, and I go off on the inequity of the criminal justice system, of how one of the three co-defendants in my case never spent a day in prison because his family could afford a competent attorney while I had to rely on a court-appointed lawyer who got me twenty-eight years. When I finish, Robert, a man in motion, sits stock-still.

We talk some more and Robert invites me to work with him as a sort of personal assistant—turning on the lights, answering the phone, cleaning and supplying the break room, keeping his schedule updated.

"But that's not your job," he says. "Your job is to find a position in the legal world because that's your dream, your passion. You're going to be a lawyer. What job would best prepare you for that?"

"Becoming an investigator," I say. "Helping an attorney find the facts in a case. Going into the field, interviewing witnesses. I believe the best attorneys have had firsthand experience in the field. Good attorneys are good investigators."

"Okay. While you're working here, look into law firms that hire investigators. When you find something, come back and talk to me. We'll figure it out from there. One more thing. I'd like to share your story. It's important that people hear it."

Linda was right, I think as I thank Robert. I do need to tell my story.

I create a routine—roll out of bed, shower, homework, work, more homework, class, *more* homework, bed, toss, turn, begin the next day. Tuesday? Wednesday? What day is it? I'm starting not to know.

I work for Robert and gradually bank parts of each paycheck. Months pass. I begin fall semester at South Suburban with Linda smiling and slashing her signature at the bottom of my fall schedule.

"All As again, I know," I say, trying not to shout in triumph.

"I expect that by now," she says. "Not why I'm smiling."

She flips my schedule around so I can read it.

"Math," she says. "Finally caught up to you. You need three math classes to get your degree. Enjoy."

Turns out, I actually do enjoy math, but not as much as my new apartment.

Yes, apartment.

My first home of my own.

Nothing great—first floor, one bedroom, in a sketchy part of the South Side. My apartment comes with appliances that usually work, an old fridge, a small stove. I have to furnish everything else. One of my aunties donates an old couch. I can't afford a chair. I hit Walmart and buy a small TV, a printer, a mattress, and a box spring. My mother gives me a pot and a pan. I buy plastic dishes and plastic cups that I wash and reuse.

I am so proud and so happy.

I still don't sleep. I still check the locks on the windows and doors. I still keep my head on a swivel when I go outside.

But I have my own place.

Warp speed.

As I power to the end of the semester at South Suburban, I lose my grip on time. I'm always inside a book, underlining sentences, highlighting paragraphs, scribbling notes in the margins. Studying, memorizing, learning, pulling As, even in math. I apply for my bachelor's to Roosevelt University, downtown, near the lake. One day, a bulging envelope arrives in the mail. Roosevelt has accepted me and offered me a full scholarship. I show the letter to my mother, who cries, then bring it to Linda Bathgate and show her. She beams a smile like a searchlight, and then she cries. I think about that day more than two years ago when I walked into her office and she told me to take one speech class. "See how it goes," she said.

Now I'm going for my bachelor's degree.

———

Mike Golden sets another chain in motion. He introduces me to Howard Swibel, a board member at OMD. I tell Howard my story. Howard introduces me to Mike Monico, a former prosecutor for the government. Mike Monico asks me what I want to do with my life. "I want to be an attorney," I say, and then I tell *him* my story.

"I want you to meet Carol Brook," Mike says. "She's the executive director of the Federal Defender Program. She's interviewing for investigators."

"*That's* what I want to do," I say.

"You'll have to go through several rounds of interviews," Mike says. "It's very competitive, very tough."

He pauses, laughs.

"Look who I'm talking to," he says.

I sit outside Carol Brook's office, waiting to meet her. My leg pumps. I'm afraid sweat has seeped through my suit. I check my collar and my armpits, feel no moisture, sigh in relief, then press my palms onto my knees to stop them from shaking. I haven't felt this way since— well, since my trial. "Relax, Jarrett," I murmur. "Calm yourself. Why are you so nervous?"

I know why. I want this job so bad I can taste it.

Then a short woman in her fifties pops her head out of the office. She smiles and I feel as if someone has turned up the lights.

"Jarrett?"

"Yes."

"Carol."

I stand, nearly knock over the pile of magazines in front of me.

"Come in."

I follow her into a modest office, sit next to her on a couch. She talks about Mike Monico, how much she respects him, and describes how glowingly he spoke about me. Carol speaks thoughtfully, doesn't rush or waste words. She exudes a quiet excitement, gestures expressively, speaks with such warmth and kindness about the lawyers in her office. She puts me instantly at ease. I don't want to say this to her, but she reminds me of my mother. We talk some more, and then she asks some personal questions and I tell her my story. This time the telling feels different. I don't slide by certain details. I don't try to gauge her reaction. I spend more time than usual telling her about Pops and working with inmates on their legal work. She takes it all in, digesting every moment. When I finish, she asks me questions, wants me to clarify certain events. Then she stands and looks out her window.

"I want you to talk with some of the staff," she says.

I've gotten through round one, I think.

"Great. Thank you."

"I have truly enjoyed meeting you," Carol says, extending her hand.

We shake hands.

"I'll see you again," I say, not realizing until I'm in the elevator that I meant to say, "It was nice meeting you, too."

I tell Robert about my meeting with Carol. He immediately sends me off to the library. "Research investigators," he says. "Find out what they do."

"I don't have the job yet," I say.

"Prepare," he says.

I do my homework. I study the responsibilities of being an investigator. The job requires extreme patience. You spend hours combing through police reports, court records, files, old newspaper clippings, researching anything you can about the case and the client. You also pound the pavement, locating and interviewing witnesses and serving subpoenas.

Witnesses, I think.

That word still wrecks me. If only my lawyer had hired an investigator to interview Shawn Demain. It would've changed my life.

———

Carol calls me in for a follow-up interview with someone on her staff. A week later, she calls me again and asks me to come in to see her personally. When I arrive at her office, I announce myself to the receptionist and prepare to sit and skim a magazine, but Carol appears almost immediately and waves me into her office. As I follow her, I realize that I tower over her, and I tower over nobody.

"I'll get right to it," she says. "Congratulations."

"Wait. You mean—"

"Yes. You'll be joining the Federal Defender Program. I'll be overseeing you, of course, but you'll be working with a dedicated, talented team—"

I lose it.

I fall apart.

I land heavily on the couch and lower my head into my hands, the tears storming down my face.

"I'm sorry," I say.

I try to catch my breath to stop the tears, to pull myself together, but I can only stammer; I've only cried twice in my *life*—

"It's okay," Carol says. "You're safe here."

Safe.

Is that what I feel?

She hands me a box of tissues and looks at me with concern and care. I blink through my tears and take in Carol—short dark hair, soft-spoken, a white woman I've only spoken to twice—and again I think of my mother. I trust her, I think, and I realize she's right. I do feel safe.

18.
We Need to Talk

I walk through the South Side in a suit and tie, my polished dress shoes squeaking with each step. We've come out of a muggy, rainy September, and although the sun peeks over the clouds, last night's damp air hangs like a drape, playing havoc with my limp. I stop at a corner, check the address on my paperwork, realize I've overshot the house. I retrace my steps, my foot throbbing on the broken sidewalk.

The modest houses here huddle tight, their roofs pointy as steeples, their small yards and front porches nearly touching. I pass one house, pull up at the next, the house I'm looking for. I smooth out my tie, buff my shoes on the back of my creased pants, and walk—*squeak, squeak*—to the front door.

MiAngel Cody, a lawyer in the office, sent me here to find a particular witness. From day one, MiAngel—dynamic, confident, intelligent, a *force,* the kind of lawyer I aspire to be—has taken me under her wing.

"I'm addicted to getting people out of prison," she tells me one day. "It feeds my soul."

Her passion feels palpable. I feel it because I share it. At first, Mi-

Angel had me reading files and taking notes, and then she would quiz me on the specifics of cases. If I didn't have the answer she wanted, she sent me back to the file until I found it. One day, wearing a broad smile, she sent me into the field. I've been taking the lead looking for witnesses ever since. When I go out, usually to the South Side or the West Side, I always dress up.

"Why do you wear a suit and tie?" an investigator, a white guy, in the office asks me. When he goes out, he wears sweats. If he wants to dress up, he puts on some jeans.

"When I go into these neighborhoods, I look the same as the people I'm trying to find and serve," I say. "I stand out if I wear a suit. I don't want the police to roll up on me, slam me against the hood, and put my hands behind my back because *I fit the description.*"

I don't know if the investigator understands, but I can tell by the way he nods uncomfortably that I've made my point.

When I wear a suit, the folks I talk to look at me differently.

"Who are you?" a woman asks me as she sits on her front porch. "Where did you come from?"

"I'm on a job," I say.

"What kind of job?" she says. "A young Black man out here, wearing a *suit*? I want to know about this *job*."

I do look and feel out of place. But a part of me feels as if I never left.

Grandmothers and pit bulls.

That's what I find at nearly every house, on every street.

One time, looking for an important witness, I park in front of a house on the West Side. I get out of my car and lean into the backseat to get my file. That's when I see out of the corner of my eye a blurry shape moving toward me. I hear the scraping of claws on concrete and I hear a growl. Pit bull. Charging. Larger and angrier than Cujo, his eyes fiery red slits, his mouth wide as a yawn, his fangs moist and glistening. I panic. I slam the door to the backseat and jump onto the trunk.

The dog jumps up next to me.

I shout, roll off, race to the driver's side, fling open the door, and dive into the car.

"Oh, he's fine! He won't hurt you."

The grandmother.

"Ma'am," I say, opening my window a crack, "all due respect, he seems upset."

"Nah, he's a big baby. Just don't look at him. Don't make any eye contact."

Later, with the pit bull chained up, I sit across from the grandmother, sipping tea, swapping stories about our families.

"I'll give my grandson a call for you," she says.

"It's important. Our client was accused of robbing a bank. Your grandson is my client's alibi witness. He could keep an innocent man out of prison."

"I'll definitely get in touch with him."

"Thank you."

"You're welcome. By the way, I love your suit. You say you come from the South Side?"

"Originally. I'm living downtown now. Going to school at Roosevelt University. I just started my junior year."

"Is that right? Are you married?"

"No, ma'am."

"That's surprising."

"Well, I'd better be going. Thank you for the tea."

I fish out my card, hand it to her.

"Your grandson can call me at this number."

"He's always losing his phone," she says. "Tell you what. Why don't you come back next week, same time? He'll meet you here."

When I return the following week, I see no sign of the pit bull that jumped up on the trunk of my car. I cautiously approach the front door, but before I even knock, a woman in her twenties, wearing a dress, opens the door. The grandmother appears behind her.

"Oh, I see you've met my granddaughter. Come on in, Mr. Adams."

The granddaughter offers me iced tea. We sit in the living room.

We make small talk for an hour as I wait for the grandson to show up. He never does.

"I don't know what happened to him," the grandmother says.

"As I mentioned, he's our client's alibi witness. I have to talk to him."

"We told him you'd be here. He said he would come. You might have to wait until *dinner* until he gets here. You like pork chops?"

"I'm sorry, I have to be at class."

"Well, then, come back next week. I'll be sure he gets the message. I know he'll want to help you."

The following week when I return, a different granddaughter also wearing a dress answers the door. She pours iced tea. We talk. The grandmother makes herself scarce. The grandson never shows.

"It's really urgent that I speak with your grandson," I say, getting ready to go.

"Come back next week. He'll be here."

The next week, a *third* granddaughter invites me in. More iced tea—I'm drowning in iced tea—more small talk, no grandson, a different set of excuses.

As I leave, I tell the grandmother that I'm seeing someone so I'm afraid, sadly, that I can't be fixed up with her granddaughters.

"That's a shame," she says. "I guess I'll go let the dog out."

I laugh and, thankfully, she does, too.

"I do need to talk to your grandson," I say.

"He got a new cell phone," she says, scribbling the number on the back of my card.

Back at the office, I finally connect with the grandson, who confirms he spent the night of the bank robbery with our client. Locating this witness results in clearing our client and my first big win as an investigator. I feel triumphant and valued.

This case gets me thinking about all the grandmothers and granddaughters I've come in contact with since I've been an investigator. Overall, I see very few young women and almost no men my age in these neighborhoods. Because of poor education, lack of opportunity, exposure to violence, and a pervasive sense of hopelessness, these men so often make the dead-end journey from the streets to prison, and even, tragically, to their graves. I have seen how the police look at young Black men in these neighborhoods. They see criminals instead of young men of promise. Too frequently, they act accordingly. As a consequence, the criminal justice system has not only decimated the population of young Black men in communities of color but also profoundly affected young Black women, upending the family structure.

In another era, at another time, the young men might have gone to war. These men have gone to prison. I think about the entire generation of men I saw locked up with me—grandfathers, fathers, sons, *grandsons*. It's no wonder that with so few men available Black women sometimes end up with men who may not appreciate their full value. It's not their fault. With so few men, they have few choices.

The closer I work with the lawyers in this office, the more I respect them. They work harder than any group of people I've seen. They inspire me. I strive to keep pace with them. When I become a lawyer myself, I want them to consider me an equal. For now, I can only do what I can do, which is work harder than any other investigator on the staff. I come in before the office opens, work all day, go to class, come back in at night, and stay late. I become tight with the cleaning crew. Many nights, I sit at my desk poring over files to the hum of a vacuum cleaner or floor buffer.

I've also recently moved to an apartment two blocks from the office and a couple blocks from Roosevelt. A strategic move. Walk out my front door and I'm a five-minute walk from either school or the office. Exactly how I want it. No wasted time.

As the holidays approach, I notice how the lawyers in the office turn to me first on complicated cases. I have become the office's go-to investigator. That only makes me work harder. One evening, as I focus on a confusing police report, Carol comes out of her office and drifts toward my desk. She smiles.

"You work late," she says.

"Yeah, this case is a bear. A lot of discrepancies."

"No, I mean you always work late."

"Well, you know, with school—"

"You have plans for the holidays?"

"No. I'll probably just work."

Her eyes shade in concern. "Make sure you eat, get enough sleep. Do you get enough sleep?"

I shrug. "I sleep."

She smiles thinly, a look that I read as "I don't believe you."

"Take care of yourself," she says.

"I will."

As she leaves, I think, she sounds a lot like—

My mother.

We get a case.

Two guys rob a bank on the Northwest Side of Chicago, an impoverished, rough part of town. They hit the bank, indicating guns in their pockets, scarves wrapped around their faces. They stuff their pockets with money, run out of the bank, and scramble into a car parked in an alley, their getaway car, just as the bank manager presses the silent alarm signaling the police. In the alley, the dude behind the wheel turns the key and steps on the gas. He grins because they've pulled off the perfect crime.

Except the car doesn't start.

The robbers abandon the car and start walking, their jackets bulging with bills, arguing over what they should do next. By this time, the police have blanketed the neighborhood. In a matter of minutes, the police stop Mel, a jittery, suspicious-looking guy with stacks of money spilling out of his pockets who's hiding, poorly, in somebody's backyard. They start questioning him.

"Bank robbery?" Mel says. "I don't know anything about no bank robbery. I'm always around here. Ask anybody. This is my neighborhood. I just happened to be in the vicinity of the bank when all the commotion started."

They don't believe him. They take him in, compare Mel with the surveillance footage from the bank.

"You can't see that guy's face," Mel says. "The video's too grainy."

"You're the same height, you have the same build, you have the same mannerisms."

"I don't care," Mel says. "That ain't me. I had nothing to do with no bank robbery."

"What about the money in your pockets?"

"That's my money. I hate banks. Don't trust them. I never go into a bank. I keep my money on me."

The police have heard enough. They charge him. One of the top lawyers in our office brings me on as the investigator. I go through Mel's file, find one crazy, inconsistent statement after another.

I sit down with Mel. He admits that he has been known to do drugs.

"But I don't rob banks, man," Mel says.

"You deal?"

"Just to pay the rent. Minor stuff."

"How much do you use?"

"Recreational. That's all. Look, this is total *bull.* They want to send me away for *bank robbery*? Look at me. Some pot, some blow, dabble in crack, *dabble,* but I would never rob a bank."

Then I drop the bomb on him.

"They found the scarf, Mel."

He studies the wall behind me.

"What scarf?"

"The scarf the dude who robbed the bank wore."

"So?"

"We want to have the scarf tested. If they don't find your DNA, we can make a tremendous case. You'll walk."

I pause.

"But if they do find your DNA—"

"Yeah?"

"You can't come back from that."

Mel coughs, paws at his face. "I just want to get out of here, man."

"So, you're good with getting that scarf tested?"

"*Yeah*. I didn't do it, man. You won't find nothing on that scarf."

I lean forward and lower my voice.

"You have to listen to me very carefully."

I wait for Mel to stop squirming and to focus on what I'm about to say.

"What about the car?"

"Car?"

"It's stolen and your fingerprints are all over it. Come on, man. You have to level with me."

Mel scratches his head with both hands.

"I can't help you unless you tell me the truth," I say.

"I know."

"The other dude's a hardened criminal. He has a record long as his leg."

"I don't know nothing about that."

"I'm waiting," I say. "For the truth."

Mel takes a very long, very slow breath.

"I admit I have had some struggles with addiction. I don't really know this guy. He calls me, asks if I can help him out with something. I say, with what? He says, a pickup. He says he'll pay me. So, why not? 'I need a car,' he says. So, I get a car."

Mel's head moves back and forth like a windshield wiper.

"Man, okay, listen, I've been on drugs my whole life. I have done some dealing. Okay, fine. I deal. But I don't rob banks. I don't hurt people. I don't put people in harm's way. That's not me. I had no idea he was going to rob a bank."

"So, you were not inside the bank?"

"No, man, *no*." Mel's lip quivers and he starts to cry.

"I didn't know what he was gonna do," he says, blubbering.

Now he begins to weep. He buries his head in the crook of his arm.

"Look, man," he says, his voice trembling between sobs. "I'll do anything for a couple of dollars. I was getting sick from heroin, so I just went to pick him up. I needed a fix. I knew he was going into the bank. I thought he was making a withdrawal."

"Well, he was," I say.

Mel wails. I reach into my pocket and hand him my handkerchief. He honks into it, hands it back.

"Keep it," I say. He waves a thank-you with my balled-up handkerchief, then sobs silently.

Back at the office, I describe my interview to the lawyer.

"He got caught up in this robbery," I say.

"Wrong place, wrong time," she says. "Is that what you see here?"

"Yeah. The getaway car wouldn't start."

"You can't make this stuff up," the lawyer says.

As it turns out, you can.

The DNA results come back.

The scarf we found in the bank is swimming with Mel's DNA.

Mel was the guy in the surveillance video—the one who wore the scarf over his face and robbed the bank.

I interview him again and tell him we have his DNA all over the scarf.

"Yeah, that was me," he says. "I never robbed a bank *before,* though."

"You played me," I say.

He shrugs. "I'm sorry."

"You're *sorry*? I was trying to help you."

"I needed the money. I was desperate. I've been hooked on heroin my whole life. My mother was an addict. I was strung out in the *womb.*"

I look at Mel. I don't know what to believe. I know this much: he lied to me.

"I'm really sorry," he says again. "My addiction has led me to make the worst decisions."

I head back to the office, ducking my head as a raw and cold December wind cuts into me. I wanted to believe him so much. I gave him the benefit of every doubt. What an actor, I think. I feel so embarrassed.

"It happens," the lawyer I'm working with says when I tell her how Mel lied.

"I will never let that happen to me again," I say.

"Lesson learned," she says. "Part of your education."

I slump into my chair. An immense wave of exhaustion suddenly rolls over me. I could fall asleep right here. I could take a three-day nap.

It's not enough to work hard, I realize. I have to become more precise. I have to take my time and go through every fact, every facet, listen to every moment on every tape, examine every line in every transcript, and then do it all over again, and *then* maybe I'll be able to decide if I think someone is innocent.

No. I have to do better than that.

From now on, I have to *know*.

How can I achieve that? What lesson have I learned?

"Slow down, Jarrett," I murmur. "You have to *slow down*."

I close my eyes, try to fight off the exhaustion, can't.

I sleep in my chair until the cleaning crew wakes me up.

I have a job. I have insurance. I have survived ten years behind bars. I have come out with a toughness few people understand—at least an outer toughness. I am sailing toward my bachelor's degree, and I will continue on to law school. And still—I check the locks on my windows and doors. When I go out, I still keep my head on a swivel, peek over my shoulder, look at faces, hands, shadows. Once, when I started dating someone, she said to me at dinner, "Why are you always checking out other women?"

"What? I'm not checking out other women. I'm—"

I stop myself. I can't explain what I go through every time I step outside. It sounds too insane, too paranoid. It would be easier to say, "Yeah, you're right, I'm checking out other women. I'll stop."

We break off seeing each other after that. I stop dating, and I do work harder, if that's possible. I learn to enjoy the pleasure of my own company. Easier that way.

———

Carol invites my mother to our office Christmas party. I introduce her to everyone, and then as I mingle with the lawyers, I see that Carol and my mother have gone off together and sit huddled intensely in a corner. They nod conspiratorially, they look over at me, they laugh, they both dab at tears, and at the end of their conversation they hug.

That is so touching, I think. The two of them together, connecting like old friends.

Then a cloud of dread appears in my mind and parks itself over me.

Uh-oh, I think. I believe I have just witnessed the first meeting of the mothers' mafia.

"We need to talk."

Four words you never want to hear from your boss.

I follow Carol into her office, wondering if this has anything to do with Mel and his Academy Award–winning performance.

"Shut the door."

The only words worse than those first four words.

"Sit down," Carol says.

I sit. I accept Carol's offer of a glass of water.

"If I need to talk to you privately, I know I can find you here every night after everyone else has gone," she says.

"I like it here at night. Quiet. No distractions. I can get a lot done."

"I'm glad I'm not paying you by the hour."

I laugh, nervously.

"So," Carol says, settling into the couch. "We're going to have a conversation, and it's not going to be a short conversation."

"Okay—"

I guzzle half the water.

"Your mother and I have been talking."

"I know. I saw you two at the Christmas party."

"That's when we *started* talking."

I jerk forward in my chair, nearly spill the rest of the water.

"You've been in touch since?"

"Oh, yes."

"I had no idea."

"We see the same things. She sees them at home. I see them at work. We think—"

I laugh. I have to.

"Two mothers," I say. "Two of the most powerful human beings on earth tag-teaming me."

Now Carol laughs.

She settles on the couch, takes a moment.

"Jarrett, you work at a million miles an hour. You never take breaks. You hardly ever go out. Your mother wanted you to take a break after you graduated from South Suburban, but you wouldn't."

"I wanted to keep going year-round. I have a lot of catching up to do."

"But you've earned vacation time. You can take a day here and there. She says you don't sleep. You get anxious. Sometimes you have a short fuse."

I go quiet.

"I want to talk to you about therapy," Carol says. "A lot of people go to therapy. It can be very helpful. *I* went to therapy."

"You did?"

"I did. It's not a bad thing. There's no stigma about therapy."

"Maybe not in your neighborhood."

We both laugh at that.

"You've gone through something unimaginable," she says. "It would do you good to talk to somebody."

"This isn't a job requirement, is it?"

"It's a strong suggestion."

"Sounds like a job requirement."

"Call it a mother's wish."

"Which one?"

"Both," Carol says.

I shake my head. I know I can't win.

She hands me a slip of paper with a list of names.

"Here are three therapists. All excellent. I researched them. They're all within walking distance of the office, and they're all in network covered by our health insurance."

"Those copays though—"

"I'll reimburse them."

"But the time—"

"One hour a week at most. I want you to take an hour away from work, here and there, anyway."

"For myself."

"That's what you'd be doing. Taking an hour for yourself."

"Not exactly a vacation."

"Worth more than a vacation right now."

I lean back and sigh heavily.

"Why do I think I don't have a choice?"

"You always have a choice. You know that. That's how it works around here. I'll never force you to do anything."

She smiles.

"Yeah," I say. "I don't have a choice."

I take the paper from her, look over the three names.

"Oh, by the way," Carol says. "I want you to make an appointment for your foot."

"My mother told you about my foot?"

"Yes. We think you broke it."

"What else have you two discussed?"

"Oh, look at the time," Carol says, abruptly standing.

Two weeks later, I sit across from Peter, bearded, soft-spoken but direct, his eyes alive with intelligence, kindness, and laser focus. In some way, he reminds me of Pops. We've both done our homework. Peter knows my story. He's read an article that appeared in the newspaper after I graduated from South Suburban. I've found out on the Internet that he has treated people who survived the Holocaust.

Survivors of trauma, I think. Is that who I am?

We start slow. I'm sure Peter senses my resistance to this whole idea. That's not even accurate. I don't want to be here at all. For starters, I'm not crazy. That's why people go into therapy, right? I've *felt* crazy at times. But I'm tough, motivated, *driven*. I, too, am a survivor.

To my surprise, Peter doesn't ask me about prison at all. He asks about my family, my grandparents, my father, my brother, my aunts, my mother. He asks me what it was like growing up in my neighborhood. He gets me to talk about who I am, how I see myself, what I want to achieve. He probes and asks me to tell him what I have lost. I talk about my passion for school. The session flies by. I leave feeling worn out from talking so much. I don't feel—different.

The second and third sessions, he asks me about the night of the party, the stupid decision I made to go, the guilt I feel for destroying my mother's life. Then I talk about prison. Peter watches me carefully, never dropping eye contact, his listening active, alive. When I describe an event from that night, or something significant that happened during my incarceration, he asks, "How did that make you feel?"

That's what shrinks always say, I think as I leave after my third session. I don't know if this is working. I don't feel any sort of change. I wonder if I should even continue. Then I picture what Carol and my mother would say if I quit. The last thing I want to do is incur the wrath of the mothers' mafia. I'll stick it out a few more weeks. See where it goes.

The fourth session, Peter gets specific. He asks questions that trigger deep feelings, feelings that I have kept so buried I never knew they existed. At one point, Peter asks me, "Are you angry?"

The very question angers me.

"Yes. I'm angry."

"At whom?"

I think about Rovaughn and Dimitri and young Black men in general and how being Black in our neighborhood—being Black in *Chicago*—defined us as criminals. The emotion bubbles up, churns inside me, threatens to boil over. I feel raw, revealed.

"Mostly I'm angry at myself for what I did to my mother."

"That's it," Peter says. "I'm restricting you. Cutting you off."

"From what?"

"I am not going to allow you to say one more time that going to that party ruined your mother's life, that it was your fault."

"It was, though. My mother warned me constantly—"

"Do you know how many teenagers lie to their parents and sneak out to parties? Do you know how many teenagers go to parties and drink and smoke weed—and have sex?"

"They don't get charged with rape because they're Black. They don't go through a system that ignores all justice along the way. The only way they see justice is if they can afford to *buy* it."

"You have a right to feel angry. You should feel angry."

"Oh, I'm angry."

"Good. And you're dealing with it—by the work you're doing and by going on to law school. But we're not talking about your anger."

"We're not?"

"We're talking about your *guilt*. That's not an emotion. It's a choice."

I pause. I feel tears welling up. I breathe, smother the tears.

"You need to stop feeling that you have to pay your mother back. You know the only way you'll pay her back?"

I wait for him to answer his question.

"I'm not answering the question for you," he says, softly. "You have to."

"I don't know the answer," I say.

"You do. Take a shot."

"I really don't—"

"Why are you here? Who sent you?"

"My mother."

"Why?"

"Because she's worried about me. She's worried about my mental state."

And then I whisper into the floor, "She wants me to be okay."

"So—?"

"I guess—if I get healthy mentally, that's how I pay her back."

"Congratulations," Peter says.

I don't cry. I blink, and a feeling of relief comes over me.

"I see."

I leave feeling wrung out. But beginning at that session, something clicks. I return to Peter's office feeling both eager and filled with dread. What will I unearth this time? I take a deep breath and dive. I allow myself to feel, to confront, and to continue to *see*. He shows me how emotions work and how, for the last ten years, I have forced my mind to suppress them.

"Your mind signals everything in your body," he says. "Stress level, blood pressure, heart rate. Your brain triggers all that. You are putting a tremendous amount of pressure on yourself, especially on the idea that you have to catch up. You have to reconfigure your time frame. You cannot catch up overnight. You have to find a way to turn off that switch."

"Turn off the switch," I say, taking that in.

"When you went to prison, you were a kid. You had to turn on a switch to survive."

He's right. I was on high alert all the time.

"Now that you're out, in order to heal yourself, you have to find a way to turn off that switch."

"It's hard," I say.

"Very hard. Many people never do it."

"I had to turn it on in prison," I say, "to desensitize myself."

"I know," Peter says.

"You see and experience things that aren't normal, but they become normal because you see them every day, sometimes every hour. That's your normal. I know segregation isn't normal. It's not healthy. It's cruel. But to survive, I had to find a way to become healthy in isolation."

"That's what you're doing right now," Peter says.

He pauses.

"You still have the mentality of surviving in a kind of isolation. Isolation has become your comfort zone. You're still in isolation."

"How so?"

"You isolate yourself in school and work. You think that's how you're going to catch up. Being in isolation and going at a thousand miles an hour."

"Well—"

I start to object. Then I realize that is exactly what I am doing.

"You're right," I say.

"It's different now. This is another life. You're still operating on your old normal. You've still got that old switch turned on. You have to find a new switch."

"What is my new switch?"

"I can't tell you. I don't know. Only you do. But you can't find it until you turn the old one off."

This resonates.

"And you know what happens when you always go at a thousand miles?"

"You lose control," I say.

"And then?"

"You crash."

I see Peter for the next two years, all through my time at Roosevelt. Gradually, I start to feel calmer, less anxious. I carry less guilt. I understand that part of why I keep living, working, and going to school at such an accelerated speed is that I see my mother and my aunts aging. I want to hurry so they can watch me graduate from college and go on to law school. It means so much to me. I will be the first in my mother's and father's line of succession to graduate from college. I want them to share that moment with me. I continue to drive myself hard. I study for the Law School Admission Test and do well enough to receive a scholarship to Loyola University Law School.

I walk in my graduation at Roosevelt University, wearing my cap, my gown, my Li'l Johnnie Cochran glasses, and a purple sash across my chest signifying that I have earned a bachelor's degree with honors. I collect my diploma and smile at all the cameras and phones my family and friends point at me. I hold my diploma aloft like a championship trophy—which in a way it is—murmuring a silent thank-you to every angel who helped carry me here and walked by my side.

19.
So, What Are You Going to Do?

We pull off the expressway, our summer intern Ricardo Arroyo and I, heading into a neighborhood of narrow streets, dirt patches instead of front yards, houses dark and crumbling, boarded up and abandoned.

"Where are we?" Ricardo asks as I park on a street across from a foreboding, three-story weathered brick apartment complex.

"Englewood," I say.

"Looks bleak. Depressed."

"It's also dangerous. We're going to serve our subpoenas and get out of here before we get shot at."

"In daylight?"

"The light doesn't matter. Just watch yourself."

Ricardo chuckles. "I come from a rough part of Boston. I know tough neighborhoods."

"Not like this," I say.

We get out of the car, and I lead Ricardo to the side of the apartment complex. Several young men conduct drug deals, a few in the shadows of the apartment's entranceways, others right out in the open.

"Open-air drug market," I say.

"Brazen," Ricardo says.

"You know the difference between crack and opioids? Choice. White kid gets strung out on opioids? That's his *addiction*. Get him help. Black kid gets strung out on crack? That's his choice. We got politicians up in arms because oxycodone has invaded their neighborhoods. *Help.* Save the suburbs. I don't see politicians coming down here."

I shrug helplessly at the teenagers buying and selling crack right in front of us.

Suddenly a kid no older than twelve buzzes by on a bicycle. He carries an automatic weapon slung over his shoulder.

I can hear Ricardo's breathing change, quicken.

"He's got an assault rifle," he says.

"Security," I say.

"He's *twelve*." Ricardo looks at me.

"They start them young down here."

"Maybe we should go back to the car."

"Definitely. We serve and split."

We knock on a dozen doors in the apartment complex. Ricardo walks so close behind me he's practically climbing up my back.

As we head back to the car, I can't help asking him, "Is this like Boston?"

"No, man. This isn't like any place."

Soon, a lawyer in our office brings me onto a case.

Two Chicago police officers pull over Philip, our client, on a routine traffic violation. According to the police report, Philip bursts out of his car and starts running. The cops run after him, chase him through the streets, but Philip finds an extra gear and the cops lose him. They return to the car, trace it back to Philip, and arrest him, an obese man in his fifties with breathing problems.

"I want you on this case, Jarrett," the lawyer in our office says. "There's something about this Philip guy. I think he's telling the truth."

"Meaning?"

"He said he was nowhere near that car, that area. He says the cops arrested the wrong man."

I interview Philip, his girth filling up the interrogation room as I sit across from him.

"Listen to me, man," he says, mopping his face with a handkerchief. "I'm a grown man. I admit that when I was younger, I did some stupid stuff."

"We all did," I say.

"That's over, man. I got a house and two daughters. I bought this car for my daughters to share. I always keep the keys in it. My daughters got these little boyfriends, you know? I make them keep in touch with me when they go out so I know how they're getting around. I don't know who those police was chasing, but it wasn't me."

"Where were you that night?"

"Home. I didn't go out. Nobody came to see me."

"Let me look into this," I say.

After the debacle with Mel, the bank robber who played me with his performance, I have determined that I will go over every single piece of information until I'm absolutely sure of a client's innocence. Triple sure. I dive into Philip's paperwork as if I were studying for a final. I read all the transcripts and police reports, and then I listen to hours of police scanner recordings. I listen every day, all day, for two weeks straight. I don't know exactly what I'm listening for, but I'll know it when I hear it. The truth—if it's there—will jump up and bite me.

Two weeks in, I hear it.

A time discrepancy.

The police say they dispatched officers to Philip's house two hours after they started chasing him, plenty of time for him to get home, change into his pajamas, and sleepily answer his door.

But on the recording, the police dispatched officers to Philip's house *fifteen minutes* after they started chasing him.

When I interview Philip again, I go over the timeline.

"Fifteen minutes?" he says, and roars with laughter. "Look at me. I'm *fat*. I'm out of shape. Do you think I can outrun anybody? Do you think I could sprint down some street, jump over a fence, come all the way back here to my house, take off my clothes, and throw on my pajamas in *fifteen minutes*? I'd be dead from a heart attack."

"I believe you," I say.

As I sit with Philip, I realize a sad, enraging fact.

The police had a crime to solve. They didn't have a criminal, so they created one.

Does it happen all the time? No.

But it happens.

I deliver my evidence to the lawyer in our office.

"You found the discrepancy," he says. "You're a miracle worker."

"It wasn't a miracle," I say. "Time and effort."

Our lawyer presents the evidence. The prosecutor dismisses the charges.

The police officers don't get suspended, disciplined, slapped on the wrist.

They go back on the job.

As if nothing happened.

Three months before orientation, but it feels as if law school were a day away, looming, bearing down on me. For my mental health, I probably should take a day off here, a long weekend there, but I don't. Law school will cost more than undergrad, so I increase my hours at work. With a push and letters of recommendation from MiAngel and Carol, I've also applied for the prestigious Chicago Bar Foundation Abraham Lincoln Marovitz Public Interest Law Scholarship, awarded yearly to one incoming Chicago-area law student who is committed to helping vulnerable people with their legal needs. A long shot, I admit, but why not go for it? *Let somebody else tell you no.*

One day, I'm walking into work when the receptionist at the front desk stops me.

"You got a message from Judge Williams. She wants you to go over to her chambers."

"Really? When?"

"Now."

I almost say, "Judge Ann Claire Williams, one of the most prominent judges in the country, the first African American to serve on the Seventh Circuit, wants to see *me*? Why?" I hold my tongue, backpedal, head out the door, and walk to the courthouse. On the way, I try not to speculate why Judge Williams has asked for me. I'll find out soon enough. One thing I've been working on in therapy—*try to obsess less.* But I do recall that the last time I got a note telling me to meet somebody at a government building, I ended up in prison for ten years. Thinking about that triggers a sense memory and my nerves kick in. As I walk into the courthouse, my hands start shaking.

The judge's assistant, Deborah, escorts me to Judge Williams's chambers the instant I arrive. I walk in and a stylishly dressed, striking woman with short-cropped hair stands at her desk and moves toward me.

"Mr. Adams."

"Judge Williams," I say, "I'm honored to meet you."

"Well, I'm honored to meet *you*."

She beams a wide smile.

"Thank you," I say, and then I blurt, "Why?"

She roars. "The Marovitz Scholarship. I'm on the three-person selection committee."

I nod. I have a feeling that her vote carries a lot of weight.

"So, I drew the first third of the alphabet. Yours was the first application I read."

"Right. Adams," I say.

"I read your application and that was it. I said, 'Okay, I'm done. I've made my decision.' Everyone else agreed."

"I don't know what to say." I start to laugh. "I'm kind of speechless. Thank you."

"You deserve it. Now, I wanted to ask you something."

"Anything."

"Would you be willing to tell your story at a few events in the city?"

"Of course."

"I helped start this organization, the Just the Beginning Foundation. We try to get kids of color from low-income neighborhoods interested in the law. I'm thinking that you could be sort of an ambassador."

"I'd be honored."

We talk for a while about how that would work. Judge Williams mentions another organization that she started twenty years ago to help law students of color pass the bar, Minority Legal Education Resources.

"I can have you speak to them, too," she says. "A few folks at a time. I just want people to meet you and hear your story."

It all sounds unreal, incredible, a golden opportunity. I say all this to Judge Williams, and after I leave, I mentally replay my meeting with her; then I do it again and again. I keep hitting rewind in my mind.

"Did that really happen?" I take a walk around the block before I can come back to earth and return to the office.

Only after I sit at my desk and start plowing into a paper mountain of police reports do I answer that question.

"Yes. It really did happen."

Judge Williams invites me to attend an event at the law offices of Perkins Coie, a major downtown law firm. She introduces me and then, to my shock, asks me to say a few words. I'm thrown off for a second, but I don't think it shows. After my brief speech, I'm standing off to the side, surveying the room, sipping a soda, when I see—this woman.

She's around my age, impeccably dressed, curvaceous. I look at her and I swear she's bathed in light. Then she faces me and smiles, and my knees buckle. I feel as if I have to hold on to something or I will fall over. It's as if I black out for a second. She's not just beautiful; she's beyond that. She's celestial. And I believe, ridiculous as this sounds, that she is—the one. In the two seconds she looks at me, not even at me, in my direction, this thought—this certainty—crackles through my mind like a lightning bolt.

I don't know if she heard me speak, if my speech made any impact on her whatsoever, but I know this. I have to go over to her. I have to meet her. I clear my throat and walk toward her, tentatively. It takes only a few seconds to cross the room, but it feels as if time has stopped. And then I'm next to her. I start to introduce myself, but I first look at her hand.

No ring.

She's not married.

Yes, I say, hopefully to myself.

"I'm Jarrett."

"I know. That was a good speech."

"Thank you, I—"

She turns away, engages with somebody else.

"Adams," I say, making sure she can hear. "Jarrett Adams."

"Joi Thomas," she says, turning back to me.

"Nice to meet you, Joi."

She turns away again.

I understand. I get it. She's a lawyer here, and I haven't even started law school. Out of my league, right?

No way. I'll see you again, Joi. I can promise you that.

That's what I say to myself as she exits the room, without giving me a second look, her back to me, gone, the light extinguished.

For now.

A few weeks later, the Just the Beginning Foundation holds its annual fundraiser and gala in the Marriott hotel ballroom, downtown. Eight hundred people will attend, a gathering of lawyers, judges, and politicians from all over the country. I'm flattered and only slightly intimidated when Judge Williams asks me to speak on behalf of several scholarship recipients.

"You're ready for this," she says.

"I am," I say, thinking, thank God for that speech class at South Suburban and Judge Williams putting me in front of at least a dozen groups before this, rehearsals for tonight.

"Joi Thomas will be the emcee," Judge Williams says. "I believe you met her at Perkins Coie. She'll call you about the speaking order."

"Oh," I say, trying to sound nonchalant. "Great. Terrific. Nice."

Judge Williams tilts her head, narrows her eyes. "You all right?"

"No, no, yeah."

A few days later, Joi calls. I pace in my apartment, pressing my cell phone against my ear, changing ears constantly because I'm sweating. I wonder if she feels the same connection, the same chemistry. We talk for about a minute, and I realize she has absolutely no idea who I am. She doesn't remember meeting me, she doesn't know anything about me, and she's not thrilled that Judge Williams has invited me to speak.

"You're a law student?" she says.

"Yes, I'm starting at Loyola in a couple of weeks."

"You're a *first-year* law student?"

"Well, I mean, yeah."

"You realize what this event is?"

"I know it's sort of a big deal—"

"*Sort* of? Every major federal and state judge of color in the *nation* will be there. You'll be speaking in front of eight hundred people. Are you sure you're ready for this?"

"Definitely. I got this."

My confidence silences her.

"Okay. Well. Good."

"You know, we've met before."

"We have?"

"At Perkins Coie. I spoke—"

"Oh, that's my other line. Sorry. I have to take this."

Click.

She's gone.

————

At the gala, I find myself seated at a round table next to Johney and Yvette, a married couple from Detroit, guests of their daughter. At first, I doubt I'll have much to say to them, but within minutes we're talking, joking, laughing, gossiping as if we were seated at our own private table of four.

During the programs, I keep an eye on Joi, who seems to be both emcee and producer. She introduces some of the speakers, but sometimes she disappears. I assume she's running around backstage, putting out fires, making sure the evening stays on track. At a certain point, with Joi nowhere around, someone introduces me to speak. I excuse myself from my new friends at the table and make my way to the dais, my eyes searching for Joi while at the same time feeling all eyes on me. "Who is this young man?" I hear somebody say, and then I begin speaking.

In the next three minutes, my limit, I tell my story and reveal my goals, to become a lawyer and mentor Black youth, helping them become part of the legal field.

I finish speaking, and the ballroom goes silent. For a second, I wonder if my microphone cut out and nobody heard a word I said. And then applause erupts, cascading toward me, people cheer, and everyone in the room, all eight hundred people, rise to their feet. I bow my head slightly, press my fist to my chest, thanking them from my heart, and then I weave my way through the guests who are still standing and applauding, until I arrive at my table, where my new friends hug me, clasping me in their arms, their words commingled with the applause.

"That was so moving, so inspirational," Johney says. "You have to stick around afterward. We want you to meet my daughter."

No, thanks, I think, remembering the grandmothers I met when I went into the field to serve subpoenas. That's the last thing in the world I want.

"You're not going anywhere, Jarrett. You're sticking around. Promise us."

"I promise," I say.

The speeches end. The gala concludes. Judge Williams gives a few final words of appreciation, and the guests begin to disperse. As promised, I hang back with the married couple, sharing another laugh, and then we exchange our contact information.

"Lil Moma, Daddy, how did you like it?"

I look up.

"Jarrett Adams, meet our daughter—"

"Joi," I say.

"You've met?"

"Yes," we say at the same time, and we both can't help laughing.

"Don't lose track of this young man," her father says.

A week later, I hit her up for lunch.

"My folks love you," she says.

"That's a start," I say.

She wears a smart-looking business suit as if she were meeting with a client. I wear a sport coat, blue button-down shirt, no tie, pressed slacks. Joi picks up the menu and frowns.

"I thought we were meeting for coffee."

Coffee? I think. I specifically said lunch, as in, would you like to have lunch—as in, would you like to go out on a *date*?

At least that's what I meant.

She places the menu on the table, folds her hands.

"I wish I'd heard your speech," she says. "I had to deal with an issue backstage."

"That's okay."

"Everyone loved it. My folks *loved* it."

"They love me; they loved my speech. I'm doing really well with your parents."

She laughs. "Scoring a lot of points with Johney and Yvette."

Then she sighs and does something with her posture, sits up straighter, more formally, a move that I know signals bad news.

"I like you," she says.

"Uh-oh. The kiss of death," I say.

"No, I do, honestly. But you need to focus on your first year of law school."

"Check, please," I say, pretending to signal our waiter.

She laughs.

"Seriously, I know what first year is like. It's *beyond*."

"Beyond?"

"Beyond intense, beyond stressful, beyond the amount of work you can imagine. I don't know how you will be able to go to law school and keep your job. Or least keep a full-time job."

"I'm used to stressful situations," I say.

"Fair point."

"So, you're letting me down easy."

"I think you have an unbelievable future. As a friend, I want you to concentrate on that, fully."

"That is what a friend would say."

"Good. Friends?"

She extends her hand. I take it and we shake. I hold on longer than a typical handshake, longer than a *friend*. I notice that she doesn't let go until the waiter arrives to take our order. Not exactly a friend move on her part, either.

She's instituting a hiatus. That's how I see it.

I will focus on my first year of law school. Smart advice. But there's no way I'm letting her go.

"I just want to remind you," I say, "your father told you to keep track of me."

"I always listen to my dad," she says, smiling.

One day, hurrying into work, I stand aside to allow a mail carrier to walk by. As he does, our eyes meet.

"Jarrett?"

I recognize him now. Mr. Hill. Rovaughn's dad.

"Mr. Hill."

"How are you, Jarrett?"

"I'm good." I pause. "I've been meaning to reach out to Rovaughn. I know it's been a while—"

Mr. Hill stops me. "It's okay." He shakes his head. "What you went through? What you *all* went through? I can't imagine."

I look at Mr. Hill and I see the same anguish in his eyes and the same deep lines etched in his face that my mother still carries.

"He didn't go through what you and Dimitri did, but he *felt* it."

Mr. Hill fixes his eyes on the sidewalk.

I think about Rovaughn. He never talked about going into the army, but after they dropped the charges against him, he enlisted. Maybe he wanted to escape.

Mr. Hill brings up his gaze to meet mine. His eyes have filled up.

"So, what about you? What are you doing downtown?"

"Actually, I work here. And I'm about to start law school. I want to become the kind of lawyer I wish I had."

"That's something," Mr. Hill says.

He grips my hand.

"I'm proud of you, Jarrett," he says. "Don't stop. You keep going."

"I will."

The first day of orientation at Loyola University Law School, I take a seat in a large auditorium, a mix of excitement and nervousness pumping through me, followed by an almost impossible surge of pride. I am a young Black man in law school. I don't puff my chest, but I don't even attempt to smother my smile. I scan the auditorium to take the measure of my classmates, to see who they are, to see whom I will be spending so much of my waking hours with for the next three years. As I look at them, another emotion edges its way in—sadness. In our class of three hundred, I see only a handful of Black men.

We have to do way better than that. If we can't get an equal representation of Black and white students in our law schools, how will we ever achieve equality in our criminal justice system? Without a strong number of lawyers, judges, politicians, and advocates coming from our neighborhoods, how will we effect change in those neighborhoods? I want to work on fixing those inequities, on leveling the playing field.

Five minutes into law school and I have placed even more pressure on myself to become an attorney and make a difference.

It begins. We don't test the water, get our feet wet. We dive in. Or maybe we're pushed. Here it comes, just as Joi said: beyond. The infamous work, pressure, and stress of first year. I sailed through my undergraduate classes. I worked hard, put in long hours, but I never felt overwhelmed or overmatched. Law school is a whole new ball game—more demanding, harder, more competitive, my classmates more engaged, intelligent, and motivated. I feel as if I've gone from Triple-A to the major leagues.

I am battle tested, though. I know how to do this, how to attack every task, how to attain my goal, which appears like a mountaintop in the distance. I glance at that mountaintop, acknowledge it, commit to conquering it, then focus not on the peak but on the *middle* of the mountain. I've learned that I need to break each task into parts, starting at the bottom and then working my way up methodically—to the middle. Once I arrive at the center, the peak won't appear so far away, so unreachable.

My workday breaks down the same way as undergrad—work all day, go into the field, return to the office, go right from there to class usually starting at 5:30, ending at 10:00, four or five nights a week. After each class, I duck into the law library, find my spot in the corner, hunker down, and stay there studying until the cleaning crew or janitor kicks me out on their way home. I make friends with my classmates, occasionally meeting for a beer or a bite to eat, but mostly I lock myself away and work. That's the key to this. I may not be the most brilliant law student in my class, but nobody will ever outwork me. I tell myself that the bars and clubs will be there when I graduate from law school in three years.

And of course, I think about Joi. I make a decision. I'll put her out of my mind, concentrate completely on my classes. I do, mostly. I text her once in a while. She texts me back. That's all I need. For now.

A couple months into first year, I learn that I have been accepted to a program that spends part of the summer on the Loyola campus—in *Rome*. I tell Carol the news.

"Good thing I banked those vacation days," I say.

"You'll never use them all up. I have a crazy idea. Why don't you take a *vacation*?"

"Nah," I say. "Saving up for next year's program abroad."

"Where's that going to be?"

"China."

"You're going to need a passport."

I go to the main post office downtown, fill out the paperwork, and prepare to pose for my passport photo. The post office clerk instructs me to take off my glasses and look serious. I nod and close my eyes. For a moment, I see myself as a seventeen-year-old inmate in Cook County Jail, posing for another photo. My mug shot. I blink furiously.

"Sir? You ready?"

I snap back to the present, to this post office.

Here I am, I think, in law school, getting my first passport so in a few months I can travel to Rome.

"Sir?" the clerk says.

"Yeah?"

"You're not supposed to smile."

"I want you on this," MiAngel says, plopping a bulging file folder onto my desk. "Unless you don't have time."

"I got nothing but time," I say. "First year of law school is a *breeze*."

"Good." She smiles. "Then you can be the lead investigator. You've been on a roll."

"I got lucky," I say. "Who do we have here?"

I read the client's name on the file's tab.

"Reynolds Wintersmith."

"He's doing life for dealing crack and cocaine," MiAngel says.

I open the file and I read aloud, "First time offender. Conspiracy to sell drugs." I look up. "Life in prison?"

"President Obama has gotten into this. He wants to commute these egregious sentences. I think we can get Reynolds clemency."

"I'm having a hard time wrapping my head around this," I say. "A first-time offender gets *life* for dealing drugs?"

"He's already done nineteen years."

"This is some racist bull—."

"Dig in," MiAngel says.

As I leaf through Reynolds's file, I think about the case before this, resulting in a win for a client. The feds arrested our client as part of a sting operation known as a fake stash house.

The sting works this way: A federal informant infiltrates a group of people who have recently been released from prison. The ex-cons, struggling to reenter society, find few jobs available to them, almost all of them through temp agencies. I know these jobs well—minimum wage, inhumane working conditions. The federal informant, working next to the ex-cons, looks for a suspect. He's a hunter stalking prey. He identifies the most vulnerable person and makes his move. In this case, our client's brother.

"Hey, man," the informant says. "I'm sick of this temp agency work. It's brutal."

"I know, man, but what's our choice?"

"Well, I heard something."

"Yeah? What?"

"You have to be a certain type. Someone willing to take a risk."

"You got my attention."

"Okay, there's this stash house run by a bunch of strung-out drug dealers. We hit them. Fast, easy. Take the money and run. What do you think?"

"It's tempting."

"Think about it."

"I thought about it. I'm in."

"Good. But."

"Always a 'but.'"

"You have to put together your own crew and use your own guns."

"That's a lot."

"No risk, no reward."

"A onetime deal?"

"One time. That's it. You give me the word, I'll set it up."

Our client's brother puts together a group of guys and gets some guns. The informant tells him the address of the fake stash house, usually a vacant apartment building or warehouse. Our client, sixteen years old, a kid who looks up to his brother, begs him to go along. His brother relents, allows him to drive the car to the spot of the fake drug stash house.

"Stay in the car and don't move," the brother tells our client, and he and his gang hit the stash house. They charge in, guns drawn, and find themselves facing an army of federal agents—and no drugs. Ghost dope, we call it. The feds arrest everyone, including our client, the kid brother who is sitting in the car. He has no weapon, no involvement in the stickup, has no idea what's going on. Doesn't matter that he has no record. Nothing matters. The kid brother gets fifteen years in federal prison for being part of a drug-dealing conspiracy, even though there are no drugs. We claim that our client is collateral damage of the fake stash house sting operation. We prove that there were no drugs, that he was literally along for the ride. He's not a criminal, we argue. He's a victim. A disposable young Black man.

Prey.

A lenient judge goes easy on him.

He gives our client only five years.

I have trouble calling that a win.

I read Reynolds Wintersmith's file for hours, scribbling notes on a legal pad, rubbing the bridge of my nose, stretching, getting up to pace when I need a break or when I need a moment to absorb the unbelievable account of his story. I feel as if I were reading an offbeat, twisted, sad crime novel.

Reynolds's conviction came in 1994 as part of our country's notorious "war on drugs," a faulty belief that this so-called war would result in safer communities. Reynolds, then seventeen years old, was named as part of a gang conspiracy and received a life sentence for dealing crack. At the time, he lived with his family in Rockford, a small, depressed city in the far northern part of Illinois. Reynolds grew up in a world of crime and drug dealing. His grandmother ran a house of prostitution and dealt drugs. His sister had a relationship and kids with the main drug dealer in Rockford. Most upsetting and harrowing of all, Reynolds's mother died of a heroin overdose one night as he and his family spread out in their living room watching movies. In the police report, the first responder reported that he found a woman lying dead on the floor, surrounded by her kids, who had been asleep next to her.

Reynolds didn't deny that gangs and drugs were all around him. He couldn't deny that he lived on the periphery of the drug world. He even admitted that he dabbled in selling drugs. On occasion, he took a phone call for his sister's boyfriend or drove his flashy car around town. But he stayed on the sidelines.

In 1994, the feds hit Rockford hard and disassembled the drug dealer's operation. They took Reynolds down with them. He happened to be there, barely inside the circle of the conspiracy, a bit player. But based on the sentencing guidelines, the judge gave Reynolds the harshest penalty. He had no choice. He had to follow the rules.

"There ought to be some latitude when you have a seventeen-year-old who gets involved," the judge said before sentencing our client to life in prison. "It gives me pause to think this was the intent of Congress to put somebody away for the rest of their life, but in any event it's there."

Gavel slammed down. Reynolds gets life.

———

I wake up early one morning, chug a cup of coffee, and start my drive up to Rockford, a good two hours from Chicago. To prepare our defense, I have to tell the Reynolds Wintersmith story in detail, using documents, pathologists' reports, death certificates, my job to create a narrative that will resonate, that will set him free. I go directly to the Winnebago County Coroner's Office, located in a lumpy-looking building in downtown Rockford. I introduce myself to the receptionist, who sends me to a different floor to talk to another receptionist, who sends me *back* to the first receptionist.

Worse than the DMV, I think, but I smile at the receptionist and shake my head. "Y'all whacking me back and forth like a tennis ball."

She tries not to laugh, but I see through her. She's someone's mom, or grandma. I relate to that type, and she relates to me.

"What do you need?" she asks me.

"A file," I say, and I tell her the documentation I'm looking for.

"That's *old*. I'm sure they transferred those records to an electronic system, probably stored it away somewhere in the basement."

"Meaning?"

"It would be nearly *impossible* to find."

She emphasizes the word, indicating that she has ended the conversation and I have been dismissed.

I don't move.

I smile, adjust my glasses.

"In other words, the file exists—somewhere in the basement," I say.

"Possibly. I don't know for sure."

I tilt my head, glance at the nameplate in front of her.

"Martha."

"I'm picking up something in your voice, Martha. Are you from Chicago?"

"You have a good ear," she says, grinning. "South Side."

"Where about? I'm from the South Side originally."

We play the geography game, name a certain park, a certain street, a market, places we both know.

"How long you been up here?" I ask.

She waves the thought away with her hand. "Too long."

"Well, it's different, I can see that."

"Oh, yeah." She pauses, smiles, remembering. "You know what I miss? Garrett's popcorn."

"The best," I say.

"Nothing like it," she says. "Oprah called it her favorite food a while back."

"I don't doubt that. I watched every Cubs game on TV sitting on my granddad's lap, both of us eating from a tin of Garrett's."

"Now you got me craving some Garrett's."

"Me, too." We laugh, and I say, "Martha, you wouldn't want to double-check and see if you could find that file?"

"Charmer," she says.

She picks up a phone and makes a call. I hear a loud, annoyed voice crackling through on the other end. Martha rolls her eyes, shakes her head, murmurs, "Thank you," and hangs up.

"Yeah," she says, "they couldn't find it." She drops her eyes, pretends to file a paper.

They didn't look.

Martha and I both know that.

A month later, I go back to Rockford. I block out a whole day. I talk to Reynolds's family and interview his sister. Then I go to the Rockford Public Library and spend hours scrolling through microfiche, reading and copying news articles about Reynolds Wintersmith, his family, their history, and Rockford in the 1990s. I create a profile of Reynolds—a young man who was born into a world of drugs, a world he didn't choose. He knew nothing else yet managed to keep his involvement in that world minimal. At the end of the day, I return to the county coroner's office and pay another visit to Martha.

"Just checking back," I say to her. "Remember me?"

"Mr. South Side. How you doing?"

"Not bad. Yourself?"

"Can't complain. Well, I could—"

"I hear you. Hey, I thought I'd take a chance that you might have found that file."

"No," she says. "No luck. Haven't found it."

Again, we both know she hasn't looked.

"I figured," I say. "Those files can be tricky to find. They play hide-and-seek on you. Oh, I almost forgot."

I reach into my bag and bring out a blue tin and place it on her desk.

"Garrett's popcorn." Martha's mouth drops open in shock. "You didn't."

"I thought that since I was making the trip back up here, I wanted to give you this. You spent all that time with me before. I wanted to say thanks."

"So unnecessary," she says. "I wish I could open it up now and share it but, you know, work rules—"

"No worries," I say. "More for you."

"*Thank* you," Martha says. She looks as if she might cry.

"Let me know if it's as good as you remembered. Nice seeing you again."

I start to leave, stop at the door, turn, and take a few steps back in. "If by some chance, you happen to decide to take another look for that file—"

"I'll let you know," she says.

"My card," I say, snapping it down in front of her.

"I have it from the last time," Martha says.

I smile and wave.

I've also taped a card to the outside of the Garrett's tin and placed another one inside the cellophane.

She definitely has my number.

Two weeks later, Martha calls.

"That Garrett's," she says. "To *die*. I did share it with my niece. Not all of it, though, not all of it."

"I bought some for myself," I say. "I couldn't resist."

"Well, okay, I happened to be down in the basement, and I looked for the file you asked for."

"You did?"

"I found it. It was in a big three-drawer file cabinet, way back in the far corner of the basement."

I switch the phone to my other ear and start pacing as I talk.

"So, you found the file?"

"Yeah. In that cabinet."

"That is really good news."

"One small problem. The file cabinet was locked."

No.

I stop pacing, pull up in the corner, lower my head into my free hand.

"I had the key, though," she adds.

"Martha," I say, pacing frantically. "You're torturing me. Did you find that file?"

"I did. It's all here. Pretty sure I got everything you need."

"I'll be there in the morning," I say.

"Is Garrett's still in business?"

I almost want to sing. "Martha, I got you covered."

MiAngel submits the request for Reynolds's clemency, a petition containing the argument and all the background information, documentation, and the narrative I've constructed. We tell Reynolds Wintersmith's story.

The week before Christmas 2013 at a news conference, President Obama commutes our client's sentence along with seven others'. He says, "Commuting the sentences of these eight Americans is an important step toward restoring fundamental ideals of justice and fairness."

After serving twenty years in federal prison, Reynolds Wintersmith will be coming home.

Merry Christmas.

I feel validated.

More so, I feel as if I have played a part in righting a wrong.

Reynolds committed a crime. Barely. He was caught and convicted. But the judge admitted, on the record, he was sentenced brutally, unfairly. Rightly convicted; wrongfully—egregiously—sentenced. For too many in the Black community, that has become the way of life.

That Christmas break, I drive four and a half hours to visit Reynolds at the federal prison in Greenville, Illinois. The Bureau of Prisons is preparing his release, which will occur in three months. Moving justice along, especially within the prison bureaucracy, always takes longer than you think.

Reynolds and I sit in a visiting room and we talk, keeping our voices low. We don't discuss his case. We talk about our prison experiences. We talk about how each of us survived. And we talk about his return, how he will reenter society. His eyes glisten as he swats at the tears that course down his cheeks.

He says prison has hardened him, changed him, but I recognize the determined look in his eye. I know he has had battles inside, a few literal ones for sure, but I'm certain he has fought some that were emotional and psychological. Those battles will continue.

"So, what are you going to do?" I ask.

Reynolds bites his lip and with conviction says, "I'm going to go to school. I'm going to get a degree. I'm going to make something of myself."

"Never lose sight of that goal. Grab it. Hold on to it."

Reynolds keeps his word. He keeps his promise to himself.

When he gets out of prison, he goes to school, and he begins mentoring kids. He works with kids who live in areas overrun with drugs, those who are vulnerable and naive the way he was. The next time we talk I learn that he's on his way to achieving his goal, earning a college degree.

So many young Black men like Reynolds Wintersmith have been ripped from their families and their neighborhoods and thrown away for no good reason, or no reason at all. They are now gone, lost, rotting in prisons. I was fortunate. I fought my way to a second chance. Sadly, that rarely happens. We don't know whom we're throwing away. Of the 2.3 million people who are incarcerated, 750,000 are Black men. The numbers are so disproportionate they scream. That has to change.

20.
The Return

The summer after my first year of law school, I go to Rome. My head is a camera, snapping shot after shot, a pastiche of images exploding too fast. I can't take it all in. It's too much—the ancient city in ruins, the enormity of our world's history, the thrum and rumble of Rome's streets, how humble and minuscule I feel seeing the pope at the Vatican, the exquisite taste of fish seemingly plucked right out of the sea, drizzled with olive oil, salt, and simply grilled. I vow to come back.

One day, I get a surprise email. After my work on the Reynolds Wintersmith case, MiAngel and other lawyers in the office nominated me for the National Defender Investigator Association's Investigator of the Year Award. Again, vowing not to obsess, I've put the thought of winning out of my mind. Or tried to. Didn't always succeed. Now, reading this email, I find out that I've won.

I'm overwhelmed by the honor.

I send thank-you emails to everyone who nominated me. Then I reread the first email again, savoring every line. I can't wait to tell my mom. And then I think I can't wait to share the news with Joi.

Yes. Joi. We've kept our distance except for a few sporadic texts and emails. But I've thought about her, a lot, wondering if she's thought about me a little. Returning to Chicago, I hit her up again, tell her about the award on a phone call as casually as I can, even though I'm bursting with excitement about winning. From there, we start texting more intensely. The texts became phone calls that became dates that became overnights that became weekends, and then over the holidays we became a couple. It's destiny, I think, if you believe in such things, and I do.

When the second year of law school ends, Loyola offers a program in China, and Joi and I go together. Now a world traveler, I'm certain I know my way around a map and refuse to ask directions, and Joi and I get hopelessly lost. Two young Chinese students save us. I gawk at the sheer enormity of the landscape, the number of people, the culture, the epic achievement of the Great Wall.

Third year of law school starts, my fellowship at the Federal Defender Progam ends, and I go to work at Loevy & Loevy, a civil rights firm. Right after the New Year, I head abroad again, this time for three weeks in London, where I will research and start writing my law school thesis. I practically live at the Old Bailey, the Central Criminal Court of England and Wales. I spend much of my time on the balcony overlooking the gallery of the main courtroom. At first, I'm thrown off by all the barristers—lawyers—wearing white powdered wigs. As part of the course, I put one on myself. I want to say I look dignified, but when I show it to Joi, she cracks up.

I become fascinated by the differences between the British criminal justice system and ours. At one point, I'm assigned to follow a particular barrister while she works two different cases, one as a prosecutor, one as a defense attorney. As I observe her, I'm struck by how effectively she argues both sides. That's how it works in Britain. Our system in the United States has become adversarial, emphasizing winning, not fairness. In Britain, barristers need to show balance and have empathy for both sides of the law, which we don't do.

We put our focus and our money into one side—incarceration. The United States recently quadrupled the budget on corrections. That makes no sense. We should be putting more money into education—early childhood through high school—for kids who live in poor neighborhoods. Studies show that educational programs reduce crime. We should be investing in those programs and in teachers, not in prisons. As I discovered when I got put into segregation twice for no reason, when you build prisons, you have to fill the beds. I go back to my room and jot down notes for my thesis, which I title "An Adversarial System Robs the Justice System of Justice."

I return from London, work on my thesis, complete my courses, and realize I'm too late to apply for a traditional clerkship. I talk to Steve Art, my supervising attorney at Loevy & Loevy. He suggests I ask Judge Williams if she'll create a public interest fellowship for me on the condition that I find my own funding.

"Steve, I'm going to need something like twenty grand."

"I know."

"Where am I going to get twenty thousand dollars?"

Steve shrugs. "We'll do a GoFundMe campaign."

"Go Fund Jarrett for a fellowship?"

"Catchy."

We set it up. We don't raise twenty. We raise *thirty*. Judge Williams creates the fellowship, and I go to work as a law clerk, as I discover, an extremely rare position for a person of color.

At my law school graduation, I walk feeling a sense of accomplishment if not completion. I have finished seven years of school while working full-time. I have fallen in love. I have traveled the world. I have won awards. I have worked with prominent judges and attorneys, but I have so much more to do. I know I'm just beginning. It's as if I have climbed a set of steep stairs, only to find a door to an unknown room facing me. Then I hear my name. I glance at my small cheering section of family and friends. I step forward, accept my law school diploma, and shake hands with the dean of the law school.

———

That summer, I begin the final leg of my journey. Passing the bar, getting a job, practicing law. Being a lawyer.

Being a lawyer.

That is who I am, in my essence, at my core.

A lawyer.

But it's more than that.

I imagine a little kid sitting on his front porch in a neighborhood like the one I grew up in and I want to say to him, "If I made it, you can, too. Your success is not limited to becoming a ballplayer or an entertainer. You have other options. You can find other dreams."

Commuting from Chicago to the Southern District of New York, I work my clerkship with the Honorable Judge Deborah Batts. One day, back in Chicago, as I sift through some paperwork in the courtroom at the Seventh Circuit, the court calls a case out of Milwaukee. The attorney steps to the lectern and introduces himself.

Rob Henak.

I jerk my head in his direction.

The attorney, a sturdy-looking man with a friendly face and a wide smile, begins arguing his case.

I have never met Rob in person, but I will never forget working with him on my habeas petition when I was in prison. I picture all the letters we exchanged, his red lines slathering the pages of my drafts so much that it seemed as if he'd dunked them into a can of red paint. He started the process of my reversal. He accepted a fee much lower than he deserved, and he helped me beyond any thanks I could give him.

The hearing ends. As Rob approaches the elevator, I catch up to him.

"Hey, Rob," I say.

"Yes?"

"Jarrett Adams."

He pauses for a second, fighting to recall the name.

"Remember me? You helped me when I was locked up."

He drops his briefcase.

"Jarrett." He grips my hand with both of his. "Of course, I remember you." He pulls away, takes me in, that wide smile spread across his face. "Are you—?"

"I just finished law school."

We stand by the elevator, talking lawyer to *lawyer,* oblivious to the people swirling around us.

A couple months later, I propose to Joi. I whisk her away to the Dominican Republic, plan a romantic getaway, strategize the perfect time to pop the question. In a comedy of errors, almost everything goes wrong with my plan, except for the most critical part. She says yes.

We plan a romantic, exotic destination wedding in Costa Rica. But my family squelches that idea. They hold an intervention.

"We thought you'd all like to go to Costa Rica," I say.

My mother and aunts respond in a chorus.

"Uh-uh. No. Not gonna happen."

I look at Joi helplessly. I give it one last feeble shot.

"Costa Rica is so—?"

"Do you not read the *news*?" my aunt Honey says.

"Yes. You know I do."

"I'm seventy-eight, she's seventy. We are not getting on a plane and going to some *exotic* place so we can get that Zika virus."

A long pause.

"We're all going to be part of this thing. You're getting married *here* so we can all pitch in and help. We've waited too long to see this day."

I look at Joi again. She shakes her head, trying to contain herself. For a second, I wonder if she's crying, and then I realize she's trying not to burst out laughing.

"Okay, let's forget Costa Rica, and let's say, for argument's sake, we agree on Detroit—"

"*No.* Pick some place in the middle."

Now I shake my head. Joi takes my hand and smiles at my family. "That's exactly what I was thinking."

We end up getting married twice.

First Judge Williams marries us in her chambers in the Seventh Circuit.

As Joi and I walk out of the courthouse, I pause. This place, I think. This is where the judge granted my certificate of appealability, where Judge Williams gave me a fellowship, and now where I got married. Surreal. Storybook.

We hold our second wedding ceremony in Michigan City, Indiana, midway between Chicago and Detroit. After repeating my second, even more emphatic "I do," I careen from guest to guest, embracing friends and family, losing myself in a constant pulsing of pure love. At one point, I see my mother standing with Carol Brook, the two women in tears, propping each other up. My two mothers—the godmothers of the mothers' mafia—cling to each other and sob.

"Look at our boy," one of them says—maybe my mother, maybe Carol. It doesn't matter.

In the summer of 2016, my fellowship with Judge Williams concludes, and I take a job with the Innocence Project in New York, working cases of people who have been wrongfully convicted. As I begin the work, I think about the scores of letters I wrote in prison, asking lawyers for help. Now I find myself in a position to answer letters from inmates. In some weird way, I feel as if I were looking in a mirror at my younger self.

Vanessa Potkin, the head of the litigation department, hires me, and an attorney named Bryce Benjet takes me under his wing. For the first eight months, I do nothing but read and analyze cases and learn how to litigate by going to court and watching. Bryce makes certain that I spend as much time as possible in court.

"If you're not around water," he says, "you can't expect to get wet."

One day, I enter the courtroom to observe a case being litigated. I head to the first two rows, where the attorneys always sit. A burly guard—a white man—follows me all the way to my seat.

"These rows are reserved for attorneys," he says. "You have to sit in the back row."

I want to shout, "Back of the bus, right?"

But I exhale slowly to compose myself, reach into my wallet, and hand the guard my ID. He looks at it for a long time, deciding, I believe, if the ID is fake.

"Okay," he mutters, giving back my ID.

I know. Black people can't be lawyers. They're the *defendants,* right?

I almost say that.

"**Y**ou're ready," Bryce says.

He assigns me as co-counsel with him and another attorney on our case with Richard Beranek, a case we're confident we can win. Richard, who has a record of sexual assault, has been convicted of a rape he insists he did not commit. He's currently serving a life sentence for that crime at Green Bay Correctional Institution. A prison I know too well. Now, practically ten years to the month that a judge overturned my case in Wisconsin, I sit in another Wisconsin courtroom awaiting our evidentiary hearing on Richard Beranek. I sit between Bryce and our other co-counsel from the Wisconsin Innocence Project, Keith Findley, the same attorney who argued my case ten years ago in the Seventh Circuit, which led to my release. Neither of us can stop grinning.

"Crazy," I say for about the tenth time.

"Talk about coming full circle," Keith says.

Keith and I have stayed in touch over the years through text and email and occasional phone calls. We've both had an inkling we would someday meet as lawyers and possibly work together on a case. And now here we are.

Crazy.

"I thought you said you would never again set foot in the state of Wisconsin," Keith says.

"I said I would only set foot in this state again—as an *attorney*."

He asks me to catch him up on my past few years. I tell him about Rome, China, London. I tell him about Joi and living in New York.

"It's just crazy that I'm sitting here with you, on this side of the fence."

"Did you tell your mother you were going back to Wisconsin?"

"Oh, man, that was a hard conversation."

"What did she say?"

"She said, 'The minute you get out of that courtroom, you go right back to the hotel room and you stay there. You don't answer the door, you don't answer the phone, you don't do anything. You hear? Don't even get *ice*.'"

Keith cracks up.

"She was serious," I say.

"I remember you."

The night before the hearing, Richard Beranek, late fifties, his pale white skin nearly transparent, his eyes placid blue and penetrating, leans into me and offers up a thin smile.

"From where?" I say.

"Gladiator School."

"Green Bay."

"I met you in the law library," he says.

I search my memory. "I don't think I did any legal work for you."

Richard keeps his narrow smile locked in. "No. The line was too long."

"Now I remember. I couldn't get to you. Well, Richard, I got to you now."

Richard's smile fades.

"I want you to know something," he says.

He waits so long to speak I wonder if he's forgotten his thought.

Then he leans in further and says in a hushed voice, "I am not lying. I admitted when I was guilty before. I *pleaded* guilty. I can understand how you could believe that I'm lying now. But I'm not. I didn't do it."

"I know you didn't do it," I say. "That's why I'm here."

"Okay," Richard says. Satisfied, he leans back in his chair.

I flip through Richard's paperwork and frown at a number on the first page. I've read the number before. I want to verify it with Richard.

"The Innocence Project started with you—how long ago?"

Richard Beranek stares into me with his placid blue eyes. "Eight years."

"Wow. I know how hard it is to wait. I certainly know that."

"I'm not going anywhere," he says.

I don't dare go out of my hotel room. I don't care if I'm well into my thirties, I am going to listen to my mother. I stay in my hotel room and I pace. I stop at the window, spread the curtains, peer outside. Then I pace back across the room, sit at the edge of the bed, pick up the TV remote, and flip through channels, not concentrating, my mind on the past.

I picture myself in prison, sitting in the law library. Li'l Johnnie Cochran–Looking Mofo with the Glasses. My reputation, my jacket, which evolved into my identity. I learned a valuable lesson then that holds to this day. Prosecutors and judges rush to convict. But overturning an unfair conviction takes forever. There are no shortcuts. You are attempting to prove that something a court determined to be true is actually a *lie*. There is no direct path to that. You go forward, backward, sideways, and sometimes you go in circles. You take one step forward, five steps back. Emotions rip at you. Your client's and yours. Frustration. Fear. Rage. Sometimes all at once. The only way to ease those emotions is with patience. You need so much patience. Even more, you need faith.

I think about Dimitri. He never caught a break. He filed too late for his appeal. He finally got released from prison three months after I did. To this day, he remains labeled a sex offender. I wish I could defend him as his attorney, but because he and I were part of the same case, that would be a conflict of interest. I do advocate for him, speaking on his behalf, giving him my opinion, trying to guide him through the process of removing that stain permanently from his record. When we speak, I hear his frustration and rage. I leave every conversation feeling his emotions and thinking—

Three young Black men.

Three defendants accused of the same crime.

Three different outcomes.

All innocent.

Eighteen years after being convicted of a crime he never committed, Dimitri is still paying the consequences of a breach of justice, of blatant racism, of a broken, biased system. He's not asking for anything extreme or outlandish. He simply wants equal justice. That's all. No more. But no less.

Sitting on the edge of the bed in this hotel room, having just taken on my first client as a lawyer, I consider that term—"equal justice." Those two words should be the core of our judicial system. A given, not an aspiration. The criminal justice system spends as much money as it needs to get a conviction. Instead, the system should spend that amount of money on getting it *right*.

Eighteen years have passed.

Still no complete exoneration for Dimitri. To this day, he remains a sex offender, his name on a registry, for no reason.

How do I tell Dimitri to be patient?

How do I tell him to have faith?

A man rapes a woman at knifepoint. She smells alcohol on his breath. He'd been drinking. She can't identify him at first because he made her turn away. A year later, after two tries, she identifies Richard from a photograph. He fits the profile. He'd been convicted of sexual assault before. That time, he'd been drinking and admitted his crime. He owned it. He said he did it and he had to do something about his drinking.

But he insists he didn't do this rape. He swears he was nowhere near the scene of the crime. He was in a different *county*. The FBI finds a man's hair in her bedroom. The hair goes into evidence. The hair sits in an evidence room for nearly thirty years, unclaimed, untested for DNA.

We go through the evidence and discover the hair that was found in the bedroom. We ask that we do a DNA test on that hair. While we wait for a response, we do a DNA test on Richard's hair.

The court resists. We have to petition and fight to get the hair in the bedroom tested. They argue that the hair should not be admissible as "new evidence." We win that battle. We test the two hair strands. To a 99.99 percent certainty, lab experts determine that the DNA found on the hair in the bedroom does not match Richard Beranek's.

It takes one year to bring Richard to this evidentiary hearing. By now, my improbable journey from wrongful conviction to lawyer has drawn the attention of the national media. NBC News and Lester Holt follow me, Keith, and Richard into the courtroom in Wisconsin. When the segment airs, the four-minute story shows me meeting with Richard in a legal visit and sitting in court about to hear the judge's decision. By necessity, it leaves out the grunt work that got us to that point. You don't see me months before, poring over two thousand pages of paperwork, police reports, witness testimonies, slogging through eight years of documents and court filings. Since my days as an investigator, I have learned to be methodical and meticulous. I live by this credo: do your job, take all the time you need, and get it *right*. No wonder they call my profession the "practice of law." This job will never be perfect; it will always be a process. One night, late, my eyes blurry from reading court transcripts, I say aloud to the empty room, "Man, Bryce, my first time out, you really threw me into the deep end. Remind me to thank you."

I mean that.

———

In 2017, based on the new DNA evidence we provide, the court in Wisconsin reverses Richard Beranek's rape charges and releases him.

I have won my first case.

21.
Forward

In the fall of 2017, I come to a momentous decision. I decide to start my own practice. The Innocence Project takes on cases based on DNA evidence. I've learned that a number of wrongful convictions are simply not DNA based. I see a need to venture out and tackle those cases as well. I know that starting my own practice is risky, that you don't make big money by righting wrongful conviction cases. I'm not looking to make a killing. I'm looking to make a living.

I need seed money, but not one bank will give me a loan. I can't prove that the color of my skin has anything to do with loan officers turning down my applications, but I don't meet one loan officer who looks like me. I decide to forgo renting an office and set up shop at home. I hang my own shingle—the "Law Office of Jarrett Adams"—in a corner of our apartment. Almost immediately, I take on the cases of Terence Richardson and Ferrone Claiborne. Despite being found not guilty of murdering a police officer in rural Virginia, Terence and Ferrone are serving life in prison on a completely fabricated drug conspiracy charge.

The very next night, I lie in bed and stare at the ceiling. My first case, on my own. I know my clients are innocent, but even so I have to consider it a long shot. All attempts to exonerate innocent people or reduce extreme sentences are long shots. I murmur this to Joi before we go to bed, my anxiety pulsing through the room.

"They *are* long shots," she says. "But without you, they have no shot at all."

"I don't know if this is going to work, Joi. Did I do the right thing? My desk is a piece of wood and some cinder blocks in the corner of our living room. Maybe I made a mistake."

"Listen to me." Joi rolls over, leans on her elbow, and looks me in the eye. "Do you have trust and faith in yourself?"

"You know I do."

"Do you have trust and faith in God?"

"Yes."

"You can't have it both ways. Either you believe in yourself and in God and you believe this is going to work, or you don't. Which is it?"

Before I answer, my wife nestles into my side.

"Do everything the way you always do, with all your heart and all your passion, and it will work out."

I stare at the ceiling. She rolls over on her side. After a while, I hear the soft hum of her breathing. She's out. I lean over and kiss her forehead.

"I'm not doing this for the money anyway," I say.

February 2020.

"Man, man, man."

I wait on the line for Mr. Claiborne, Ferrone's father, to catch his breath and for his sobs to stop. The man has gone through so much while his son sits in prison. Now I've told him that we still have a long way to go.

"I'm sorry, Jarrett," he says after a while.

"It's okay, Mr. Claiborne, take your time."

"How—" Mr. Claiborne swallows and then whispers into the phone. "How much longer, Jarrett?"

"Maybe another year."

"I can't do that. Ferrone keeps calling me, asking me for money to help him out. I can't—I can't tell him I don't *have* any more money. It's gone. All of it. You know how much I spent over the past twenty-five years trying to get him out? Take a guess."

"I couldn't, Mr. Claiborne."

"Three hundred thousand dollars. That's all of it. Everything I have. Every dime. I drained my savings, my retirement. Liquidated my 401(k). I have no more money."

"I'm so sorry. I don't know what to say. I wish I could make the court move faster."

"What do I tell Ferrone? He calls me and he screams, 'Why is this taking so long? I'm innocent. I didn't do anything. Where are the results? I need to see *results*.'"

I close my eyes and shake my head. I really don't have an answer. I say the only thing I can.

"Tell him to please try to hang in there. We may have gotten a break. A new prosecutor has been assigned the case. An African American. Maybe she'll be sympathetic."

The line goes quiet. I hear the echo of Mr. Claiborne sniffling. I know how he feels. I heard the same anguish in my mother's voice as she waited for something—anything—positive to happen in my case. I also know what Mr. Claiborne is going through financially. I watched my family burn through money they didn't have to pay for my lawyer and to post my bonds. I don't know what to say to Mr. Claiborne, how to calm or encourage him. I know personally what it feels like to hemorrhage money. I have been working Ferrone's and Terence's cases pro bono. I pay my paralegal, who has a family, out of my own pocket.

But I refuse to rush. We have to play this right. We have to file when we have everything lined up perfectly. *When you file is as crucial as what you file.* I've learned that lesson—that strategy—by observing lawyers such as MiAngel and Bryce. We have to file when I know we can win. I know we can win with this new prosecutor. And I do know how hard it is to wait. And wait. And wait for what feels like *never*. Every day that passes is another day without justice.

"We have to be on the same page, Mr. Claiborne. We have to form a united front. You have to tell Ferrone to have faith. Tell him to pray. Tell him it worked for me. God continues to save me in spite of myself."

"Please, Jarrett," Mr. Claiborne says, his tears coming again, his voice raw. "I just want my son to come home before I die."

To replenish his retirement account, Mr. Claiborne signs up for extra hours at the plant where he works, putting aside fears of the pandemic. I continue working the case. Then I get a call from one of his relatives.

Mr. Claiborne has contracted COVID-19.

As I write these words, he is on a ventilator, clinging to his life.

I pray that he survives to see his son released from prison.

March 2020.

Madison, Wisconsin.

My client list has grown. I have received a number of calls from the families of inmates in Wisconsin. Others come from inmates I remember from my time in prison. More than ten years after my release, they remain locked away in Waupun, or Dodge, or Green Bay for nonfatal offenses. Some have been incarcerated for decades. I know these people. I talked to them. I played basketball with them. By now, many have become the walking dead. They wake up, slouch to the chow hall, pick at their food, return to their cells, and drop onto their cots, curled up like snails, waiting for time to pass, for time to end. They have waved the white flag on their lives. I have never seen prison as a place for corrections. I see it as a warehouse for human beings.

I get these calls and hear their stories, and I know I have to help them. After the first few calls, I realized that I'm doing exactly what I did when I earned my nickname Li'l Johnnie Cochran–Looking Mofo with the Glasses. I've outgrown the "Li'l" part and become a card-carrying lawyer, but I'm still helping inmates with their legal work, still breaking it down for them, still hearing the voice of the first inmate I helped: "He good with the legal work."

I stop to take in the grandeur of the Wisconsin State Capitol. An imposing dome lords above four ground-level wings that spread in each direction. A bronze statue of a woman holding a globe stands on the very top of the dome. She symbolizes the state motto: "Forward."

I smile.

"Forward."

That could be my motto.

I take Joi's hand and we walk inside the statehouse and into a courtroom. I pause again at the courtroom door, this time to gather myself.

"Surreal," I say to Joi.

A few minutes later, I stand in line with six other attorneys who will be admitted to the State Bar of Wisconsin. A judge says my name and calls the lawyer I have asked to administer my lawyer's oath, the man who will swear me in.

Keith Findley.

I turn and face him. He smiles as if we were in on some private joke, which, in some way, we are. Keith has fought for me, and we've fought battles together. We have vowed to continue to try to do right, or at the very least to try to undo wrongs.

Before reading the lawyer's oath, Keith speaks to everyone assembled in the courtroom: "No one is more deserving than Jarrett Adams to be admitted to the Wisconsin State Bar. No one has traveled a more circuitous route. Jarrett is a man of great perseverance and great moral character. I am honored to call him my friend and to administer the lawyer's oath."

Keith turns back to me. I shift my weight, and for one moment my body hits pause and a memory seeps in. I see myself on the last day I spent in a Wisconsin jail. I promised myself and my mother that if

I ever came back to the state of Wisconsin, it would be as a lawyer. I have kept that promise and begun working on another promise I made to myself and to God. In prison, I met dozens of men who were much more than their convictions. As a member of the State Bar of Wisconsin, I want to chip away at the stigmas attached to these men until they are defined not by what they have done but by who they are now and who they may become.

And then I see myself as a twenty-seven-year-old, walking through my neighborhood, remembering the changes I saw on those streets. Drugs came in and burned through our neighborhood like a raging fire. Buildings were abandoned and boarded up. Homes became crack houses. Crack ripped families apart. Crack divided us, bankrupted us, killed us. Then an army of police rushed in, took us away, incarcerated us, with society's approval. We became disposable. We became invisible.

My attention shifts back to the courtroom, where the same system that disposed of me is about to proclaim me a lawyer. I accept that change—real change—will come slowly, one tiny step at a time. But you have to commit to taking that step. I picture my grandfather Buddy, and I hear him say, "You got to keep going, Jarrett. You can't go back. Keep moving forward."

I look Keith Findley in the eye, exhale, and blink back my tears. Then I raise my right hand.

ACKNOWLEDGMENTS

"You armed me with strength for the battle."

PSALM 18:39

Without hesitation, I first thank God for gifting me with the resilience to struggle, survive, sustain, strive, and then thrive. There were times along my journey when I questioned my faith and asked, *why me?*, not realizing that you ordered each step, and when I was unable to walk, you carried me.

Mom, I've never forgotten the words I said to you that day in court. I rise every day aiming to make sure that I leave a lasting mark on the same system that stole as much from you as it did from me. I am fueled by your endless love, your unbreakable belief in the man you raised me to be, your undeniable selflessness, and your unbreakable strength. *Thank you* will never be enough.

To my family—Sugar, Honey, Bill, Harold, my aunts, uncles, cousins, brothers, and sisters—I never stood alone on my journey and cannot thank you enough for your endless support and encouragement. We've shared many frustrations, disappointments, and tears of pain. I'm extremely grateful to now share in this moment of joy and gratitude with each of you.

To my Joi—you are simply extraordinary. It takes a wife like you to unveil the soul of a man like me. I do not thank you nearly enough as I should and yet you give endlessly and pour into me and my vision constantly. You showed me how to transform from a sole man on a mission to one-half of an unstoppable team. I'm grateful to your family for helping to craft the woman who makes me better every day. God blesses me in unbelievable ways through you. With God and our hustle, there is nothing impossible for us.

To my fellow "Jailhouse Lawyers"—keep up the fight. I acknowledge and salute you for your tenacity, passion, and determination to overcome despite the odds being stacked against you—against us!

To the people who made *Redeeming Justice* possible, starting with the team at CAA, especially Anthony Mattero, my superb agent. You believed in me and my story from the very beginning and found us the perfect home. Thank you.

To everyone at Convergent: Tina Constable, who supported and encouraged me from proposal all the way through production; to all those in editorial, publicity, and marketing; and a huge shout-out to Derek Reed—thoughtful and thorough reader, gifted editor, constant champion—countless, heartfelt thanks.

Finally, to Alan Eisenstock—simply put, there's no book without you. Your artistry turned this lawyer into an author. Thank you for helping me tell my story.

My journey has been blessed by several individuals who have helped clear a path forward and sometimes create one when the road seemed to run out. To the Honorable Judge Ann Claire Williams, Deborah Batts and Patricia Holmes, Keith Findley, John Pray, Barry Scheck, Peter Neufeld, Carol Brook, MiAngel Cody, Mike Golden, Mike Monico, Linda Mattox, Linda Bathgate, and many more professors, mentors, colleagues and role models whom I've been blessed by along the way. Your contributions have led me to where I am today. I'm forever grateful to each of you for your choice to step up, instead of standing aside. I commit to paying it forward and never forgetting to reach back and lift someone else up.

ABOUT THE AUTHOR

Jarrett Adams was falsely accused at the age of seventeen and ultimately wrongfully convicted and sentenced to twenty-eight years in a maximum-security prison. After serving nearly ten years behind bars and filing multiple appeals, Jarrett was exonerated with the assistance of the Wisconsin Innocence Project.

Jarrett used the injustice he endured as inspiration to become an advocate for the underserved and often uncounted. As a first step, he earned his Juris Doctor from Loyola University Chicago School of Law in May 2015 and started a public interest law fellowship with Ann Claire Williams, judge for the Seventh Circuit U.S. Court of Appeals. This is the same court that reversed Jarrett's conviction because of his trial lawyer's constitutional deficiencies. Jarrett also clerked in the U.S. District Court for the Southern District of New York with the late Honorable Deborah Batts.

Jarrett's remarkable story has captured both local and national media attention. An adjunct professor at the Loyola University Law School from 2014 to 2015, Jarrett is a recipient of the 2012 Chicago Bar Foundation's Abraham Lincoln Marovitz Public Interest Law Scholarship.

He also won the National Defender Investigator Association's Investigator of the Year Award for his work with the clemency petition of Reynolds Wintersmith ultimately granted by President Obama.

Jarrett launched the Law Office of Jarrett Adams, PLLC, in 2017 and practices in both federal and state court throughout the country. His story of incarceration, exoneration, and redemption has been featured widely in the media, and he has become a sought-after motivational speaker for athletes, students, inmates, attorneys, and others.

ABOUT THE TYPE

This book was set in Minion, a 1990 Adobe Originals typeface by Robert Slimbach. Minion is inspired by classical, old-style typefaces of the late Renaissance, a period of elegant and beautiful type designs. Created primarily for text setting, Minion combines the aesthetic and functional qualities that make text type highly readable with the versatility of digital technology.